The Revd Dr Sharon Moughtin-Mumby is the director of Diddy Disciples, which she set up at St Peter's, Walworth, South London, when her own wriggly children were three, three and two, and going to church with them felt impossible! Sharon is an Anglican priest and a respected Bible scholar with a strong interest in Bible translation, imagery, art and biblical languages. Before ordination, she was the tutor in Old Testament studies at Ripon College Cuddesdon. She continues to have a passion for education, particularly during the formative early years of life, and loves exploring new, ancient and imaginative ways of engaging with the Bible and worshipping alongside young children.

For my inspirational daughters, Joy, Anastasia and Zoe, and my husband, colleague and friend, Andrew

'This is a book for those who take children seriously. A wonderful, practical resource for those who want to nurture children to be disciples in their own right: to pray, to engage with Scripture, to contribute to worship, to play their part as children of God. A must-read for those who work and volunteer with very young children.'

The Most Revd Justin Welby, Archbishop of Canterbury

'We all think we know that biblical scholarship and Sunday School teaching belong in different worlds. *Diddy Disciples* shows that we are wrong. Sharon Moughtin-Mumby brings the wisdom of a professional biblical scholar to the task of communicating the essence of the Bible to very young children, unveiling the depths of biblical stories for young disciples. Very user-friendly material from which adults can learn too.'

The Revd John Barton, Emeritus Professor, University of Oxford

'*Diddy Disciples* is an invaluable blend of Sharon Moughtin-Mumby's reflective practice and contemporary thinking about childhood spirituality. The result is an exceptional and inspiring resource for churches working with the very youngest children. A powerful case for seeing why the very young deserve the very best, and this is a well-tested method for doing that.'

Dr Rebecca Nye, Godly Play expert and researcher and consultant in children's spirituality

'*Diddy Disciples* is brilliant: a rich resource for leaders, simple and accessible for young children, inviting them into a lifelong journey of faith. Highly commended.'

The Rt Revd Dr Steven Croft, Bishop of Oxford

'I'm excited by *Diddy Disciples*! It's a celebration of Psalm 8.2 and all that babies and toddlers bring to worship. Movement, stories, actions and songs combine in carefully crafted sessions to draw groups into a new way of worshipping that will enrich everyone involved. I can't wait to start using it.'

The Revd Mary Hawes, National Children and Youth Adviser, The Church of England

'When Jesus taught, he often used a language that was unafraid to hover rather than land. Through imaginative and playful provocation, he was opening up spaces for his listeners to move into. This is exactly what *Diddy Disciples* does. It takes for granted the fact that young children are intelligent and perceptive, and it therefore doesn't look down on them. Neither does it pretend that Christian faith is anything but a rich, complex and teasing migration towards the love and mystery of God, where questions can be as vital as insights. This is a liberating combination for everyone involved.'

The Revd Canon Mark Oakley, Chancellor of St Paul's Cathedral

'Diddy Disciples [the programme] is being taken up enthusiastically by a growing number of parishes in the Diocese of Southwark. Helping young children grow into the fullness of Christ through creative, age-appropriate engagement is a wonderful journey of adventure and discovery; and this book, which I gladly commend, will be an essential resource for anyone starting out on that path.'

The Rt Revd Christopher Chessun, Bishop of Southwark

'I am very happy to support [the] Diddy Disciples [programme]. I was particularly encouraged and impressed by the way in which the biblical approach is intelligent and searching, without being above the heads of those for whom it is intended, or condescending to them. Similarly, the programme is firmly connected with the liturgical life of the Church, and this is something that is particularly important in a time when there seems to be widespread enthusiasm for separating all-age worship from good liturgy.'

The Most Revd Dr Richard Clarke, Archbishop of Armagh and Primate of All Ireland

'Our young children love joining in with the simple songs and actions at Diddy Disciples, and before we know it they (and I) have a real understanding of the church liturgy. *Diddy Disciples* gives all types of children a chance to engage in a variety of activities: the chatty ones can sing, the active ones can move, the creative ones can get arty but the highlight of the week is always "What's in the Box?"

I love preparing Diddy Disciples as it is all done for me – I just pick up the book and off I go. If I can't remember a tune, I either hum it and it comes back to me or one of the children sings it for me, as they all know the nursery rhyme tunes. The crafts are all very basic and the children seem to like to be able to "make it their own". Before I did Diddy Disciples I used to spend hours preparing complicated crafts that took the children two minutes to complete, leaving them bored and me frazzled!!'

Charlotte Chappell, Diddy Disciples leader, Christ Church Aughton, Liverpool

'This is a serious book: serious about children; serious about worship; serious about spirituality; serious about God. Sharon Moughtin-Mumby draws upon her own experience as a priest, a parent and a theologian, and on the time-honoured shape of the liturgy, to create patterns for worship that honour God, by enabling the tiniest worshippers to hear the word and respond in praise. She offers enchanting and creative resources that will help to build the Church.'

Gill Ambrose, Consultant to the Liturgical Commission and Chair of Godly Play UK

'Anyone involved in education would agree that the early years in a child's life are crucial for laying the foundations of learning. We so often underestimate children's abilities and needs. *Diddy Disciples* is the resource I have been waiting for; a superb treasure trove of meaningful, interesting and challenging activities for pre-school children in our churches. Whether at a weekday event or Sunday School, *Diddy Disciples* provides singing, texts and ideas that link with the Church's year and provide the building blocks for Christian education. This is an essential resource for every church school, parish and Christian nursery. [The] Diddy Disciples [programme] has been road-tested in a real parish with real children. It demands nothing more than the resources available in any parish or setting. It is properly theological and completely age appropriate. If children are to experience proper faith development and to grow as disciples, it is just material like this that will give the resources needed. A lifetime of Christian discipleship is built on solid foundations. *Diddy Disciples* provides that resource.'

Fr Richard Peers, Director of Education, Diocese of Liverpool

Diddy Disciples
Book 1: September to December

Worship and storytelling resources for babies, toddlers and young children

Sharon Moughtin-Mumby

First published in Great Britain in 2017

Society for Promoting Christian Knowledge
36 Causton Street
London SW1P 4ST
www.spck.org.uk

British Library Cataloguing-in-Publication Data
A catalogue record for this book is available from the British Library

ISBN 978–0–281–07435–8
eBook ISBN 978–0–281–07436–5

Designed by Melissa Brunelli
Typeset by Fakenham Prepress Solutions, Fakenham, Norfolk NR21 8NN
First printed in Great Britain by Ashford Colour Press
Subsequently digitally reprinted in Great Britain

eBook by Fakenham Prepress Solutions, Fakenham, Norfolk NR21 8NN

Produced on paper from sustainable forests

CONTENTS

Part 3: Additional information and resources

ACKNOWLEDGEMENTS

Diddy Disciples would never have happened without the children of St Peter's, Walworth. Many of the words, phrases, actions, symbols and ideas in Diddy Disciples came from them, as well as all the illustrations for the book cover, icons and templates. As the project's gone on, I've really come to see the Diddy Disciples themselves as a little editorial team, giving me helpful comments and suggestions as we've gone along! Thank you, little sisters and brothers, for your energy, insights, playfulness and willingness to share your gifts.

Regular Diddy contributors from St Peter's Church

Aaron, Abbey, Abigail, Abu, Adammah, Aimee, Albert, Alex, Alfred, Alice, Amy, Anastasia, Anna, Ariyanna, Austin, Ava, Bernice, Bella, Cameron, Chelsea, Christian, Cleo, Daijuan, Decory, Daniel, Daniel, Deborah, Demari, Dickson, Eden, Efe, Elijah, Emerald, Emmanuel, Emmanuella, Eri, Ezra, Fire, Gavin, Geoffrey, Gladys, Golden, Gracie, Imani, Isaac, Isabella, Isla, James, Jayden, Jessica, Jo Jo, Joseph, Jovianni, Joy, Jude, Justin, Kaiden, Keisha, Khari, Latif, Latoya, Libby, Lily, Lorien, Louise, Lucas, Maryam, Mary, Maxwell, Micah, Michael, Mitchell, Mofiyin, Nancy, Naomi, Otter, Philip, Ryan, Samson, Sasha, Sepphorah, Shemaiah, Shane, Shannon, Sophia, Susan, Temitope, Timi, Ximena, Zoe, Zoe, Zoey.

Diddy contributors and friends from St Peter's School

Aamilah, Aania, Abass, Abigail, Abu, Adiss, Adonia, Ainhoa, Akil, Alfie, Alicia, Alieu, Alisha, Amaya, Amelia, Amir, Amy, Andres, Aneesa, Ansel, Ashleigh, Austin, Ayla-May, Biola, Brigitte, Chelsea, Christian, Cleo, Crystal, Daijuan, Daniel, Darcey, David, Deborah, Dickson, Divine, Dylan, Eden, Eleanor, Eleil, Elijah, Elissa, Eliza, Elizabeth, Emerald, Emil, Emmanuel, Emmanuelle, Enoch, Ephraim, Ethan, Fabrice, Fraser, Gavin, Grace, Harry, Ibrahim, Isab, Isabella, Isaiah, Jaida, Jake, James, Jasmine, Jeffrey, Jessica, Jhon, Joel, Joel, Joel, Josephine, Jovianni, Joyce, Jude, Julia, Juliet, Kai, Kayleigh, Keisha, King, Kofi, Kwabena, Kwaku, Kwame, Lateef, Leonard, Lily-Rose, Luke, Madox, Mahlon, Maisie, Maja, Ma'khadijah, Marlon, Mason, Michael, Michelle, Mitchell, Moremi, Muhammed, Mya, Nancy, Nathaniel, Osariemen, Pearl, Philip, Reggie, Rhys, Rosa, Rukaiya, Ryleigh, Samuel, Saoirse, Sarah, Selleh, Shalom, Soufriere, Stanley, Sultan, Susan, Victory, Ya-Kai, Ya-Sapor, Zayden, Zephaniah, Zoe, Zoe.

The amazing Diddy illustrators from St Peter's Church and School

Abigail, Amelia, Anastasia, Bella, Christian, Daijuan, Darcey, Eden, Elijah, Gavin, Harry, Isabella, Isla, Jessica, Joy, Julia, Kayleigh, Marlon, Mya, Michael, Mitchell, Nancy, Pearl, Philip, Samson, Samuel, Susan, Susannah, Zoe, Zoey.

It's a special pleasure to thank the congregation, PCC, wardens, staff and clergy team of St Peter's, Walworth, for giving me the space to play and experiment, and the support to make Diddy Disciples possible. Particular thanks go to Gene, Kate, Doreen, Aisha, Dipo, Femi, Clare, Lucia, Lady, Laura, Chris, Ian, Theo, Eileen, Novelette, Donna, Robert, Beryl, Lahan, Mary, Catherine, Michael, Alan, and Andrew. Thank you also to St Peter's School for making Tuesday Diddy Disciples in the sanctuary such a rich time of worship and development, especially Laura, Debbie, Julie, Tracy, Sue, Deborah, Linda, Audrey, Marcia, Wendy, Charlie, Laura, and their head teacher, Anne-Marie Bahlol.

Huge thanks go to Christopher Chessun, Bishop of Southwark, for his unwavering support and encouragement. He was the first bishop to preside at Diddy Disciples and has given his permission for us to share communion with even our youngest baptized disciples as part of their faith journey. Thank you also to Jane Steen, the first archdeacon to preside at Diddy Disciples: the children still talk about her visit.

There are many others who've been a great support to the project behind the scenes. It's impossible to mention them all here, but special thanks go to Niall Sloane, Daniel Trott, Sister Carolin Clare OSC, Alison Seaman, Richard Peers, Hugh Ridsdill-Smith, Alex Lawson, Beth Hayward, Sarah Strandoo, Sarah O'Donoghue and Charlotte Chappell.

Thank you also to the team at SPCK for their guidance, experience and patience in the often challenging task of turning a vision into print, especially Tracey Messenger, Steve Gove and Rima Devereaux.

Finally, I would like to thank Andrew, who's been part of Diddy Disciples from the very beginning: reading, listening, commenting, critiquing, encouraging, consoling, challenging, inspiring and fielding random questions. Diddy Disciples wouldn't be what it is without him. Andrew, thank you!

Part 1
Introducing
Diddy Disciples

INTRODUCTION

What is Diddy Disciples?

Diddy Disciples is a collection of Bible storytelling, prayer and worship materials especially designed for babies, toddlers and young children. The materials aim to create a space for children to encounter God for themselves, inviting them to discover, explore and take an active part not only in telling Bible stories but in all forms of Christian worship. Diddy Disciples uses movement, imagination, our faces and bodies, symbols, creative activities, music and song to encourage and enable young children to participate fully.

Diddy Disciples is designed to be flexible and can be used in a variety of settings. Alongside the Bible Storytelling materials, a range of worship resources are set out in different 'Building Blocks' that your group can choose from to build its own sessions.

Why not just have a crèche for very young children?

Diddy Disciples grew from the realization of just how important the early years of a person's life are. During these first years, our sense of who we are, where we belong and how we fit in are shaped, as well as our interests, learning styles and attitudes. Diddy Disciples is based on the belief that, if we aim to build up a people of God who take part fully in worship, who are willing to lead and open to seeing how the stories we tell from the Bible are relevant to the way we live life, then this approach must begin during these first years. To put it another way, people who learn to 'sit still and be quiet' in church during the early years of their life are more likely to continue to 'sit still and be quiet' in church as adults, not becoming actively involved, or at least needing a lot of support to move beyond that way of being.

In the last few decades, we've become increasingly aware of the importance of exposing our children to music, singing and the rhythms of human language from the earliest age, even from the womb. We recognize that encouraging a baby or toddler to take part actively in talking, singing, making music, clapping, turning the pages of a book, even playing an instrument has a lifelong impact on that child's relationship to music and language. We don't wait until children have reached an age when they can be expected to fully grasp what is going on before we invite them to join in. We talk to children long

before they understand the words because we know that they understand the tone, the relationship, and will in their own time become active in speech and language. We understand that it's by making those first babbles, banging that first drum, turning that page, or moving in time to a beat that children start their journey towards a lifelong learning and love of language and music. Of course, we can begin to learn a new language or instrument as adults, but most would recognize that this is a far greater challenge and requires far more determination. Diddy Disciples is based on the belief that, if we hope for our children to embark on a lifelong journey as part of God's people – so that the language of faith becomes a 'first language', or 'mother tongue', for them – this journey can and should begin from the womb. Diddy Disciples was developed to help create a space for children to embark on that journey alongside others from the very earliest age.

Isn't babies, toddlers and young children quite a wide age group?

Diddy Disciples grew out of Sunday morning worship with babies and young children at the main Sunday communion service at St Peter's, Walworth, in London, England. We began by welcoming children over the age of two and a half. Soon, however, we decided to include babies, who arrived en masse at Advent along with their parents or carers, giving us a timely reminder in the run-up to Christmas of how much change babies can bring with them! Once we'd settled back into a pattern and rhythm, we found that the babies brought a great deal to our group.

> **Tip**
>
> For tips on how to involve babies actively, see 'Including babies in mixed groups' on p. 232.

For babies, Diddy Disciples represents an immersive approach to worship. They're not expected to follow and understand every word, but they are included as a full part of the group, drawn into the experience that is taking place around them, and encouraged to participate and lead in their own ways (which usually involves using their bodies). Being actively included from the very beginning is important in itself. As part of God's family, these babies take part in the family's activities, just as at home they spend some time simply immersed in the melee of family life. At the same time, by being immersed in activities that are especially designed for the first years of life – alongside children only a little older than they are – these babies and toddlers are also given the opportunity to gradually develop skills that will deepen their experience over time. At St Peter's, Walworth, the babies' parents and carers speak movingly of what their children gain from the experience of being included in worship. The babies' verbal understanding may be limited, but they respond actively to the music, the movement, the actions, and the sense of being part of something important. Most of all they understand what it is to be included, for their contribution to be both expected and to make a difference.

The inclusion of babies in our group has also been beneficial for the children over the age of four. The revolutionary, 'topsy turvy' idea that they might learn from a baby doesn't pass them by: they love finding out what unorthodox uses the babies can make of their imaginative aids and imitating them. Some lovely friendships between babies and young children have emerged from their worship together, and these often continue beyond worship. Including babies in Diddy Disciples has also been beneficial for our parents and carers, who no longer spend the adult sermon either 'shushing' their children or segregated into a crèche area where it can be difficult for them to feel an active part of the church. We've found that many adults themselves find the worship and Bible storytelling meaningful, and are often moved by the experience of worshipping alongside – and being led by – the youngest of children.

Much of the material in the main volume is designed for a mixed group like that at St Peter's, or for groups with children over the age of two and a half. Groups that include *only* children under the age of three might find it helpful to look at 'Bible storytelling with babies and toddlers' (p. 233).

> " From around 9 months of age, Ezra loved to join in the New Start sign in the Sorry Song, and soon began singing along with his own harmonies. Now 18 months old, he can be heard in the main church service singing along joyfully, again with his own harmonies. Ezra almost certainly has no grasp of any of the words in those hymns at all, but he has grasped the most important thing: the song of the Church is *his* song and it's important for him to join in. "

How do we know which Bible story to tell each week?

Diddy Disciples is organized into units of up to six sessions, with each unit covering an important biblical theme. In creating each unit, we asked: if we could only tell six stories to encapsulate this theme, what would they be? The Bible stories are then carefully ordered to help the children to build – week by week – their understanding and engagement with that theme. At the same time, each week's story is designed to stand alone, so that children joining or visiting the group, and those who can't be there every week, can be fully involved in the storytelling for whichever session they attend.

The units can be worked through in any order (with weeks missed out where appropriate for your group). However, they're designed so that churches who would like to follow the seasons of the liturgical year can do so. The connections to the liturgical year are indicated in brackets in the list below, but don't need to be kept by groups for whom this isn't relevant.

The units in this first volume are:
- Jesus' Wonderful Love (Green Time/ Ordinary Time)
- God the Maker (around Harvest in Green Time/Ordinary Time)
- In November We Remember (Green Time/Ordinary Time or Kingdom Season, in November)
- Getting Ready for Baby Jesus (Advent and Christmas)

Note: The storytelling material for All Saints (week 1 of the In November We Remember unit) can also be adapted for patronal festivals or saints' days.

The units in the second volume will include:
- Jesus, Light of the World! (Epiphany)
- John the Baptist (the weeks before Lent)
- The Journey to the Cross (Lent)
- Jesus is Alive! Alleluia! (Easter)
- The Day of Pentecost and Trinity Sunday
- Let Your Kingdom Come! (Green Time/ Ordinary Time between July and November)
- God's Best Friend, Moses (Green Time/ Ordinary Time between July and November)

Does Diddy Disciples follow the lectionary?

Diddy Disciples began by following the *Common Worship* lectionary. In practice, however, we found that the lectionary's tendency to move around themes and/or biblical books made it hard for young children to find a pattern. After some experimentation, we decided that working in units that could be matched to the Church's seasons worked best. We found that carefully ordering the biblical stories within the units helped to deepen our children's worship, brought a greater understanding

to their engagement with the Bible, and opened up the space for them to meet with God. Matching these units to the seasons and their broader themes meant that our worship in Diddy Disciples took place in time to the rhythm of the liturgical year, but in a way that was specially formed and shaped for young children.

Note: Book 1 begins with material that is appropriate for Green Time/Ordinary Time in September (rather than with the beginning of the liturgical year in Advent), as we recognize that many children's groups will be structured to work in time with the school year as well as the liturgical year.

BUILD YOUR OWN DIDDY DISCIPLES SESSION

Diddy Disciples isn't just Bible storytelling. The Building Blocks provide a wide range of prayer, worship and creative materials to resource and nurture your group's time with God. Different groups work in different ways and so the idea is that you can choose Building Blocks and options that are appropriate for your group to build your own service.

> **Tip**
>
> The material includes Building Blocks for every part of a communion service or a Service of the Word. However, it was never envisaged that any group would attempt to use all these Building Blocks each Sunday. That would be far too much for children and leaders alike!

Broadly, there are four types of Building Blocks:

Preparation Blocks: these work well before the Bible storytelling

Interactive Bible Storytelling: this is central to Diddy Disciples

Prayer Blocks: these work best immediately after the Bible storytelling. They're more substantial, so we recommend you choose only one of these at a time

Response Blocks: these work well after the Bible storytelling

The idea is for your group to explore the material and decide which Building Blocks you'd like to use for your session. Each Building Block comes with a range of options, which allows you to choose according to your tradition, time limitations, leaders, children, space and resources. Whatever choices you make, we advise that you stick to those choices for one whole unit (unless you intend to build gradually) so your group can enter into a rhythm. This will encourage participation and allow for deeper engagement among the children and adults.

At this point, you have a choice. You can:

- dip straight into the material itself by choosing a unit. The first unit – Jesus' Wonderful Love – starts on p. 29;
- read a step-by-step guide to the Building Blocks including practical tips from p. 217;
- continue reading to see how three different groups built three different sessions from the Building Blocks.

> **Tip**
>
> You may want to use one of the first two samples as a 'quick start' guide for building your own first session. Sample 2 is particularly suited for new groups starting on Sunday mornings.

Sample 1: A simple and short weekday session

Sample 2: A session for a Sunday morning group who are just starting out with Diddy Disciples and adding Building Blocks gradually

Sample 3: A session for a well-established group held during a communion service on Sunday

> **Tip**
>
> Remember to look at 'Bible storytelling with babies and toddlers' (pp. 233–53) if your group is made up only of babies and very young children.

Welcome

Getting Ready for Bible Storytelling

Thank You God

Creative Response

Getting Ready to Worship

Interactive Bible Storytelling

Prayers for Other People

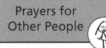
Sharing God's Peace

Introducing the Unit

Gathering Song

Saying Sorry to God

God Gives Us a New Start

Taking God's Love into the World

Sample 1: A simple and short weekday session

Starting simple can be very helpful. Here's the kind of 20-minute session that we hold with the nursery and reception classes at St Peter's Church of England Primary School.

| Introducing the Unit | Gathering Song | Getting Ready for Bible Storytelling | Interactive Bible Storytelling | Taking God's Love into the World |

This is how the session looks in practice:

God the Maker unit: Week 1

Introducing the Unit

Starting this week, we're going to tell
stories about God the Maker who made the whole world!

Gathering Song: Option 1

→ Song: 'It's raining, it's raining!' Words © Sharon Moughtin-Mumby
→ Tune: 'A-Tisket, A-Tasket' (traditional). For the music see p. 85, or for a taster see the Diddy Disciples website.

Our world can have lots of different weather!
Who can tell us what the weather is like today?

Invite a child to respond.

If you're using imaginative aids, ask two or three children to give them out at this point. Then invite the children to warm up their imaginations by exploring actions for different kinds of weather: rainy, snowy, windy, sunny, cloudy, rainbows, chilly, stormy (thunder and lightning), etc.

God the Maker made the weather!
Let's thank God for every kind of weather
with our God the Maker song.

> This Gathering Song and its introduction remain the same for the six weeks of the unit.

Introduce each verse by inviting the children to show the kind of weather mentioned with their imaginative aids or their bodies, as exemplified below.

Let's start off by imagining it's raining outside!
Can you show me rain?

Continue with the action as you sing:
It's *raining*, it's *raining*!
Outside it is *raining*!
God the Maker made the world.
Thank you, God the Maker!

Now let's imagine it's sunny outside!
Can you show me sunny?

Continue with the action as you sing:
It's *sunny*, it's *sunny*!

Outside it is *sunny*!
God the Maker made the world.
Thank you, God the Maker!

Look! I can see a rainbow!
Can you show me a rainbow!
Let's sing 'a rainbow, a rainbow!
Outside there's a rainbow!'

Continue with the action as you sing:
A rainbow, a rainbow!
Outside there's a rainbow!
God the Maker made the world.
Thank you, God the Maker!

Oh my goodness, now there's thunder!
Can you show me thunder with your feet?
And lightning! Can you show me lightning?
It's stormy!

Continue with the action as you sing:
It's *stormy*, it's *stormy*!
Outside it is *stormy*!
God the Maker made the world.
Thank you, God the Maker!

Wow! Now there's snow,
Soft, beautiful snow, falling all around.
Can you show me snow?

Continue with the action as you sing:
It's *snowing*, it's *snowing*!
Outside it is *snowing*!
God the Maker made the world.
Thank you, God the Maker!

And now listen.
Hand over your ear. Lead the children in blowing.

Can you hear that?
Lead the children in blowing louder and louder.
It's windy outside! Can you show me wind?

Continue with the action as you sing:
It's *windy*, it's *windy*!
Outside it is *windy*!
God the Maker made the world.
Thank you, God the Maker!

Yawn. Who's feeling tired after all that weather?
Let's sit back in our place and go to sleep . . .
Lead the children in being sleepy.

Look! *Point up.* Outside the stars are twinkling. *Twinkle hands*
Can you show me the twinkling stars?

Lead the children in twinkling with hands as you sing quietly and sleepily.
It's *starry*, it's *starry*,
Outside it is *starry*.
God the Maker made the world.
Thank you, God the Maker!

End by falling asleep quietly and peacefully.

Getting Ready for Bible Storytelling: Option 1

→ **Action: opening your group's box and naming this week's object**

Invite one of the children to open the box. Inside will be pictures of different kinds of weather.

What's in the box? *Ask the child to respond.*

Invite the children to name the different kinds of weather on the pictures.

Interactive Bible Storytelling: God the Maker, week 3

→ **Song: 'Everything in all the world sings "Alleluia!"' Words © Sharon Moughtin-Mumby**
→ **Tune: 'Old Macdonald had a farm' (traditional). For the music see p. 112, or for a taster see the Diddy Disciples website.**

Tip

The group sings a song based on Psalm 148, exploring how all the different kinds of weather sing 'Alleluia!' to the tune of 'Old Macdonald had a farm'. To see the full material, go to p. 110.

Taking God's Love into the World

→ **Matthew 5.14–16**
→ **Song: 'This little light of mine' (traditional)**
→ **Tune: Traditional. For a taster, see the Diddy Disciples website. For tips on teaching songs for the first time, see p. 215.**
→ **Guide: p. 232**

> This closing song and its introduction remain the same for every session.

Our time together is coming to an end.

Invite the children to sit in a circle for a moment of quiet.

God has lit a little light of love inside all of us.
Trace a circle on your heart.
Let's make our finger into a candle.
Bring your finger from your heart and hold it out.
Let's be God and light our little light of love together, after three.
Lead the children in lighting their finger candle by striking an imaginary match in the air on three and pretending to light your finger.
1, 2, 3 . . . Tssss!

Let's imagine God's love shining and dancing like light in us.

Wave your finger in front of you as you sing.
This little light of mine, I'm gonna let it shine!
This little light of mine, I'm gonna let it shine!
This little light of mine, I'm gonna let it shine!
Let it shine, let it shine, let it shine!

Blow on your finger as if blowing out a candle on 'puff'. Then hold it up high.

Won't let no one *puff* **it out! I'm gonna let it shine!**

Won't let no one *puff* **it out! I'm gonna let it shine!**

Won't let no one *puff* **it out! I'm gonna let it shine!**

Let it shine, let it shine, let it shine!

Hold your finger behind a cupped hand, then take your cupped hand away to reveal the 'candle' and hold it high!

Hide it under a bushel? No! I'm gonna let it shine!

Hide it under a bushel? No! I'm gonna let it shine!

Hide it under a bushel? No! I'm gonna let it shine!

Let it shine, let it shine, let it shine!

Lead the children in placing your finger back on your heart.

Now let's put our little light of love

back in our hearts, where it belongs.

Let's remember to let our little light shine

in all our playing and working today . . .

Tip

A simple session like this, without any time for Creative Responses set aside within the session itself, involves almost no preparation and lasts 20 minutes. Something similar may be just right for your group. Alternatively, in time, you might like to explore the wealth of options that Diddy Disciples has to offer. This might be particularly the case if you meet during Sunday worship, or want to create a service for or with young children. If it feels that it's getting too complicated, however, it might be worth returning to a simple pattern like this for a time. The important thing is to work out what's best for your children, adults and leaders: there's no right or wrong pattern.

Sample 2: A session for a group just starting out with Diddy Disciples

Christ Church, Aughton is a thriving parish church with an evangelical tradition in the west Lancashire market town of Ormskirk. The church has a strong emphasis on ministry with children and young people not just on Sundays but throughout the week, with numerous uniformed groups. Services are generally relaxed and interactive, with lots of use of music and movement. Christ Church is interested in exploring Diddy Disciples with its young children on Sundays and its babies and toddlers in midweek groups, with the hope of building stronger bridges between what takes place in the children's groups and in all-age Sunday services.

The following shape is the one that we built together for the first few sessions of Diddy Disciples for young children on a Sunday at Christ Church, Aughton.

As the group gains in confidence, they aim to add Building Blocks gradually, keeping an eye on how the children and leaders respond.

Then . . .

This is how one of the sessions would look in practice.

Jesus' Wonderful Love unit: Week 1

Welcome

Welcome your group.

Let's start by going round the circle
and saying our name out loud.
My name's _____.

Go round the circle so that every adult and child has the chance to say his or her name (and introduce any dolls, teddies or toys). If any of the children don't want to say their name or aren't able to, you (or a parent or carer) could say it for them and wave.

It's time to sing our Welcome Song!

Welcome Song: Option 1

→ Song: 'The Diddy Disciples welcome song'. Words © Sharon Moughtin-Mumby
→ Tune: 'Glory, glory, alleluia!' (traditional). For the music see p. 259, or for a taster see the Diddy Disciples website. For tips on teaching songs for the first time, see p. 215.

> This Welcome Song remains the same for every session. Different Gathering Songs are available for different groups.

Go around the circle the same way as above. See if you can remember each other's names and insert them into the song.

Welcome *Name 1* to-o *Christ Church!*
Welcome *Name 2* to-o *Christ Church!*
Welcome *Name 3* to-o *Christ Church!*
You are welcome in the name of the Lord!

Introducing the Unit: Option 1

Starting this week, we're going to tell
some of the amazing stories that Jesus told.
Lots of these stories are about how much Jesus loves us.

Gathering Song: Option 1

→ Song: 'Look how much Jesus loves me!' Words © Sharon Moughtin-Mumby
→ Tune: 'Here we go Looby Loo' (traditional). For the music, see p. 33 or for a taster see the Diddy Disciples website.

Let's show how much Jesus loves us
with our bodies!

Let's stretch up as high as we can to the stars . . .
'Higher than the stars!'
Now down as low, low, low as we can . . .
'Deeper than the sea!'
And now let's stretch out as wide as we can . . .
'Wider than the sky!'

Let's make a big shape with our body!
Bigger! Even bigger!
'Look how much Jesus loves me!'
Let's sing our song about how much Jesus loves us.

> This introductory song remains the same throughout the six-week unit. The group has no imaginative aids yet and so they make up body actions together for the song. Different Gathering Songs are available for different groups.

Higher than the stars! *Stretch up on tiptoes and reach high with 'twinkle' hands*
Deeper than the sea! *Crouch down and reach low, rippling fingers like water*
Wider than the sky! . . . *Stand and stretch arms out*
You may find it helpful to pause at this point each time to remind the children to make a 'big shape' with their body: 'Big Shape!'
Look how much Jesus loves me! *Big shape*

Jesus doesn't just love us
when we're calm and well behaved!
Jesus loves us all the time!

Either: invite the children to choose which feelings they'd like to explore.

How are you feeling today?

Or: Let's all be cross! Can you show me cross?

Lead the children in singing along with their chosen facial expression and action.

Example:

When I'm feeling cross! *Cross action and face*
When I'm feeling cross! *Cross action and face*
When I'm feeling cross! . . . *Cross action and face*
Spoken: Big shape!
Look how much Jesus loves me! *Big shape*

Repeat for different feelings, inviting the children to explore a range of positive and negative emotions. For instance:

When I'm feeling happy . . .
When I'm feeling sad . . .
When I'm feeling surprised . . .
When I'm feeling scared . . .
When I'm feeling excited . . .
When I'm feeling lonely . . .
When I'm feeling poorly . . .

You may like to repeat the 'Higher than the stars' refrain after each verse or after every couple of verses.

You may like to end with:
So many different feelings!
Yawn. I'm feeling tired after all that. Are you?
Can you show me tired?
Let's all go to sleep and sing again.
This time at the end we won't make our big shape.
Let's fall fast asleep instead . . .
When I'm feeling tired,
when I'm feeling tired,
when I'm feeling tired,
look how much Jesus loves me! *Yawn*

Sing more reflectively while still miming falling asleep. Slow down towards the end as if going to sleep at night.

Higher than the stars!
Deeper than the sea!
Wider than the sky!
Look how much Jesus loves me . . .
End with a moment of sleepy silence

Interactive Bible Storytelling: Jesus' Wonderful Love, week 1

→ Luke 15.3–7
→ Song: 'The lost sheep song'. Words © Sharon Moughtin-Mumby
→ Tune: 'Little Bo Peep' (traditional). For the music see p. 54, or for a taster see the Diddy Disciples website.

> The group tells Jesus' parable of the Lost Sheep through a song to the tune of 'Little Bo Peep'. To see the full material, go to p. 54.

Thank You, God: Option 1

→ Song: 'My hands were made for love'. Words © Sharon Moughtin-Mumby
→ Tune: 'Hickory, dickory, dock' (traditional). For the music, see p. 262, or for a taster see the Diddy Disciples website. For tips on teaching songs for the first time, see p. 215.

> ### Tip
>
> For the first few weeks – while they're settling – the group don't use this Building Block. However, once the children and leaders are feeling confident, they plan to introduce it.

Invite the children to sit in a circle for a moment of quiet.

It's time to remember all the things we've done this week.
It's time to say 'thank you' to God
for when we've been part of showing God's love.

Let's wiggle our fingers!
I wonder when you've shown love
with your hands this week?

> This time of prayer remains the same for at least six weeks and can be used for any unit. There are different Prayer Building Blocks available.

Wiggle fingers as you sing.
My hands were made for love!
My hands were made for love!
Thank you for the love they've shown.
My hands were made for love!

Let's wiggle our feet!
I wonder when you've shown love
with your feet this week?

Wiggle feet as you sing.
My feet were made for love!
My feet were made for love!
Thank you for the love they've shown.
My feet were made for love!

Let's put our hands gently on our neck.
Let's sing 'Ahhh!'
Ahhhhh!
Can you feel your throat vibrating and dancing?
I wonder when you've shown love
with your voice this week?

Hold your neck and feel your voice 'dancing' as you sing.
My voice was made for love!
My voice was made for love!
Thank you for the love it's shown.
My voice was made for love!

Creative Response

As Christ Church Aughton are used to using print-and-go style material with their young children, they choose this option to begin with, as well as providing paper and pencils that the children can use however they wish and a table for playdough. For the sensory explorers, the group provides some plastic sheep from a farm set, along with some building bricks. In time, they plan to add to their resources for sensory explorers.

Sharing God's Peace: Option 1

→ Song: 'I've got peace like a river' (traditional). Isaiah 66.12, NIV
→ Tune: Traditional. For a taster, see the Diddy Disciples website. For tips on teaching songs for the first time, see p. 215.

> This closing song remains the same for every session. Different Peace Songs are available for different groups.

Hold one end of the peace cloth (see Guide, p. 231) and ask one of the older children or an adult to hold the other end. Start singing the Peace Song. As the children begin to gather, invite them to join in holding a small section of the cloth, raising and lowering it so it 'flows' like a river as you sing together.

I've got peace like a river,
I've got peace like a river,
I've got peace like a river in my soul.
I've got peace like a river,
I've got peace like a river,
I've got peace like a river in my soul.

Sample 3: A session for a well-established group held during a communion service

Many of the children at St Peter's are now very familiar with Diddy Disciples worship, so we can include quite a few Building Blocks. Material like the Welcome Song, the Sign of the Cross and the Prayers for Other People take hardly any time at all for us now and tend to settle the group, as they know exactly what they are doing. It was not like this to begin with! It will take a while for a new group to build up to holding a service like this, as everything that is new will take much longer than you expect. But, in time, it is possible: we hold a session like this every week with between 25 and 35 babies, toddlers and young children.

Getting Ready for Baby Jesus! unit: Week 2

Welcome Song: Option 2

→ **Song: 'You are welcome in the name of the Lord' (traditional)**
→ **Tune: Traditional. For the music see p. 262, or for a taster see the Diddy Disciples website. For tips on teaching songs for the first time, see p. 215.**

Welcome to *St Peter's*!
Let's wave with one hand. *Lead waving*
Then with our other hand. *Lead waving*
Then let's choose someone and show God's 'glory'!
Move arms up and down in front of you with fingers wiggling, palms facing out, towards one person.
And someone else! *Repeat*
Then let's wave with both hands all around the circle.
Lead waving.

We're ready to sing!

This Welcome Song remains the same for every session throughout the year. Different Welcome Songs are available for different groups.

You are welcome in the name of the Lord!
Wave with right hand to one person.
You are welcome in the name of the Lord!
Wave with left hand to another person.

I can see all over you, the glory of the Lord!

Move arms up and down in front of you with fingers wiggling, palms facing out, towards one person and then another.

You are welcome in the name of the Lord!

Wave with both hands all around the circle.

Getting Ready to Worship: Option 1

→ **Psalm 139.4**
→ **Action: The sign of the cross. Words © Sharon Moughtin-Mumby**

Invite the children to make the sign of the cross slowly with you. As the children become more confident, invite a child to lead the action as the whole group says the words and makes the sign of the cross.

> This action remains the same for every session throughout the year. Different options are available for different groups.

In my head,	*touch head*
in my heart,	*touch chest*
and all around me,	*touch shoulders one by one*
Jesus is here.	*open hands in front facing upwards*

Introducing the Unit: Option 2

→ **Focus: the liturgical colour, purple**

Who can tell us what colour season we're in now?

> *If appropriate:* You may have seen it in church.

The colour purple
reminds us it's time to 'get ready'!
Baby Jesus is coming at Christmas!

> *If appropriate:* Let's all look out for purple when we go back into church.
> *Or:* Let's remember to look and see what colour we're in next time we go into church.

Gathering Song: Option 1

→ **'Busy, busy, busy, getting ready for Christmas!' Words © Sharon Moughtin-Mumby**
→ **Tune: 'What shall we do with the drunken sailor?' (traditional). For the music see p. 171, or for a taster see the Diddy Disciples website.**

Baby Jesus is the Light of the World!
Let's close our eyes and feel the dark . . .

> This introduction and Gathering Song remain the same for the whole unit.

We're waiting for Baby Jesus, the Light of the World,
to shine in the darkness!
Let's open our eyes again.

You might like to show the children a picture of the sun rising, if you used one in the storytelling for week 1.

Like we wait for the sun to 'dawn',
to come up, in the morning.

If you're using imaginative aids, ask two or three children to give them out.

Let's show the sun 'dawning' with our bodies.
Let's crouch down low . . .
Let's close our eyes . . . it's dark!

Let's show the sun coming up and up and out . . .
in the morning.
Lead the children in showing the sun rising with your hands as you stand up.

The sun is 'dawning'!
Now let's do that as we sing our song,
'Jesus, Light of the World'.

Je-sus, Light of the World, *Sun dawning action*
Je-sus, Light of the World, *Sun dawning action*
Je-sus, Light of the World, is *Sun dawning action*
dawning in the darkness! *Sun dawning action*

Getting ready for Christmas can be very busy!
What have we been doing to get ready for Christmas?

Either invite the children to make suggestions, or choose from the suggestions below. For each activity sing the 'Busy, busy, busy, getting ready for Christmas' verse with an appropriate action designed by the children, followed by the 'Jesus, Light of the World' refrain.
- *hanging lights on the Christmas Tree . . . (we use lights at Christmas to remember that Jesus is the Light of the World!)*
- *opening our Advent calendars*
- *writing Christmas cards*
- *cleaning our home*
- *baking and cooking*
- *wrapping presents*
- *dancing at parties*

Busy, busy, busy, getting ready for Christmas!
Busy, busy, busy, getting ready for Christmas!
Busy, busy, busy, getting ready for Christmas!
The Light of the World is dawning! *Sun dawning action*

Je-sus, Light of the World, *Sun dawning action*
Je-sus, Light of the World, *Sun dawning action*
Je-sus, Light of the World, is *Sun dawning action*
dawning in the darkness! *Sun dawning action*

Getting ready for Christmas can be very busy!
You might see your parents or carers at home running around
and getting very busy!

> *If appropriate:* Or your teachers at school getting stressed
> about the Christmas/Nativity play!

Let's all look busy and stressed like the adults!
Lead children in waving imaginative aids or arms around madly and running on the spot.

Let's sing 'Busy, busy, busy, getting ready for Christmas!' again.

Busy, busy, busy, getting ready for Christmas!
Busy, busy, busy, getting ready for Christmas!
Busy, busy, busy, getting ready for Christmas!
The Light of the World is dawning!

Je-sus, Light of the World, *Sun dawning action*
Je-sus, Light of the World, *Sun dawning action*
Je-sus, Light of the World, is *Sun dawning action*
dawning in the darkness! *Sun dawning action*

My goodness, that was busy!
Who's feeling tired?
When we're getting ready for Christmas
it can get really busy and really exciting!

Who's excited about Christmas?
In all the busyness,
let's remember to also have time for some quiet.
Let's remember to get ready for the very special baby
that's coming: Baby Jesus.

Let's sit quietly now and close our eyes . . .
Let's imagine holding Baby Jesus in our arms
and singing to him quietly and gently.
Baby Jesus will be born at Christmas!

Lead the children in rocking a baby and singing quietly.
Je-sus, Light of the World,
Je-sus, Light of the World,
Je-sus, Light of the World, is
dawning in the darkness!

One of the ways we get ready inside *Trace a circle on your heart*
is to tell stories about Baby Jesus.
We're going to tell one of those stories today.

Interactive Bible Storytelling: Getting Ready for Baby Jesus, week 2

→ Luke 1.26–38
→ '"Yes!" said Mary'. Words © Sharon Moughtin-Mumby
→ Tune: '"Pop!" goes the weasel' (traditional). For the music, see p. 195, or for a taster see the Diddy Disciples website.

> The group tells the story of the angel Gabriel visiting Mary through a song to the tune of
> '"Pop!" goes the weasel'. To see the full material, go to p. 196.

Prayers for Other People: Option 1

→ Ephesians 6.18; Jeremiah 29.7; Nehemiah 1.11
→ Song: 'Jesus, hear our prayer!' Words © Sharon Moughtin-Mumby
→ Tune: 'Brown girl in the ring' (traditional). For the music see p. 260, or for a taster see the Diddy Disciples website. For tips on teaching songs for the first time, see p. 215. For similar words designed to fit with the alternative tune 'He's got the whole world in his hands', see p. 261.

For the world:	**Jesus, hear our prayer!**
Make a circle shape	*Open hands upwards to God*
For the Church:	**Jesus, hear our prayer!**
Praying hands	*Open hands upwards to God*
For our place, *Walworth**:	**Jesus, hear our prayer!**
Hands down moving out in	*Open hands upwards to God*
a semi-circle to show the land around us	
Lord Jesus, hear our prayer. Amen.	
Open hands upwards to God	

* *Insert local area/school/church/community/parish.*

For the sick and lonely:	**Jesus, hear our prayer!**
Fingers showing tears falling	*Open hands upwards to God*
down cheeks	
For our friends and family:	**Jesus, hear our prayer!**
Arms around yourself	*Open hands upwards to God*
For ourselves:	**Jesus, hear our prayer!**
Both hands on heart	*Open hands upwards to God*
Lord Jesus, hear our prayer. Amen.	
Open hands upwards to God.	

Let's close our eyes for a moment.
I wonder if there's someone special
you'd like to pray for?
Let's imagine them now.

Now, let's imagine Jesus coming to them.
Does Jesus say anything?
Does Jesus do anything?
Let's open our eyes.

Prayer Action: Option 3

→ **John 8.12; Matthew 4.16**
→ **Action: placing lit candles (battery tealights) on a world map**

> ### Tip
>
> At St Peter's, Walworth, we've used a map jigsaw (the children can also explore it afterwards). We ask an adult to light the battery tealights in advance as we've found younger children can be distracted by attempts to light the tealights themselves.

Place your world map in the centre of the circle.

This is a map of the world.
Jesus is the Light of the World!

Show the children one or more baskets/trays holding lit battery tealights.

Now as we pray, we're going to turn the lights off
for a moment and look at these candles here.

In a moment, *Name* and *Name*
are going to bring round these candles.
If you like, you could take one.
Let's sing as we wait in the dark.
Let's hold our hands out gently like this *Model cupped hands*
as we wait for Jesus to shine in our world.

Hum the tune together, with the words 'Jesus, hear our prayer!' as a refrain, until all the children and adults who wish to take tealights have done so.

> *If appropriate:*
> At the moment, there's fighting in the world
> here and here. *As leader, place a candle on the chosen locations.*
> *Name the countries or areas if appropriate.*
>
> There's been *an earthquake [or other disaster]*
> here. *As leader, place a candle.*
> There are people who *have no homes* here. *As leader, place a candle.*
> There are people who need our prayers all over the world.

As we sing again, let's put our lights on the world.
You can put your little light anywhere you like.
Let's ask God to hear our lights as prayers for the world.

Hum the tune together, with the words 'Jesus, hear our prayer!' as a refrain, as you lead the children in placing the candles on the map. We've found that asking the children to do this in age groups helps, as the older children tend to be more intent on finding a location than the others. We invite babies first, then nursery and reception children, then Year 1 and upwards (including the adults). Once all the children and adults who wish to place a candle have done so, end with the final verse of the 'Jesus, hear our prayer!' song.

Take our prayers:	**Jesus, hear our prayer!**
Hands together gently	*Open hands upwards to God*

Make them holy:	Jesus, hear our prayer!
Hands together gently	*Open hands upwards to God*
Make them beautiful:	**Jesus, hear our prayer!**
Hands together gently	*Open hands upwards to God*

Lord Jesus, hear our prayer! Amen.
Hands together gently, then open hands upwards to God.

Creative Response

> A range of simple starter ideas are provided for the children to choose from, including simple sensory responses that are also accessible to babies and toddlers.

Sharing God's Peace: Option 2

→ Song: 'Peace is flowing like a river' (traditional). Isaiah 66.12, NIV
→ Tune: Traditional. For a taster, see the Diddy Disciples website. For tips on teaching songs for the first time, see p. 215.

Hold one end of the peace cloth (see Guide, p. 231) and ask one of the older children or an adult to hold the other end. Start singing the Peace Song. As the children begin to gather, invite them to join in holding a small section of the cloth, raising and lowering it so it 'flows' like a river as you sing together.

Peace is flowing like a river,
flowing out through you and me.
Spreading out into the desert,
setting all the captives free.

> As the group is about to rejoin the adults for communion, we continue with the words of the Peace. This Peace Song and the Peace remain the same for every session.

The peace of the Lord be always with you.
Hold hands open to the children.

And also with you.
Invite the children to open their hands towards you.

Let's shake hands or hug each other
and say 'Peace be with you' as a sign of God's peace.
Lead the children in giving and receiving the Peace.

Tip

Immediately following this at St Peter's, we lead the children back to join the rest of the congregation to continue our worship with the Eucharistic Prayer. Some generous and faithful volunteers, including teenagers, return later to tidy the room.

Deciding what's right for your group

The three samples outlined on the previous pages are very different in character, as they've been chosen to suit very different situations and very different groups. Diddy Disciples provides lots of options within the Building Blocks so your group can decide what works best for your particular setting. We suggest you start small and simple and build gradually as your children and leaders become more familiar with the material. We also suggest that, where possible, your choices reflect the choices of your adult or all-age church, helping children (and parents and carers) to join up the dots. If you meet during a Sunday morning service, it's particularly helpful to build a session that reflects the shape of that service. In other words, if it's a Service of the Word, make your children's session into a Service of the Word, if it's a communion service, then build a communion service for your children (up to the Peace, at which you can rejoin the wider congregation to share communion together). If your church uses liturgical colours, then use liturgical colours; if your church has an informal prayer time, then have an informal prayer time, etc.

Starting Diddy Disciples for the first time

When starting Diddy Disciples for the first time with new children and leaders, please remember to take it easy! For the first three or four weeks, everything will take longer than you expect. As a leader you'll be having to remember and respond to lots of new things: how you use the space, what the tunes are, what comes next, etc. These will soon become second nature – a bit like riding a bike – but to begin with, it can seem a lot to take in.

The children will also not yet know what to expect: from their point of view, there'll be no pattern to the session and many or all of the words will be unknown. Imagine starting a brand new service where none of the congregation has ever attended before! In time, the rhythm and pattern of Diddy Disciples will allow both leaders and children to become more confident and fluent in using the material: it's then that the space to worship will begin to open up. In the meantime, it makes sense to cut the material right down and focus on a small number of Building Blocks, as illustrated in Sample 2 above. You can always add more Building Blocks (adding one at a time will help) once everyone has relaxed into the rhythm of your time together.

Similarly, Diddy Disciples provides a whole range of Creative Response starter ideas at the end of each unit. But, unless you're used to preparing for multiple activities, we would recommend providing just one or two options for the first couple of weeks – as well as free use of paper and crayons/pencils or an open-ended activity such as playdough or building bricks – while you find your rhythm. This may help to ease the transition while everything is still new.

DIDDY DISCIPLES: SEVEN PRINCIPLES

Before turning to the Diddy Disciples material itself, it's worth outlining seven important aspects that are key to understanding the material. However, if you prefer, you can turn straight to the material itself from p. 29 onwards.

1 Diddy Disciples celebrates movement

Diddy Disciples accepts and celebrates body language as the first language of many young children, as well as encouraging (in very small doses!) their use of words and stillness before God. Babies can become fluent in reading facial expressions from a very young age. Many babies love copying other people's expressions and gain a great deal from doing so. As children grow, they become increasingly confident and fluent in their body language, using their bodies to express themselves and their internal thoughts and feelings far more naturally and readily than through words. 'Having a go' and getting actively involved is a vital part of learning and developing for children. Diddy Disciples provides countless opportunities to worship God and tell Bible stories through movement. It celebrates contributions from children and babies through body movements, hand actions or facial expressions in all sorts of ways.

When children do offer verbal responses or contributions, this is wonderful! In accordance with Rebecca Nye and Godly Play,[1] Diddy Disciples stresses the importance of valuing and celebrating any contribution that a child might offer. Even if the words don't make complete sense to us at the moment – or their relevance is unclear from our point of view – the observations of children are to be celebrated. The fact that anyone feels able to let their voice be heard before God and God's people and is willing to risk a contribution is in itself a cause for celebration. And there is often much that we have to learn from the youngest of children about God and how God sees the world. The speech of young children can often be like the tip of an iceberg: much more can be going on beneath the surface than we could ever imagine. For these reasons – and many more – we aim to respond to children's verbal contributions as we would to a colleague or leader in the church. Instead of 'Well done!' or 'That's right!' we tend to say 'Thank you!' or another response we might also offer an adult who has led or contributed.

2 Diddy Disciples celebrates repetition: 'Again! Again!'

Finding a pattern and rhythm is key to Diddy Disciples. It's for this reason we recommend that you keep the structure of your session the same for a whole unit, no matter which Building Blocks and options you choose.

- A clear, familiar pattern begins to give children the confidence to take part fully and join in, rather than having to wait or watch because they're not sure what's happening next.

- A familiar pattern creates opportunities for children to lead. Even very young children can be invited to take part in making shapes with ribbons or scarves, or making up actions for the songs or stories. It may be as simple as asking a child to lead the group in smiling, or (if they're very shy!) in putting their hands over their eyes.

- Repeating words and songs can help children who aren't fluent in English (whether due to their age, the fact that English isn't their first language, or because they have special needs). It can help them to start making sense of the shape of the sounds they hear, as they have a repeated chance to match them with the movements they see, the music, and their overall experience of the worship.

- Returning to certain words, actions, symbols and themes, week after week, gives all children the opportunity to build up layers of understanding. It can help children begin to appreciate that some words – perhaps especially words that are used of God – contain lots of different meanings that are interesting and meaningful to discover.

- A familiar pattern takes the pressure off the person leading worship. Leading Diddy Disciples for the first few times can feel challenging. Once you're in the rhythm, however, it is liberating to know that almost all of the next week's worship will be familiar.

- Clear expectations and boundaries can really help with behaviour management. Diddy Disciples moves between periods of movement and (short) periods of silence and calm. As the children become familiar with this, it becomes much easier for them to remain quiet for a short time when appropriate.

3 Diddy Disciples celebrates our voices

Singing plays an important role in Diddy Disciples worship. Almost all the songs are based on well-known tunes, either from church settings or nursery rhymes. Don't worry as a leader about whether you feel you're a good singer or not. This kind of singing is just to get the group started: it's more like singing along with the hymns at church, or singing to your child at home, than giving a performance.

Diddy Disciples encourages singing in worship for all sorts of reasons:

- Singing is something we do together: it gives the children an opportunity to feel what it's like to be part of God's family.

- Singing uses words but isn't completely dependent on words. Songs can provide all sorts of clues to help with meanings: through the shape of the tune, rhymes, rhythm, pitch and volume, as well as through movement and actions. Young children can be really good at picking up on these clues even when they're not fluent in speaking English.

- Repetitive songs give children a chance to join in with the words, without needing to read.

- Singing tends to attract and keep children's attention far more easily than words alone.

- Singing encourages us to bring body and soul together and can help us tune into our feelings before God. It can be a spiritual experience, lifting our focus beyond ourselves and opening us up to God.

In all these ways, singing enables babies and children, even the very youngest, to join in worshipping God at a level that is appropriate to them: from listening and swaying, through moving and dancing, to joining in with the actions and even with some of the words.

> Thomas (aged six) has autism. His favourite moment during our session at school is when we begin to sing our Closing Song, 'This little light of mine'. Thomas doesn't tend to talk much in or out of worship, but he knows 'This little light of mine' and joins in joyfully and in full voice every week. Whenever he sees me enter the classroom he breaks into song and waves his finger in the air to show his 'little light', and his face lights up to match. Any mention of 'light' during the session will also prompt him to begin to sing as he leads the whole group in making the connection between the 'light' in the storytelling and the 'light' that we'll sing about at the end of our session.

4 Diddy Disciples celebrates children's spirituality

Diddy Disciples is strongly influenced by Rebecca Nye's work on children's spirituality (a very accessible must-read for anyone working with children).[2] Diddy Disciples takes seriously research indicating that children have a sense of God and spirituality from before birth, as well as those biblical stories which speak of our relationship with God from inside the womb. We believe it's the Church's responsibility to try to make connections with and nurture children's already-present spirituality, rather than to attempt to build spirituality from scratch. Imagination is one place in which children's spirituality can be witnessed, shared and nurtured. For this reason, there is a strong ethos of fostering imagination throughout the material in all sorts of ways.

> 'Jesus said: "Truly I tell you, unless you change and become like children, you will never enter the kingdom of heaven."' (MATTHEW 18.3)

5 Diddy Disciples celebrates being part of the Church

At St Peter's, Walworth, we wanted church, not an alternative to church, for young children and babies. We see our babies and children as full members of our worshipping community: they are disciples too, albeit little disciples, 'Diddy Disciples'. We wanted material that was not only designed for young children but would help them understand and take part in our other services in church, that would help them to join up the dots between their sessions and the worship of the Church as a whole. In the words of Rebecca Nye, we wanted to be part of building 'two-way bridges between the child's spiritual insights and the traditional spiritual language of the church'.[3] It was also very important for us to recognize that Diddy Disciples was the weekly worship of many adults (whether as leaders or parents or carers of small children). For these reasons, a distinct feature of Diddy Disciples is the consistent attempt to make lots of connections with the kind of language that we hear in church. Some of this language can be poetic in feel, although it is tailored for very young children. It felt important to us to recognize that babies and young children can appreciate and enjoy language as poetic and beautiful from the youngest age (just think of the number of picture books in poetic form there are for young children).

For groups who wish to avoid 'churchy' language entirely, there are alternative options available in Diddy Disciples. But for churches that use *Common Worship* or BCP 2004 (Church of Ireland) – and hope that their children will be able to join in at a main church service as well as taking part in their children's session – there are a whole host of ways to encourage connections. Diddy Disciples offers children and babies the opportunity to experience and learn the rhythm of the Church's worship from the very youngest age: to appreciate that there are times of joy and singing; times to lead, and times to be led; times to take turns; times of quiet and internal reflection; times of bustle and activity. To put it another way, Diddy Disciples is not *playing* at being church, it is *being* the Church. For this reason, Diddy Disciples also provides children and babies with plenty of opportunities to lead. At St Peter's, it has been important for us to provide a space where babies and young children can not only take part fully, but also discover their own ministries and what they have to give. We've found that we've learned an enormous amount from these children and their insights over the years.

> **Tip**
>
> For churches that hold all-age services, it's worth noting that it's possible to borrow elements from Diddy Disciples for all-age worship.

6 Diddy Disciples celebrates learning

Diddy Disciples grew from the realization of just how important the first six years of a person's life are for shaping that person. From the very beginning, we wanted to lay foundations that would help to build up a people of God who naturally bring their life with God into their home life and work, and their home life and work into their life with God. We wanted to develop an approach that would help young children make connections between what happens in their sessions and what happens at home, school or nursery. For this reason, Diddy Disciples makes lots of links with the kinds of things that babies and young children learn in their daily lives: for instance, counting out loud, noticing different kinds of weather, and exploring the different kinds of emotions that we can feel. There are also options within the Creative Responses which encourage the children to make connections between their Bible storytelling and the kinds of things they may be learning about science, geography, maths or reading. In this way, while Diddy Disciples is about accepting children (and adults!) as they are and in no way sees worship as just another 'learning exercise' or a 'school', it recognizes that learning is a fundamental and important part of babies' and young children's lives and tries to help children make connections between their experiences of learning and their life with God.

7 Diddy Disciples celebrates our feelings and emotions

God created humans with a wide range of emotions and feelings. In the Bible, all human emotions are explored openly, and Diddy Disciples aims to follows this biblical lead. In the book of Psalms, the singers repeatedly bring feelings of anger, revenge, jealousy, hopelessness and self-hatred before God as well as their joy, praise, love, hope and thankfulness. In countless Bible stories, emotions that can be seen as negative are brought before God and transformed. To give just one example, Moses' deep anger – expressed in murderous rage – is seen by God, transformed, and used as a catalyst to set God's people free (see *Diddy Disciples: January to August*). One of my favourite moments at St Peter's each year is our telling of the story of Jesus cleansing the Temple in Lent, when the children encounter holy anger in its proper place as we're told, 'Let's all look angry like Jesus! . . . Now, really angry!' Diddy Disciples takes the examples set by the Bible seriously and aims to build a people of God who are comfortable and experienced in bringing all sorts of feelings before God, in hope and trust, ready to see even negative emotions transformed by God into something beautiful, holy and life-giving.

Early childhood is a wonderful place to begin this way of life. Young children are at a stage where they're exploring their own emotions and can sometimes be startled by the depth and complexity of those emotions. Diddy Disciples aims to open up lots of opportunities to explore all sorts of different emotions and feelings in a safe place. It hopes to create a space where children experience their negative emotions being seen, named, forgiven, and transformed by God. This aspect of Diddy Disciples is evident throughout the material, especially in the 'Interactive Bible Storytelling' and 'Saying Sorry to God' Building Blocks. For further discussion of this theme, see the Saying Sorry section in the Guide below (p. 223).

Part 2
The Diddy Disciples units
(September to December)

UNIT 1
JESUS' WONDERFUL LOVE (GREEN TIME)

The Jesus' Wonderful Love unit invites young children to take part in telling Jesus' parables about God's love for us, as well as exploring Jesus' command that his followers share that love with others.

Within this unit there are also plenty of opportunities to explore a range of emotions such as feeling lost, scared, sorry, found, lonely, treasured, guilty, surprised and joyful, and to bring these emotions before God.

> For Jesus' parables about the kingdom of God, see *Diddy Disciples: January to August*.

Section 1

The Building Blocks, Jesus' Wonderful Love unit

Pick and choose from these Building Blocks and their various options to build sessions for your group. Whatever choices you make, we suggest you keep to that pattern for the whole of the unit, as this will open up opportunities for the children to participate fully and confidently during your time together.

> **Build your own Diddy Disciples session** (p. 6) provides an overview of the Building Blocks and a short introduction to fitting them together, along with examples.
>
> **A Guide to the Building Blocks** (p. 217) provides a step-by-step guide to each Building Block.

Welcome

→ **Guide: p. 217**

Welcome your group.

Let's start by going round the circle
and saying our name out loud.
My name's _____.

Go round the circle so that every adult and child has the chance to say his or her name (and introduce any dolls, teddies or toys). If any of the children don't want to say their name or aren't able to, you (or a parent or carer) could say it for them and wave.

It's time to sing our Welcome Song!

Welcome Song: Option 1

→ **Song: 'The Diddy Disciples welcome song'. Words © Sharon Moughtin-Mumby**
→ **Tune: 'Glory, glory, alleluia!' (traditional). For the music see p. 259, or for a taster see the Diddy Disciples website. For tips on teaching songs for the first time, see p. 215.**

Go around the circle the same way as above. See if you can remember each other's names and insert them into the song.

Welcome *Name 1* to *St Peter's**
Welcome *Name 2* to *St Peter's**
Welcome *Name 3* to *St Peter's**
You are welcome in the name of the Lord!

* Insert the name of your church or children's group, or sing 'our worship'.

Welcome Song: Option 2

→ **Song: 'You are welcome in the name of the Lord' (traditional).**
→ **Tune: Traditional. For the music see p. 262, or for a taster see the Diddy Disciples website. For tips on teaching songs for the first time, see p. 215.**

Let's wave with one hand. *Lead waving*
Then with our other hand. *Lead waving*
Then let's choose someone and show them God's 'glory'!
Move arms up and down in front of you with fingers wiggling, palms facing out, towards one person.
And someone else! *Repeat*
Then let's wave with both hands all around the circle.
Lead waving.

We're ready to sing!

You are welcome in the name of the Lord!
Wave with right hand to one person.
You are welcome in the name of the Lord!
Wave with left hand to another person.
I can see all over you the glory of the Lord,
Move arms up and down in front of you with fingers wiggling, palms facing out, towards one person and then another.
You are welcome in the name of the Lord!
Wave with both hands all around the circle.

DIDDY DISCIPLES • **PART 2**

UNIT 1 • JESUS' WONDERFUL LOVE

Section 1: The Building Blocks

Getting Ready to Worship

→ **Guide: p. 218**

Choose one of the following greetings according to which is familiar in your church. (If your church uses a different greeting, you could use that here instead.)

Getting Ready to Worship: Option 1

→ **Action: The sign of the cross. Words © Sharon Moughtin-Mumby**

Invite the children to make the sign of the cross slowly with you. As the children become more confident, invite a child to lead the action as the whole group says the words and makes the sign of the cross.

In my head,	*Touch head*
in my heart,	*Touch chest*
and all around me,	*Touch shoulders one by one*
Jesus is here.	*Open hands in front facing upwards*

Getting Ready to Worship: Option 2

→ **Action: 'The Lord be with you' (open hands)**

Let's start by clenching our hands together tightly.

Lead children in clenching fists and holding them tightly against your chest in a defensive posture.

When we close ourselves up like this,
it's hard to let anyone into our heart.
It's hard even to let God into our heart!

When we get ready to worship,
we show that we're open to God and to each other.

Open your hands out, facing up.

Can you show me your open hands?
We're ready to let God and each other in!

The Lord be with you.
Hold hands open to the children.

And also with you.
Invite the children to open their hands towards you.

:::: **Tip**

The first few times you introduce this call-and-response, you may find it helpful to say, for example:

> Now it's 'my turn' *point to self,* 'your turn' *leader's hands out to group*
> When I say 'The Lord be with you', *both hands to self*
> you say 'And also with you'
> *Hold hands open to the children.*

> The Lord be with you. *Both hands to self*
> **And also with you.** *Invite the children to open their hands towards you*
> *Repeat*

::::

Introducing the Unit

→ **Guide: p. 218**

Introducing the Unit: Option 1

Week 1
Starting this week, we're going to tell
some of the amazing stories that Jesus told.
Lots of these stories are about how much Jesus loves us.

Week 2 onwards
We're telling some of the amazing stories that Jesus told.
Lots of these stories are about how much Jesus loves us.

Introducing the Unit: Option 2

→ **Focus: the liturgical colour, green**

Who can tell us what colour season we're in now?
>   *If appropriate:* You may have seen it in church.

Invite a child to respond with the colour.

At the moment, we're in Green Time!
>   *If appropriate:* Let's all look out for green when we go back into church.
>   *Or:* Let's remember to look and see what colour we're in next time we go into church.

>   *Either:*
>   In Green Time, the Church grows like a tree or flower.
>   We're the Church, so we're going to be growing, too!

>   *Or:*
>   In Green Time, everything grows, including us!

Let's show how a tree grows.
Let's curl up into a ball like a seed.
Lead the children in curling up into a ball.

First, we need to put our roots down.
Let's show our roots with our fingers.
Lead the children in wiggling fingers.

We need to let our roots grow down deep.
Lead the children in wiggling fingers down.

Then after three, let a little shoot pop up.
1, 2, 3 . . . Pop!
Poke your hands up over your head like a little shoot.

Then start to grow up tall.
Gradually stand up, swaying like a growing stalk.

Taller and taller, onto our tiptoes . . .
Reach up with pointy hands and on tiptoes.

Let's turn our faces up towards the sun!
Then let our leaves or branches spread out wide.
Arms stretch slowly outwards.

Look at those beautiful trees and flowers!
In Green Time, the whole world grows.
I wonder how you'll grow this Green Time?

Can anyone remember what our seed did first to grow?

Invite responses from the children. If they need a clue, wiggle your fingers.

First we put our roots down!
Let's wiggle our finger roots. *Lead the children in wiggling fingers*
We're going put our roots down today
by telling a story about Jesus' wonderful love!
Let's get ready for our story by singing about Jesus' love.

Gathering Song

→ **Guide: p. 219**

Gathering Song: Option 1

→ **Song: 'Look how much Jesus loves me!' Words © Sharon Moughtin-Mumby**
→ **Tune: 'Here we go Looby Loo' (traditional). For a taster see the Diddy Disciples website.**

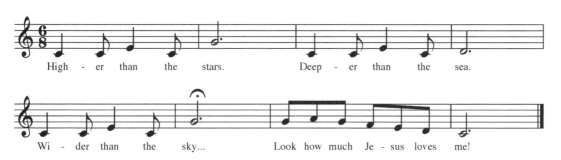

High - er than the stars. Deep - er than the sea.

Wi - der than the sky... Look how much Je - sus loves me!

If you're using imaginative aids, ask two or three children to give them out.

Let's show how much Jesus loves us
with our bodies!

::
Tip

If you're teaching this song for the first time, you may like to say these words 'my turn'/'your turn'. Once the children are familiar with the words, in following weeks they will probably join in with you as you say them.
::

If your group is using imaginative aids, encourage the children to use these in their actions throughout.

Let's stretch up as high as we can to the stars . . .
'Higher than the stars!'

Now down as low, low, low as we can . . .
'Deeper than the sea!'

And now let's stretch out as wide as we can . . .
'Wider than the sky!'

Let's make a big shape with our body!
Bigger! Even bigger!
'Look how much Jesus loves me!'

Let's sing our song about how much Jesus loves us.

Higher than the stars! *Stretch up on tiptoes and reach high with 'twinkle' hands*
Deeper than the sea! *Crouch down and reach low, rippling fingers like water*
Wider than the sky! . . . *Stand and stretch arms out*
You may find it helpful to pause at this point each time to remind the children to make a 'big shape' with their body: 'Big Shape!'
Look how much Jesus loves me! *Big shape*

Jesus doesn't just love us
when we're calm and well behaved!
Jesus loves us all the time!
Let's all be cross! Can you show me cross?

Lead the children in singing along while making their chosen facial expression and action. Example:
When I'm feeling cross, *Cross face and action*
When I'm feeling cross, *Cross face and action*
When I'm feeling cross . . . *Cross face and action*
Spoken: Big shape!
look how much Jesus loves me! *Big shape*

Repeat for different feelings, inviting the children to explore a range of positive and negative emotions. For example:
When I'm feeling happy . . .
When I'm feeling sad . . .
When I'm feeling surprised . . .
When I'm feeling scared . . .
When I'm feeling excited . . .
When I'm feeling lonely . . .
When I'm feeling poorly . . .

So many different feelings!
Yawn. I'm feeling tired after all that. Are you?
Can you show me tired?
Let's all go to sleep and sing again.
This time at the end we won't make our big shape.
Let's fall fast asleep instead . . .

When I'm feeling tired,
When I'm feeling tired,
When I'm feeling tired,
Look how much Jesus loves me! *Yawn*

Sing more reflectively while still miming falling asleep. Slow down towards the end as if going to sleep at night.

Higher than the stars!
Deeper than the sea!
Wider than the sky!
Look how much Jesus loves me . . .

End with a moment of sleepy silence.

Gathering Song: Option 2

→ Song: 'Jesus' love is so wonderful!' Words © Sharon Moughtin-Mumby
→ Tune: 'The banana boat song (Day-O)' (traditional). For a taster see the Diddy Disciples website.

Begin by encouraging the group to whisper quietly.

Jesus' love is so wonderful . . .
Jesus' love is so wonderful . . .

If you're using imaginative aids, ask two or three children to give them out. Encourage the children to warm up their imaginations by exploring making different shapes with their aids. Invite some children, one at a time, to lead the group in making a shape or action. See p. 220 for examples of actions for scarves or ribbons, but don't limit the children's imagination to these:
What else could these be?

Once the children have finished warming up . . .

We need an action for our song!
What action could show Jesus' wonderful love?

Choose an action from those the children have demonstrated.

Let's sing our song together.

Add the tune to the words (the same as for the words 'Daylight come and me want to go home')
Jesus' love is so wonderful . . . *Children's action*
Jesus' love is so wonderful . . . *Children's action*

When you're ready, start with the verses. The children may join in with the whole song, or just sing the repeated 'Jesus' love is so wonderful!'

With the tune going down . . . (as for the words 'Come Mr Tally Man, tally me banana')
Deeper than the deep, de-ep, deep sea. *Move down slowly, swaying*
Jesus' love is so wonderful! *Children's action*

Deeper than the deep, de-ep, deep sea. *Move down slowly, swaying*
Jesus' love is so wonderful! *Children's action*

Love! Jesus lo-o-ves me! *Imitate fireworks (wave scarves or ribbons above your head quickly) or similar*
Jesus' love is so wonderful! *Children's action*
Love! Jesus lo-o-ves me! *Fireworks or similar*
Jesus' love is so wonderful! *Children's action*

With the tune going up . . . (as for the words 'Six foot, seven foot, eight foot bunch')
Higher than the stars up above me. *Reach up, swaying*
Jesus' love is so wonderful! *Children's action*
Higher than the stars up above me. *Reach up, swaying*
Jesus' love is so wonderful! *Children's action*

Love! Jesus lo-o-ves me! *Fireworks or similar*
Jesus' love is so wonderful! *Children's action*
Love! Jesus lo-o-ves me! *Fireworks or similar*
Jesus' love is so wonderful! *Children's action*

Repeat the verses as you like. You can even mix the verses together, aiming for the tune to go downwards for the 'deep sea' and upwards for the 'stars up above me'.

Getting Ready for Bible Storytelling

→ **Guide: p. 221**

Getting Ready for Bible Storytelling: Option 1

→ **Action: opening your group's box and naming this week's object**

See the beginning of the weekly storytelling material for ideas of items to place in your box. Invite one of the children to open the box.

What's in the box? *Ask the child to respond.*

Getting Ready for Bible Storytelling: Option 2

→ **Song: 'Jesus, open up my eyes'. Words © Sharon Moughtin-Mumby**
→ **Tune: 'Michael, row the boat ashore' (traditional). For the music, see p. 262, or for a taster see the Diddy Disciples website.**

It's time to open the Bible.
Let's get ready!
Let's take our thumb *Lead children in showing thumb*
and draw our cross on our eyes, *Draw cross*
and our lips, *Draw cross*
and our heart. *Draw cross*
Let's ask Jesus to help us get ready to listen out for God!

Jesus, open up my eyes. Alleluia!
Trace a cross between your eyes.
Jesus, open up my lips. Alleluia!
Trace a cross on your lips.
Jesus, open up my heart. Alleluia!
Trace a cross on your heart.
Jesus, help me hear your voice. Alleluia!
Cup your hands behind your ears.

Interactive Bible Storytelling

→ Guide: p. 221

See the Bible Storytelling material in Section 2 of this unit.

Saying Sorry to God

→ Guide: p. 223

Invite the children to sit in a circle for a moment of quiet.

Jesus loves us with a wonderful love!
But we don't always share that love with each other.
Let's say sorry for the times
we haven't loved like Jesus loves.
Let's sing our Sorry Song together.

Option 1

→ Song: 'The Diddy Disciples sorry song'. Words © Sharon Moughtin-Mumby
→ Tune: © Sharon Moughtin-Mumby. For the music see p. 259, or for a taster see the Diddy Disciples website. For tips on teaching songs for the first time, see p. 215. For a description of the 'I'm Sorry' and 'New Start' signs, see p. 225 or the website.

Let's put our hands on our head.
I wonder if there's anything we've thought this week
that we wish we hadn't thought?

Lead the children in placing your hands on head, singing.
With my hands on my head,
I remember the things I've thought today,
I remember the things I wish I'd thought a different way.

I'm sorry, I'm sorry, *Diddy Disciples 'I'm Sorry' sign (see p. 225).*
I wish I could start again. *Diddy Disciples 'New Start' sign (see p. 225).*
I'm sorry, I'm sorry, *'I'm Sorry' sign.*
I wish I could start again. *Repeat 'New Start' sign.*

Let's put our hands by our mouths.
I wonder if there's anything we've said this week
that we wish we hadn't said?

With hands by mouth, singing . . .

With my hands on my mouth,
I remember the things I've said today,
I remember the things I wish I'd said a different way.

Repeat 'I'm Sorry' and 'New Start' signs as above.
I'm sorry, I'm sorry,
I wish I could start again.
I'm sorry, I'm sorry,
I wish I could start again.

Let's cross our hands on our chest.
I wonder if there's anything we've done this week
that we wish we hadn't done.

With hands crossed on chest, singing . . .
With my hands on my chest,
I remember the things I've done today,
I remember the things I wish I'd done a different way.

Repeat 'I'm Sorry' and 'New Start' signs as above.
I'm sorry, I'm sorry,
I wish I could start again.
I'm sorry, I'm sorry,
I wish I could start again.

Continue with a Saying Sorry Action or move straight to God Gives Us a New Start below.

Option 2

→ Song: 'We need a new start'. Words © Sharon Moughtin-Mumby
→ Tune: Molly Malone (traditional). For the music see p. 259, or for a taster see the Diddy Disciples website. For tips on teaching songs for the first time, see p. 215. For a description of the 'I'm Sorry' and 'New Start' signs, see p. 225 or the website.

> **Tip**
>
> This song can be sung using 'we're sorry' as indicated, or as 'I'm sorry', adapting the material accordingly.

Let's put our hands on our head.
I wonder if there's anything we've thought this week
that we wish we hadn't thought?

Lead the children in placing your hands on head, singing.
For the things we have thou-ght
that we wish we'd not thou-ght,
we're sor-ry, we're sor-ry, *Diddy Disciples 'I'm Sorry' sign twice (see p. 225).*
we need a new start. *Diddy Disciples 'New Start' sign (see p. 225).*

Let's put our hands by our mouths.
I wonder if there's anything we've said this week
that we wish we hadn't said?

With hands by mouth, singing . . .
For the things we have sa-id
that we wish we'd not sa-id,
we're sor-ry, we're sor-ry, *'I'm Sorry' sign twice.*
we need a new start. *'New Start' sign.*

Let's cross our hands on our chest.
I wonder if there's anything we've done this week
that we wish we hadn't done.

With hands crossed on chest, singing . . .
For the things we have do-ne
that we wish we'd not do-ne,
we're sor-ry, we're sor-ry, *'I'm Sorry' sign twice.*
we need a new start. *'New Start' sign.*

Continue with a Saying Sorry Action or move straight to God Gives Us a New Start below.

Saying Sorry Action

→ **Guide: p. 223**

Saying Sorry Action: Option 1

→ Psalm 103.12
→ Action: crumpling a piece of paper to show how you feel when you're cross or sad and placing it in a basket

> ### Tip
>
> This action can be used during any unit at any time of year.

Invite two children to give out a piece of paper to everyone who would like one.

Name and *Name* are going to bring round some paper.
If you like, you can take a piece of paper
and hold it in the air
to show that there are things that you wish you hadn't done.

As the paper is given out, lead the group in either

> Option 1: *singing the 'I'm sorry' refrain, or*
> Option 2: *humming the first two lines of the 'We need a new start' song, followed by singing the refrain 'We're sorry, we're sorry, we need a new start'.*

Once all the children and adults who wish to take a piece of paper have done so:
When we do things that make God or other people sad,
it can make us feel sad and cross inside.
Let's crumple our paper up to show how we can feel
when we know we've made someone feel sad.
Let's put our feelings into the paper.

Lead the children in crumpling your paper to show your feelings: crossly, with frustration, sadly, etc. For example:

I'm feeling cross with myself for making my friend feel sad.
I'm going to put my crossness into this paper.

Crumple the paper crossly.

Whatever we're feeling, we can give our feelings to God.
Name is going to bring this basket around.
If you like, you can put your paper in the basket
and give it to God.

While all the children and adults who wish to place their paper in the basket do so, lead the group in either:

> Option 1: *singing the 'I'm sorry' refrain, or*
> Option 2: *humming the first two lines of the 'We need a new start' song, followed by singing the refrain 'We're sorry, we're sorry, we need a new start'*

Place the basket in the centre of the circle or on the focal table (see p. 217).
Continue with one of the New Start Actions on p. 43.

Saying Sorry Action: Option 2

→ **Action: crumpling a piece of paper with *other* people's feelings and placing it in a basket**

> ### Tip
>
> This action can be used during any unit at any time of year.

Invite two children to give out a piece of paper to everyone who would like one.

Name and *Name* are going to bring round some paper.
If you like, you can take a piece of paper
and hold it in the air
to show that there are things that you wish you hadn't done.

As the paper is given out, lead the group in either

> Option 1: singing the 'I'm sorry' refrain, or
> Option 2: humming the first two lines of the 'We need a new start' song followed by singing the refrain 'We're sorry, we're sorry, we need a new start'

Once all the children and adults who wish to take a piece of paper have done so . . .
Sometimes we can do things that make OTHER people sad.
Let's crumple our paper up to show
how we can make other people feel when we hurt them.
Let's put their feelings into the paper.

Lead the children in crumpling your paper with feelings: e.g. crossly with frustration, or gently with sadness, etc.

We can do things that hurt other people.
The Good News is:
we can give the hurtful things we've done to God
and God will give us a new start.
Name is going to bring this basket around.
If you like, you can put your paper in the basket
and give it to God.
Let's ask God for a new start.

While all the children and adults who wish to place their paper in the basket do so, lead the group in either:

> Option 1: singing the 'I'm sorry' refrain, or
> Option 2: humming the first two lines of the 'We need a new start' song followed by singing the refrain 'We're sorry, we're sorry, we need a new start'

Place the basket in the centre of the circle or on the focal table (p. 217).

We've said sorry to God.
I wonder if there's anyone else you need to say sorry to this week?

Continue with one of the New Start Actions on p. 43.

Saying Sorry Action: Option 3

→ **Micah 7.19; Psalm 38.4; Hebrews 12.1; Matthew 11.28**
→ **Action: placing a pebble on a piece of fabric or in a bowl of water**

DIDDY DISCIPLES • **PART 2**

UNIT 1 • JESUS' WONDERFUL LOVE

Section 1: The Building Blocks

> ## Tip
>
> This action can be used during any unit at any time of year.
>
> Make sure the pebbles are large enough not to present a choking hazard and that this action is appropriate for your current group. When we began Diddy Disciples at St Peter's, Walworth, we couldn't use pebbles in case they were thrown. As the group have got more used to using objects during our prayers, we have used pebbles without any problems or distractions, but every group is different.

Invite two children to take around two baskets of pebbles to everyone who would like one.

Name and *Name* are going to bring round some pebbles.
If you like, you can take a pebble
and hold it in the air
to show there are things you wish you hadn't done.

As the pebbles are given out, lead the group in either:

> *Option 1: singing the 'I'm sorry' refrain, or*
> *Option 2: humming the first two lines of the 'We need a new start' song followed by singing the refrain 'We're sorry, we're sorry, we need a new start'*

Once all the children and adults who wish to take a pebble have done so:

Let's hold our pebble in our hand.
Lead the children in weighing the pebble in their hand.

When we do things that make God or other people sad,
it can make us feel heavy and weighed down inside
like this pebble weighs our hand down.
When we're feeling sad and heavy,
we can give our feelings to God.

Place a basket, a piece of fabric, or a bowl of water in the centre of the circle and invite the children to place their pebble within it. Or ask two children to take baskets around the circle to collect the pebbles.

> *If your group is using water, make sure it's in a container that is deep and transparent, so the children can see their pebbles sinking:*
>
> The Bible says:
> God will sink all our wrong things
> to the bottom of the sea!
> Let's put our pebbles in gently
> and watch them sink to the bottom.
> Let's imagine God sinking the wrong things we've done
> to the bottom of the sea.

Let's give our sad and heavy feelings
to God now as we sing.

While all the children and adults who wish to place their pebbles do so, lead the group in either:

> *Option 1: singing the 'I'm sorry' refrain, or*
> *Option 2: humming the first two lines of the 'We need a new start' song followed by singing the refrain 'We're sorry, we're sorry, we need a new start'*

The Good News is:
God always wants to give us a new start!

God doesn't want us to carry round
things that make us feel sad and heavy!
God takes them from us!
After three, let's jump up high
and shout 'God gives me a new start!'

1, 2, 3 . . . God gives me a new start!

Let's use our new start to share God's love this week!

Saying Sorry Action: Option 4

→ **Action: scribbling on a whiteboard/chalkboard then wiping it clean**

> **Tip**
>
> This action can be used during any unit at any time of year.

Place a single collective whiteboard/chalkboard in the centre of the circle, or ask one or more children to distribute individual smaller whiteboards/blackboards. Ask two more children to take around chalk/pens and a piece of kitchen roll to give to each child as you sing.

> **Tip**
>
> At St Peter's, Walworth, we found packs of four A4 sheets of 'Blackboard Paper' in a pound shop that we then guillotined into four smaller sheets. These worked well with a piece of white chalk, and each child was able to rub their markings off with a small (dry) piece of kitchen roll.

We all make bad choices sometimes.
When we make bad choices,
it can feel like we've made a big mess.
Let's scribble on our board
to show the mess we can make of things.

While the children and adults scribble, lead the group in either:

> *Option 1: singing the 'I'm sorry' refrain, or*
> *Option 2: humming the first two lines of the 'We need a new start' song followed by singing the refrain 'We're sorry, we're sorry, we need a new start'*

Once all the children and adults have had the chance to scribble:
Look at that mess!
Bad choices can make everything feel messy
and all tangled up.
If we all make bad choices,
the whole world can feel messy!
The Good News is:
God always wants to give us a new start!
Let's be God, and wipe our scribble away!

Lead the children in wiping away their scribble and drawing a smile on their board. If you're using a collective board, invite one or more children to wipe out the scribble on behalf of the group; then invite another child to draw a smile on the board.

Now let's draw a big smile . . .
and after three say 'God gives me/us a new start!'

1, 2, 3 . . . God gives me/us a new start!

Let's use our new start to share God's love this week!

God Gives Us a New Start

→ 2 Corinthians 5.17
→ Guide: p. 226

Every Saying Sorry time should end by assuring the children that God gives them a new start. Most Diddy Disciples Saying Sorry Actions already include this promise of a new start. If they don't – or if you've created your own Saying Sorry Action – you should choose one from the following New Start options, or create your own assurance of forgiveness. You could also choose to move straight from the Sorry Song to God's promise of a new start, without any Saying Sorry Action.

New Start Action: Option 1

→ 1 John 1.9; Psalm 147.11
→ Action: tracing a cross/smile on each other's forehead

The Good News is:
God always wants to give us a new start!
Let's turn to the person next to us
and show that God gives them a new start.
Let's take our thumb/finger *Show thumb/finger*
And draw a cross/smile on their forehead *Draw a cross/smile in the air*

> *If your group is drawing a smile, add:*
> to show that God is very happy with them!

Let's say 'God gives you a new start!'
Then let them give you a new start, too!

When the group has finished drawing a cross or smile to show each other God's new starts:

Let's use our new start to share God's love this week!

New Start Action: Option 2

→ Psalm 145.14; Luke 15.20
→ Action: standing up and hugging each other

The Good News is:
God always wants to give us a new start!
Let's help someone next to us stand up from the floor.
Then let them help you stand up too!

Lead the children in helping each other stand up.

Then let's give each other a hug and say:
'God gives you a new start!'

When the group has finished showing each other God's new starts:

Let's use our new start to share God's love this week!

New Start Action: Option 3

→ Song: 'God loves to give me a new start!' Words © Sharon Moughtin-Mumby
→ Tune: 'Give me oil in my lamp' (traditional). For the music see p. 260, or for a taster see the Diddy Disciples website. For tips on teaching songs for the first time, see p. 215

The Good News is:
God always wants to give us a new start!
Let's sing our New Start song together.

[Yes, my] God loves to give me a new start! *Trace a smile/cross on your own forehead*
How amazing is God's love for me! *Cross hands on your chest*
[Yes, my] God loves to give me a new start! *Trace a smile/cross on your own forehead*
How amazing is God's love for me!

Sing hosanna! Sing hosanna! *Wave hands in the air*
Sing hosanna to the King of kings!
Wave hands in the air followed by placing an imaginary crown on your head.
Sing hosanna! Sing hosanna! *Wave hands in the air*
Sing hosanna to the King!
Wave hands in the air followed by placing crown on head.

Introduction to Prayers

It's time for us to bring our prayers to Jesus, who loves us.

Prayers for Other People

→ **1 Timothy 2.1–2**
→ **Guide: p. 223 and p. 225**

Invite the children to sit in a circle for a moment of quiet.
Let's imagine holding our prayer gently,
Hands together gently in traditional prayer gesture, but cupped so you can imagine a prayer inside.
and then let it go up in prayer to God,
Hands opened upwards to God.

> *If you're using Option 1:*
> Jesus *Hands together, cupped*
> hear our prayer *Hands opened upwards to God*
> Let's pray . . .

Prayers for Other People: Option 1

→ **Ephesians 6.18; Jeremiah 29.7; Nehemiah 1.11**
→ **Song: 'Jesus, hear our prayer!' Words © Sharon Moughtin-Mumby**
→ **Tune: 'Brown girl in the ring' (traditional). For the music see p. 260, or for a taster see the Diddy Disciples website. For tips on teaching songs for the first time, see p. 215. For similar words designed to fit with the alternative tune 'He's got the whole world in his hands', see p. 261.**

For the world:	**Jesus, hear our prayer.**
Make a circle shape	*Open hands upwards to God*
For the Church:	**Jesus, hear our prayer.**
Praying hands	*Open hands upwards to God*
For our place, *Walworth**:	**Jesus, hear our prayer.**
Hands down moving out in	*Open hands upwards to God*
a semi-circle to indicate	
the place around us	

Lord Jesus, hear our prayer. Amen. *Open hands upwards to God*

* Insert the name of your local area/school/church/community/parish.

For the sick and lonely:	**Jesus, hear our prayer.**
Fingers showing tears falling	*Open hands upwards to God*
down cheeks	
For our friends and family:	**Jesus, hear our prayer.**
Arms around yourself	*Open hands upwards to God*
For ourselves:	**Jesus, hear our prayer.**
Both hands on heart	*Open hands upwards to God*

Lord Jesus, hear our prayer. Amen.
Open hands upwards to God.

Let's close our eyes for a moment.
I wonder if there's someone special

you'd like to pray for?
Let's imagine them now.

Let's imagine Jesus coming to them.
Does Jesus say anything?
Does Jesus do anything?

Let's open our eyes.

Continue with one of the Prayer Action options outlined below. Once the Prayer Action has been completed, you may like to use the following verse to close this time of prayer.

Take our prayers:	**Jesus, hear our prayer.**
Hands together gently	*Open hands upwards to God*
Make them holy:	**Jesus, hear our prayer.**
Hands together gently	*Open hands upwards to God*
Make them beautiful:	**Jesus, hear our prayer.**
Hands together gently	*Open hands upwards to God*

Lord Jesus, hear our prayer! Amen.
Hands together gently, then open hands upwards to God.

Prayers for Other People: Option 1b

→ Song: 'Jesus, hear our prayer!' alternative words. Words © Sharon Moughtin-Mumby
→ Tune: 'He's got the whole world' (traditional). For the music see p. 261, or for a taster see the Diddy Disciples website. For tips on teaching songs for the first time, see p. 215.

For the world and all people:	**Hear our prayer.**
Make a circle shape	*Open hands upwards to God*
For all Christians in all places:	**Hear our prayer.**
Praying hands	*Open hands upwards to God*
For the place that we live in:	**Hear our prayer.**
Hands down, moving out in a semi-circle to indicate the place around us	*Open hands upwards to God*

Lo-rd Jesus, hear our prayer.
Open hands upwards to God

For the sick and the lonely:	**Hear our prayer.**
Fingers showing tears falling down cheeks	*Open hands upwards to God*
For our friends and our family:	**Hear our prayer.**
Arms around yourself	*Open hands upwards to God*
Fo-r me and my life:	**Hear our prayer.**
Both hands on heart	*Open hands upwards to God*

Lord Jesus, hear our prayer.
Open hands upwards to God

Let's all close our eyes for a moment.
I wonder if there is someone special
you'd like to pray for?
Let's imagine them now.

Now, let's imagine Jesus coming to them.
Does Jesus say anything?
Does Jesus do anything?
Let's open our eyes.

Continue with one of the Prayer Action options outlined below. For this alternative tune, amend 'Jesus, hear our prayer!' to 'Hear our prayer!' in the refrain sung during the action. Once the Prayer Action has been completed, you may like to use the following verse to close this time of prayer.

Jesus, take our prayers.	**Hear our prayer.**
Hands together gently	*Open hands upwards to God*
Jesus, make them holy.	**Hear our prayer.**
Hands together gently	*Open hands upwards to God*
Jesus, make them lovely.	**Hear our prayer.**
Hands together gently	*Open hands upwards to God*
Lord Jesus:	**Hear our prayer.**
Hands together gently	*Open hands upwards to God*

Prayers for Other People: Option 2

→ Philippians 4.6
→ Song: 'The Diddy Disciples little prayers song'. Words © Sharon Moughtin-Mumby
→ Tune: 'Frère Jacques' (traditional). For the music see p. 258, or for a taster see the Diddy Disciples website. For tips on teaching songs for the first time, see p. 215.

These prayers are especially suited to churches that prefer less traditional prayer forms.

> *Either: choose what you'd like the group to pray for before the session.*
> *Or: ask the children at this point if there is anything or anyone that they'd like to pray for.*

Ask the children to suggest actions for the prayers. You will need two different 'thank you' suggestions and two different 'hear our prayer' suggestions. Try to encourage the offering of at least one prayer for people outside the group.

Invite the children to sing after you, repeating your words and their actions. Sometimes it might be almost impossible to fit the child's own words in! But it's really valuable to do so where possible, resisting the urge to try and 'tidy up' their suggestions. For example:

For *our foo-ood*,
For *our foo-ood*,
Thank you, God!
Thank you, God!

Fo-r *our teachers*,
Fo-r *our teachers*,
Thank you, God!
Thank you, God!

For *Nancy's Nanny*,
For *Nancy's Nanny*,
Hear our prayer!
Hear our prayer!

Fo-r *people with no homes*,
Fo-r *people with no homes*,
Hear our prayer!
Hear our prayer!

At this point, you could insert a Prayer Action, repeat the process, or move straight on to close with the following (or other words that remain the same each week).

For toda-ay,	*Point hands down for 'now'*
For toda-ay,	*Point hands down for 'now'*
Thank you, God!	*Open hands upwards to God or hands together in prayer*
Thank you, God!	*Open hands upwards to God or hands together in prayer*
Fo-r yo-ur lo-ve,	*Cross hands on chest*
Fo-r yo-ur lo-ve,	*Cross hands on chest*
Thank you, God!	*Open hands upwards to God or hands together in prayer*
Thank you, God!	*Open hands upwards to God or hands together in prayer*

Prayer Actions

→ **Guide: p. 223**

Prayer Action: Option 1

→ **1 John 4.11–12**
→ **Action: placing small paper or material hearts on a large central heart**

The small hearts can be any colour you like, but we recommend that they're all the same colour so that the children don't become distracted by having to choose. The hearts will be most visually effective if they're a different colour from the central heart.

Place a large paper or fabric heart in the centre of the circle.
Jesus loves everyone with a wonderful love.
When we pray, we can be part of
bringing Jesus' wonderful love to people.

Invite one or more children to bring round a basket of your hearts.
Name and *Name* are going to bring round some hearts now.
If you like, you can take one.
Let's ask God to see these hearts as a prayer for a special person.

Hum the tune together, with the words 'Jesus, hear our prayer!' as a refrain, until all the children and adults who wish to take a heart have done so.

When we pray for other people,
the love we show can become part of Jesus' wonderful love.
Let's add our heart prayers to Jesus' big heart.

Hum the tune together again while the group place their hearts. Larger groups may like to invite two children to carry the large heart around the circle to collect the children's hearts. This large heart can then be placed in the centre of the circle.

End this time of prayer with the final verse of the Prayer Song you've chosen.

Prayer Action: Option 2

→ **Jeremiah 31.12; Isaiah 35.1–2**
→ **Action: placing paper, fabric, wooden or real flowers in a 'garden'**

> ### Tip
>
> At St Peter's, Walworth, we use a tray filled with soil or with a brown cloth folded onto it for our 'garden'. We use daisies that we pick on the way to church as our flowers. We recommend that all the flowers offered to the children look the same so the children don't become distracted by having a choice. This action can be used during any unit at any time of year.

Show the children the flowers you have chosen in one or more baskets or trays.
Name and *Name* are going to bring round these baskets of flowers.
If you like, you can take a flower.
Let's ask God to see these flowers as a prayer for a special person.

Hum the tune together, with the words 'Jesus, hear our prayer!' as a refrain, until all the children and adults who wish to take a flower have done so. Place your 'garden' in the centre of the circle.

If you like, you can place your flower in our garden as a prayer.
As we pray, let's watch beautiful things
growing in our garden and in our lives.

Hum the tune together again while the group place their flowers. Larger groups may like to invite two children to carry the 'garden' around the circle to collect the children's flowers. This garden can then be placed in the centre of the circle.

End this time of prayer with the final verse of the Prayer Song you've chosen.

Prayer Action: Option 3

→ Isaiah 58.8; John 8.12
→ Action: placing candles (battery tealights) on a world map or piece of fabric

> **Tip**
>
> At St Peter's, Walworth, we've used a map jigsaw (which the children can also explore afterwards). At other times, we've used a laminated Peters World Map that shows the world in its proper proportions.
>
> We ask an adult to light the battery tealights in advance, as we've found younger children can be distracted by attempts to light the tealights themselves.

Show the children the lit battery tealights in one or more baskets or trays.

In a moment, *Name* and *Name*
are going to bring around these candles.
If you like, you could take one
and hold it gently in your hands like this.

Model to the children holding their tealight.

Imagine Jesus' love shining on you
and on a special person you're praying for.

Hum the tune together, with the words 'Jesus, hear our prayer!' as a refrain, until all the children and adults who wish to take tealights have done so. Then lay your fabric or map in the centre of the circle.

Jesus' love is like a beautiful light shining,
like these candles.
Our prayers can be part of sharing Jesus' light and love
with everyone around us.
As we sing, let's give our candles to God
and ask God to hear them as a prayer.

Hum the tune together, with the words 'Jesus, hear our prayer!' as a refrain, until all the children and adults who wish to place their tealights have done so. Some groups may like to invite two children to go around the circle in opposite directions with trays to collect the candles. These trays can then be placed in the centre of the circle. End this time of prayer with the final verse of the Prayer Song you've chosen.

Thank You, God

→ Ephesians 5.20
→ Guide: p. 227

Thank You, God: Option 1

→ Psalm 107.1; 1 John 4.7, 11–12
→ Song: 'My hands were made for love'. Words © Sharon Moughtin-Mumby
→ Tune: 'Hickory, dickory, dock' (traditional). For the music, see p. 262, or for a taster see the Diddy Disciples website. For tips on teaching songs for the first time, see p. 215.

Invite the children to sit in a circle for a moment of quiet.

It's time to remember all the things we've done this week.
It's time to say 'thank you' to God
for when we've been part of showing God's love.

Let's wiggle our fingers!
I wonder when you've shown love
with your hands this week?

Wiggle fingers as you sing.

My hands were made for love!
My hands were made for love!
Thank you for the love they've shown.
My hands were made for love!

Let's wiggle our feet!
I wonder when you've shown love
with your feet this week?

Wiggle feet as you sing.

My feet were made for love!
My feet were made for love!
Thank you for the love they've shown.
My feet were made for love!

Let's put our hands gently on our neck.
Let's sing 'Ahhh!'
Ahhhhh!
Can you feel your throat vibrating and dancing?
I wonder when you've shown love
with your voice this week?

Hold neck and feel your voice 'dancing' as you sing.

My voice was made for love!
My voice was made for love!
Thank you for the love it's shown.
My voice was made for love!

Thank You, God: Option 2

→ **Matthew 25.40**
→ **Song: 'For the love we've shown'. Words © Sharon Moughtin-Mumby**
→ **Tune: 'All through the night' (traditional). For the music see p. 259, or for a taster see the Diddy Disciples website. For tips on teaching songs for the first time, see p. 215.**

Most suitable for use with children over the age of four.

Invite the children to sit in a circle for a moment of quiet.

It's time to remember all the things we've done this week.
It's time to say 'thank you' to God
for when we've been part of showing God's love.

> *Either:* Let's wiggle our fingers.
> *Or:* Let's hold up our hands.

I wonder when you've shown love
with your hands this week?

> *Either:* Let's wiggle our feet.
> *Or:* Let's show our feet.

I wonder when you've shown love
with your feet this week?

Let's put our hands gently on our neck.
Let's sing 'Ahhh!'
Ahhhhh!
Can you feel your neck vibrating and dancing with your voice?
I wonder when you've shown love
with your voice this week?

Let's sing our 'thank you' song to God
for the times we've been part of sharing God's love.

For the love we've shown with our hands, *Hold hands up or wiggle fingers*
thank you, God!
For the love we've shown with our feet, *Point to feet or wiggle feet*
thank you, God!
When we love all those around us, *Cross hands on chest*
it's the same as loving Jesus!
For the love we've shown with our voice, *Hands on neck or point to singing mouth*
thank you, God!

Creative Response

→ **Guide: p. 228**

See the Creative Response starter ideas in Section 3 of this chapter.

Sharing God's Peace

→ **2 Thessalonians 3.16; Philippians 4.7**
→ **Guide: p. 231**

> This Building Block is particularly designed for children's groups that join the adult congregation to share communion, but it can also be used to end any session or Service of the Word.

Sharing God's Peace: Option 1

→ **Song: 'I've got peace like a river' (traditional). Isaiah 66.12, NIV**
→ **Tune: Traditional. For a taster, see the Diddy Disciples website. For tips on teaching songs for the first time, see p. 215.**

Either: Hold one end of the peace cloth (see Guide, p. 231) and ask one of the older children or an adult to hold the other end. Start singing the Peace Song. As the children begin to gather around the peace cloth, invite them to join in holding a small section of the cloth, raising and lowering it so it 'flows' like a river as you sing together.

Or: Invite the children to sit in a circle in the worship space. Start singing the Peace Song. As the children begin to gather, invite them to join in raising and lowering their hands like the waters of a flowing river.

I've got peace like a river,
I've got peace like a river,
I've got peace like a river in my soul.
I've got peace like a river,
I've got peace like a river,
I've got peace like a river in my soul.

As this unit has a strong focus on love, you may like to add the second verse:

I've got love like an ocean,
I've got love like an ocean,
I've got love like an ocean in my soul.
I've got love like an ocean,
I've got love like an ocean,
I've got love like an ocean in my soul.

If your group is about to rejoin the adults for communion, when all the children are gathered, continue with the words of the Peace following Option 3 below:

Sharing God's Peace: Option 2

→ Song: 'Peace is flowing like a river' (traditional). Isaiah 66.12, NIV
→ Tune: Traditional. For a taster, see the Diddy Disciples website. For tips on teaching songs for the first time, see p. 215.

Either: Hold one end of the peace cloth (see Guide, p. 231) and ask one of the older children or an adult to hold the other end. Start singing the Peace Song. As the children begin to gather, invite them to join in holding a small section of the cloth, raising and lowering it so it 'flows' like a river as you sing together.

Or: Invite the children to sit in a circle in the worship space. Start singing the Peace Song. As the children begin to gather, invite them to join in raising and lowering their hands like the waters of a flowing river.

Peace is flowing like a river,
flowing out through you and me.
Spreading out into the desert,
setting all the captives free.

As this unit has a strong focus on love, you may like to add the second verse:

Love is flowing like a river,
flowing out through you and me.
Spreading out into the desert,
setting all the captives free.

If your group is about to rejoin the adults for communion, when all the children are gathered, continue with the words of the Peace following Option 3 below:

Sharing God's Peace: Option 3

→ Song: 'I've got peace in my fingers' © 1995 Susan Salidor ASCAP
→ Tune: © 1995 Susan Salidor ASCAP
→ The words and music can be found on the album *Little Voices in My Head* by Susan Salidor, © 2003 Peach Head. They can also be found on iTunes, YouTube, or at www.susansalidor.com

Invite the children to sit in a circle in the worship space. Start singing the Peace Song. As the children begin to gather, invite them to join in with the song and actions. If your group is about to rejoin the adults for communion, when all the children are gathered, continue with the words of the Peace below:

The Peace

→ 2 Thessalonians 3.16; 1 Peter 5.14

Once you've finished singing:

The peace of the Lord be always with you.
Hold hands open to the children.

And also with you.
Invite the children to open their hands towards you.

Let's shake hands or hug each other
and say 'Peace be with you' *or whatever is said on sharing the Peace in your church* as a sign of God's peace.

Lead the children in giving and receiving the Peace. Immediately following this, at St Peter's, Walworth, we lead the children back to join the rest of the congregation to continue our worship with the Eucharistic Prayer.

Taking God's Love into the World

→ Matthew 5.14–16
→ Song: 'This little light of mine' (traditional)
→ Tune: Traditional. For a taster, see the Diddy Disciples website. For tips on teaching songs for the first time, see p. 215.
→ Guide: p. 232

This Building Block is particularly designed for standalone groups or groups that are held during a Service of the Word. Alternatively, you could use one of the Peace Songs above to end your worship.

Our time together is coming to an end.
Invite the children to sit in a circle for a moment of quiet.

God has lit a little light of love inside all of us.
Trace a circle on your heart.

Let's make our finger into a candle.
Bring your finger from your heart and hold it out.

Let's be God and light our little light of love together, after three.
Lead the children in lighting their finger candle by striking an imaginary match in the air on a count of three and pretending to light your finger.
1, 2, 3 . . . Tssss!

Let's imagine God's love shining and dancing like light in us.

Wave your finger in front of you as you sing:
This little light of mine, I'm gonna let it shine!
This little light of mine, I'm gonna let it shine!
This little light of mine, I'm gonna let it shine!
Let it shine, let it shine, let it shine!

Blow on your finger as if blowing out a candle on 'puff'. Then hold it up high.
Won't let no one *puff* **it out! I'm gonna let it shine!**
Won't let no one *puff* **it out! I'm gonna let it shine!**
Won't let no one *puff* **it out! I'm gonna let it shine!**
Let it shine, let it shine, let it shine!

Hold your finger behind a cupped hand, then take your cupped hand away to reveal the 'candle' and hold it high!
Hide it under a bushel? No! I'm gonna let it shine!
Hide it under a bushel? No! I'm gonna let it shine!
Hide it under a bushel? No! I'm gonna let it shine!
Let it shine, let it shine, let it shine!

Lead the children in placing your finger back on your heart.

Now let's put our little light of love
back in our hearts, where it belongs.
Let's remember to let our little light shine
in all our playing and working today . . .

If you're building a Service of the Word and this is your final Building Block, you may like to close with a familiar blessing, the Peace, and/or one of the following.

Either:	Praise the Lord!	*Both hands to self*
	Alleluia!	*Both arms upwards in 'V' shape*
Or:	Let us bless the Lord.	*Both hands to self*
	Thanks be to God.	*Both arms upwards in 'V' shape*
Or:	And all the people said . . .	*Both hands to self*
	Amen!	*Both arms upwards in 'V' shape*

Tip

The first few times you introduce this call-and-response, you may find it helpful to say, for example:

Now it's 'my turn' *point to self*, 'your turn' *leader's hands out to group*

When I say Praise the Lord', *both hands to self*
you say 'Alleluia!' *both arms upwards in 'V' shape*
Praise the Lord! *both hands to self*
Alleluia! *both arms upwards in 'V' shape*

Repeat.

Section 2

The Bible Storytelling material, Jesus' Wonderful Love unit

The Bible Storytelling Building Block is the focus of any Diddy Disciples session.

Week 1: The Lost Sheep

→ **Luke 15.3–7**
→ **Song: 'The lost sheep song'. Words © Sharon Moughtin-Mumby**
→ **Tune: 'Little Bo Peep' (traditional). For a taster, see the Diddy Disciples website.**

Search-ing and search - ing   ev - 'ry-where.   Rea - dy with my shep -herd's   crook. _

What is that mo - ving   o - ver there? Let's tip - toe and take   a   look!

If you're using the What's in the Box? option (p. 221): invite one of the children to open the box. Inside could be a a toy sheep, or a picture of a sheep.

What's in the box? *Ask the child to respond.*

All groups:
Today's story is all about a sheep and a shepherd.
What's a shepherd?

Invite one of the children to explain.

A shepherd is someone who looks after sheep.
To be a shepherd we need a crook! *Hold up imaginary crook*
A crook is like a big stick that shepherds use.
Can you pick your crook up and hold it?
Lead the children in picking up crook.

It's got a curly end *Indicate curly end*
to hook around the sheep's neck
and pull them away from danger.
Let's hook our sheep with our crook.
Lead the children in pretending to hook a sheep and pull it.

To tell our story we need to learn a song.
It goes like this.

Can you say these words after me?
'My turn' *point to self*, 'your turn' *leader's hands out to group*

Searching and searching everywhere. *Hand sheltering eyes, looking.*
Searching and searching everywhere. *Hand sheltering eyes, looking.*
Ready with my shepherd's crook. *Get ready to hook a sheep.*
Ready with my shepherd's crook. *Get ready to hook a sheep.*

Let's try those two lines with the tune . . .

Searching and searching everywhere. *Hand sheltering eyes, looking.*
Ready with my shepherd's crook. *Get ready to hook a sheep.*

Then 'my turn' *point to self*, 'your turn' *leader's hands out to group* again:
What is that moving over there? *Point in surprise*
What is that moving over there? *Point in surprise*
Let's tiptoe and take a look! *Tiptoe on the spot*
Let's tiptoe and take a look! *Tiptoe on the spot*

Then we all tiptoe on the spot.
Spoken in rhythm: tiptoe, tiptoe, tiptoe . . . *Tiptoe on the spot*

Let's try that all together.

Searching and searching everywhere.	*Hand sheltering eyes, looking*
Ready with my shepherd's crook.	*Get ready to hook a sheep*
What is that moving over there?	*Point in surprise*
Let's tiptoe and take a look!	*Tiptoe on the spot*
Spoken in rhythm: **tiptoe, tiptoe, tiptoe** . . .	*Tiptoe on the spot*

We're ready to tell Jesus' story:
There was a shepherd . . .
We're the shepherd and we have a hundred sheep!
We've counted all our sheep in groups of ten.
Now we need to count our last group of ten on our fingers.
Let's count together.
1, 2, 3, 4, 5, 6, 7, 8, 9 . . . *Count on fingers.*

Gasp. Where's the last sheep? It's gone!

Let's try counting the last ten again . . .
1, 2, 3, 4, 5, 6, 7, 8, 9 . . . *Count on fingers.*
Gasp. Oh no! The last sheep is gone!
The last sheep is a Lost Sheep!
What do we need to do?
We need to find the Lost Sheep!
Let's get up.
Let's pick up our shepherd's crook and let's go!

Searching and searching everywhere.	*Hand sheltering eyes, looking*
Ready with my shepherd's crook.	*Get ready to hook a sheep*
What is that moving over there?	*Point in surprise to a place in the circle*
Let's tiptoe and take a look!	*Tiptoe on the spot*
Spoken in rhythm: **tiptoe, tiptoe, tiptoe** . . .	*Tiptoe on the spot*

Do you think the sheep might be in this log pile?
Point to an imaginary log pile.

Let's have a look . . .
Lead the children in peering inside the imaginary log pile in front of them.

I can see . . .

a SNAKE!

Tsssss!! *Lead the children in making the action and sound of a snake.*

That's not my sheep! *Shake head and look surprised*

We need to keep on looking . . .

Searching and searching everywhere. *Hand sheltering eyes, looking*

Ready with my shepherd's crook. *Get ready to hook a sheep*

What is that moving over there? *Point in surprise to another part of the circle*

Let's tiptoe and take a look! *Tiptoe on the spot*

Spoken in rhythm: **tiptoe, tiptoe, tiptoe . . .** *Tiptoe on the spot*

Something's moving in that river! *Point to an imaginary river*

I hope the Lost Sheep hasn't fallen in!

Let's go and see.

Tiptoe, tiptoe, tiptoe . . . *On the spot.*

Lead the children in peering into an imaginary river in front of them.

I can see . . .

If the children interrupt you with their own idea of an animal, you could always use what they 'see' instead, here and elsewhere in the story.

a CROCODILE!

Snap! Snap! Snap!

Lead the children in making the action and sound of a crocodile.

That's not my sheep! *Shake head and look a bit scared.*

We need to keep on looking . . .

Searching and searching everywhere. *Hand sheltering eyes, looking*

Ready with my shepherd's crook. *Get ready to hook a sheep*

What is that moving over there? *Point in surprise to another part of the circle*

Let's tiptoe and take a look! *Tiptoe on the spot*

Spoken in rhythm: **tiptoe, tiptoe, tiptoe . . .** *Tiptoe on the spot*

Look! There's something moving in that tree over there.

Can sheep climb trees? *Look confused*

At least it won't be a crocodile.

Crocodiles can't climb trees!

Tiptoe, tiptoe, tiptoe . . . *On the spot*

Let's climb the tree . . . up and up and up . . .

Lead the children in climbing up into an imaginary tree then peering through the branches.

What do you think it is? . . .

I can see . . .

An OWL! *Or one of the children's choice of animals.*

Lead the children in making the action and sound of an owl, or the child's choice of other animal.

Twit twoo! Twit twoo! Twit twoo!

That's not my sheep! *Shake head*

We need to keep on looking . . .

Searching and searching everywhere. *Hand sheltering eyes, looking*

Ready with my shepherd's crook. *Get ready to hook a sheep*

What is that moving over there? *Point in surprise to another part of the circle*

Let's tiptoe and take a look! *Tiptoe on the spot*

Spoken in rhythm: **tiptoe, tiptoe, tiptoe . . .** *Tiptoe on the spot*

There's something moving in that tall grass.

Tiptoe, tiptoe, tiptoe . . . *On the spot*

Let's part the grass and look through it . . .
I can see . . . .
A LION! *Or a child's choice of animal*
Roar! Roar! Roar!

That's not my sheep! *Shake head*
We need to keep on looking . . .

This is getting a bit scary!

Searching and searching everywhere. *Hand sheltering eyes, looking*
Ready with my shepherd's crook. *Get ready to hook a sheep*
What is that moving over there? *Point in surprise to another part of the circle*
Let's tiptoe and take a look! *Tiptoe on the spot*
Spoken in rhythm: **tiptoe, tiptoe, tiptoe . . .** *Tiptoe on the spot.*

Can you see that dark cave over there? *Point*
Shall we go and have a look in there?
It's a bit scary! *Look scared*

Tiptoe, tiptoe, tiptoe . . .

I can see . . .
Sound as if it's hard to make out what it is.
Two black, blinking eyes . . .
A little white, waggly tail . . .
What do you think it is?

Accept the children's responses, but this time you will be finding the Lost Sheep, so continue with the following words:
Let's see . . .
It's the Lost Sheep!
We've found the Lost Sheep!
The shepherd picks up the Lost Sheep.
Let's pick it up ever so carefully.
The shepherd puts it gently on his shoulders.
Let's put the sheep on our shoulders, very, very gently.
Now let's carry it back safely to its flock and family.

Lead the children in tiptoeing on the spot, still carrying the sheep.

Back past the lion!
Roar! Roar! Roar!
Back past the owl!
Twit twoo! Twit twoo! Twit twoo!
Back past the crocodile!
Snap! Snap! Snap!
I don't like crocodiles!
Back past the snake!
Tssss! Tssss! Tssss!

At last, we're back home.
The Lost Sheep is a Found Sheep!
How do you think the little Lost Sheep feels?
Can you show me?
Shall we try counting the last ten sheep again on our fingers?

1, 2, 3, 4, 5, 6, 7, 8, 9, 10!

Ten sheep! How do you think the shepherd feels?
Can you show me?
Jesus said, That's how God feels when God finds you!
Joyful and happy!

Let's sit down for a moment and close our eyes.
I wonder whether you ever feel like the Lost Sheep?
Jesus said, even when you feel lost,
even when you feel like you're in a dark place,
Jesus will come searching for you.
Jesus will find you and carry you gently home.
Let's imagine Jesus coming to us now.
Let's imagine Jesus picking us up gently and carrying us home.

Invite the children to open their eyes again.

Can you show me again your face when you found the Lost Sheep?
That's how God feels when God finds you!

Week 2: The Lost Coin

→ Luke 15.8–10
→ Song: 'The lost coin song'. Words © Sharon Moughtin-Mumby
→ Tune: 'Oh dear! What can the matter be?' (traditional). For a taster, see the Diddy Disciples website.

To tell our story,
we need to learn a hunting song . . .
Can you say these words after me?
'My turn' *point to self*, 'your turn' *leader's hands out to group*

Spoken:

Oh dear! Where can my coin be? *Hands up in question*
Oh dear! Where can my coin be? *Hands up in question*
I'm turning my house upside down! *Diddy Disciples 'New Start' sign (see p. 225)*
I'm turning my house upside down! *'New Start' sign*

Let's try singing that together.

Oh dear! Where can my coin be? *Hands out in question*
Oh dear! Where can my coin be? *Hands out in question*
Oh dear! Where can my coin be? *Hands out in question*
I'm turning my house upside down! *'New Start' sign*

We're ready to tell Jesus' story.

> *If you're using the What's in the Box? option (p. 221), invite one of the children to open the box. Inside should be a coin made from a card circle covered in shiny tinfoil.*

> What's in the box? *Ask the child to respond.*

Today's story is about a coin like this.
This coin is so beautiful and shiny that it's part of a necklace,
it's a very special coin!
Let's tell the story together.

All groups:

There was a woman who had ten silver coins.

Let's imagine we have ten beautiful, shiny, silver coins.

Let's count them on our fingers.

1, 2, 3, 4, 5, 6, 7, 8, 9 . . .

Gasp. Where's the last coin?

There are only nine here!

Let's count them again.

1, 2, 3, 4, 5, 6, 7, 8, 9 . . .

Gasp. Oh no! One of them is lost!

The last coin is a Lost Coin!

What does the woman need to do?

Accept responses from the children.

Let's get up and be the woman hunting for her coin.

Let's light a lamp,

Lead the children in lighting an imaginary lamp.

Let's look in all the dark places of our house.

Ask the children to make up a lamp searching action.

Oh dear! Where can my coin be? *Lamp searching action*
Oh dear! Where can my coin be? *Lamp searching action*
Oh dear! Where can my coin be? *Lamp searching action*
I'm turning my house upside down! *'New Start' sign*

No coin!

All right, let's try sweeping all the floors, then maybe we'll find it.

Lead the children in sweeping the floor on the spot as you sing.

Oh dear! Where can my coin be? *Sweeping action*
Oh dear! Where can my coin be? *Sweeping action*
Oh dear! Where can my coin be? *Sweeping action*
I'm turning my house upside down! *'New Start' sign*

No coin! Right, that's it!

Let's make our lamp even brighter.

Lead the children in turning the lamp up to make it brighter.

Let's search carefully everywhere!

As you continue, lead the group in stretching upwards then bending downwards with hand shading eyes to search for the coin.

Let's look high . . .

And low . . .

And high . . .

And low . . .

Oh dear! Where can my coin be? *Search high then low*
Oh dear! Where can my coin be? *Search high then low*
Interrupt yourself.

Gasp. What's that? *Point to the ground*

In that dark corner over there?

It's shining! Let's see . . .

Lead the children in picking up the coin.

It's the Lost Coin! Look!

Hold the imaginary coin up joyfully. Invite the children to copy you.

We've found it!

How are you feeling now? Can you show me?

Let's count our coins again.

We have **1, 2, 3, 4, 5, 6, 7, 8, 9 . . . 10 coins!** *Joyfully!*

Let's sing again, but this time we're going to sing:

'Hooray, Hooray! I did it! I did it!

Hooray! Hooray! Hooray!'

Let's sing loud so all our friends and neighbours can hear!

Lead the children in singing and holding up the coin.

Hooray! Hooray! I did it! I did it!

Hooray! Hooray! I did it! I did it!

Hooray! Hooray! I did it! I did it!

Hooray! Hooray! Hooray!

Let's sit down for a moment.

Let's close our eyes.

Remember how you felt when you found that coin.

Jesus said that's how God feels when God finds you!

Happy and excited and full of joy!

Let's open our eyes.

So remember that feeling of joy

and keep it inside you. *Hand on chest*

We're going to sing 'Hooray! Hooray!' one more time.

We're going to be God: so excited to see us!

Let's stand up and sing so everyone can hear us.

Let's wave our hands in the air to celebrate!

Lead the children in singing and waving hands in the air:

Hooray! Hooray! I did it! I did it!

Hooray! Hooray! I did it! I did it!

Hooray! Hooray! I did it! I did it!

Hooray! Hooray! Hooray!

Week 3: The Lost Son

→ **Luke 15.11–24**

→ **Song:** 'The lost boy song'. Words © Sharon Moughtin-Mumby

→ **Tune:** 'If you're happy and you know it' (traditional). For a taster, see the Diddy Disciples website.

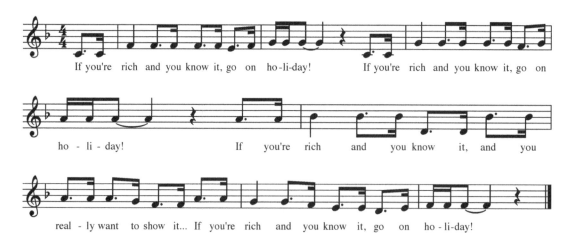

If you're rich and you know it, go on ho-li-day! If you're rich and you know it, go on ho-li-day! If you're rich and you know it, and you real-ly want to show it... If you're rich and you know it, go on ho-li-day!

If you're using the What's in the Box? option (p. 221), invite one of the children to open the box. Inside will be a picture of a child or a 'small world' child (a small plastic figure such as those from Happyland or Fisher Price, or a wooden or knitted figure).

What's in the box? *Ask the child to respond.*

Today's story is about a little boy.
Let's tell Jesus' story together.

Jesus said, 'There was a daddy with two boys.'
Let's count to two on our fingers:
1, 2.
The Littlest Boy was really bad at waiting!
Can you show me how you look when you're fed up of waiting?
Accept the children's responses.
Now show me really fed up of waiting!

The Littlest Boy was fed up of waiting to be rich.
He said to his daddy:
'I don't want to have to wait till you give me some money.
I want it NOW! Give it me NOW!'
Let's all count to three, then stamp our foot once
and shout 'Give it me now!' with our cross, waiting faces.
1, 2, 3, 'Give it me now!' *STAMP!*

If your group includes children who are unsettled by loud noises, you could teach the children how to 'air stamp', bringing your foot down as if to stamp, but stopping just short of the floor.

And, you know what?
The daddy did!
The daddy gave the Littlest Boy lots of money!
Let's hold all our money in a big sack in our hands!
Lead the children in each holding their own imaginary sack of money.

Let's look inside . . . we're rich!!!!
I wonder how the boy felt! Can you show me?
The Littlest Boy had a great time with his money!

First, he went on holiday! Who likes going on holiday?

Ask for an action for going on holiday.

Can you sing with me and use our action?
If you're rich and you know it, go on holiday!
If you're rich and you know it, go on holiday!
If you're rich and you know it,
and you really want to show it . . .
If you're rich and you know it, go on holiday!

Brilliant! Let's look in our money sack.
Lead the children in pretending to look in the sack.
Still lots of money!

Next, the Littlest Boy ate and drank all his favourite things.
Let's imagine that we have our favourite food and drink in our hands.
Mmmmm!

Ask for an action for eating and drinking.

Let's sing 'If you're rich and you know it, eat and drink'.
Use one of the children's actions for eating and drinking.
If you're rich and you know it, eat and drink!
If you're rich and you know it, eat and drink!
If you're rich and you know it,
and you really want to show it . . .
If you're rich and you know it, eat and drink!

This is fun! Let's look in our sack again.
Lead the children in pretending to look in a sack.

Still lots of money!
Who likes parties? Let's throw a party!

Ask the children to make up an action for giving a party and use it as you sing.
If you're rich and you know it, throw a party!
If you're rich and you know it, throw a party!
If you're rich and you know it,
and you really want to show it . . .
If you're rich and you know it, throw a party!

This is brilliant! What shall we do next?
Let's look in our sack.
Lead the children in pretending to look in a sack.

Oh no! There's no money left!
The Littlest Boy isn't rich any more.
The Littlest Boy is poor!
And he's far from home.
The Littlest Boy is a Lost Boy!

I wonder how the boy feels now. Can you show me?
We're going to sing 'If you're lost and you know it, shout "Help!"'

Ask the children for an action for 'Help!' and use it as you sing.
If you're lost and you know it, shout 'Help!'
If you're lost and you know it, shout 'Help!'
If you're lost and you know it,
and you really want to show it . . .
If you're lost and you know it, shout 'Help!'

But no one heard the Lost Boy. *Shake head*
And now he's hungry!
He needs some more money!
The Lost Boy looked and looked and looked.
Can you look around with me?
Lead the children looking around with your hand over your eyes.

At last, he found a job to make more money.
It was a job no one else wanted. Looking after pigs!
Let's be pigs! *Lead the children in pretending to be pigs*
Freeze!

Where the little boy came from
everyone thought pigs were dirty. *Pull a face*
Spending time with pigs made you dirty too.
But the Littlest Boy was a Lost Boy.
So he went to work with the pigs.
Let's sing 'If you're lost and you know it, clean the pigs!'

Lead the children in sweeping as you sing.
If you're lost and you know it, clean the pigs!
If you're lost and you know it, clean the pigs!
If you're lost and you know it,
and you really want to show it . . .
If you're lost and you know it, clean the pigs!

One day, the Lost Boy was really hungry. Can you show me hungry?
He looked at the pigs' food and thought, 'Maybe I should eat the pigs' food!'

Ask the children for an action for eating pigs' food.

Sing very hesitantly:
If you're lost and you know it, eat the pigs' food?!
STOP!

'No!' the Lost Boy said. *Shake head*
'I'm not going to eat pigs' food!
My daddy has lots of jobs for people.
Everyone who works for my daddy has food!
I'm going to go home and ask my daddy for a job.
I know I'm not his Littlest Boy any more, *Shake head*
but maybe I could work for him . . .'

So the Lost Boy walked all the way home.
Let's walk on the spot.
On the way, the Lost Boy thought about how sorry he was.
Let's walk home and sing 'If you're sorry and you know it, say sorry.'

If children in your group are familiar with Makaton sign actions, use the sign for 'sorry' (circling a closed fist on your chest).
Alternatively, take one hand to your mouth then remove it to show words coming from your mouth as you sing, or invite the
children to make up their own action for 'sorry'. Lead the children in making the chosen 'sorry' action as you sing.

If you're sorry and you know it, say sorry!
If you're sorry and you know it, say sorry!
If you're sorry and you know it,
and you really want to show it,
If you're sorry and you know it, say sorry!

Invite the children to sit down.

Back home, the Boy's daddy was looking out for him.
Let's be the daddy and look out with our hand shading our eyes.
We're waiting and waiting and waiting . . .
Then, one day . . . Look!
Point to the corner of the room.
It's the Lost Boy! He's coming!
What's the daddy going to do?
Rhetorical question, but if the children wish to respond, listen to their suggestions.

The daddy jumped up! *Jump up*
And ran!
After three, let's run on the spot.
1, 2, 3, run!
Freeze!
And he picked up his son in the biggest hug ever.
Can you show me a big hug in the air!
I wonder how the Lost Boy felt when his daddy hugged him?
Can you show me?

His daddy shouted, 'Let's have a party!'
And he threw the biggest party you can imagine.
Let's dance at the daddy's party!

Lead the children in continuing to dance as you sing.
If you're happy and you know it, throw a party!
If you're happy and you know it, throw a party!
If you're happy and you know it,
and you really want to show it,
If you're happy and you know it, throw a party!

Ask the children to sit for a moment of quiet.

How do you think the daddy felt when he hugged his Lost Boy?
Invite responses from the children.

Jesus said, 'The way that the daddy felt
when he hugged the Lost Boy
is the way that God feels when you come back to God.
Happy and excited and full of joy!'

Ask the children to close their eyes for a moment.

Sometimes we can feel a bit lost inside.
Sometimes we can feel like God is a long way away,
like the Lost Boy.
When we feel lost, let's remember that God is waiting for us.
God is waiting to run and hug us,
and to throw the biggest party ever!

Let's sing 'If you're happy and you know it, throw a party!' again.
This time, let's imagine God the Daddy is singing the song to us.
So happy and joyful that we're not Lost Girls and Boys any more:
we're Found Girls and Boys!
Let's dance as we sing!

If you're happy and you know it, throw a party!
If you're happy and you know it, throw a party!
If you're happy and you know it,
and you really want to show it,
If you're happy and you know it, throw a party!

Week 4: The Good Shepherd

→ **John 10.11–15**
→ **Song: 'The good shepherd song'. Words © Sharon Moughtin-Mumby**
→ **Tune: 'Mary had a little lamb' (traditional). For a taster, see the Diddy Disciples website. Alternatively, use the tune for 'Have you seen the muffin man?'**

If you're using the What's in the Box? option (p. 221), invite one of the children to open the box. Inside will be a picture of a sheep, or a toy sheep.

What's in the box? *Ask the child to respond.*

Today's story is about a little sheep.
Let's tell the story together.

To tell Jesus' story today we need to be sheep!
What do sheep say?

Can you say 'Baa, baa! Bleat! Baa, baa!'
Baa, baa! Bleat! Baa, baa! *Repeat*
Let's wiggle our tails to show we're sheep.

Can you say our sheep words and sound scared?
Don't forget to wiggle your tail to show how you're feeling!

Lead the children in sounding and looking scared as you repeat the words together, and likewise with the following emotions.
Baa, baa! Bleat! Baa, baa! *Scared*
And happy?
Baa, baa! Bleat! Baa, baa! *Happy*
And cross?
Baa, baa! Bleat! Baa, baa! *Cross*

We're ready to tell our story about a little flock of sheep.
This flock didn't have their own shepherd. *Shake head*
A different person came every day to look after them.
Let's sing 'We are all little sheep'.
Let's wiggle our tails like sheep as we sing.

We are a-ll little sheep, *Wiggle tails or other sheep action*
little sheep, little sheep!
We are a-ll little sheep!
Baa, baa! Bleat! Baa, baa!

But look! What's that over there?! *Point and look scared*
It's a wolf!
A big, bad wolf!
Hold your hands out like claws, ready to pounce.

How are you feeling?!
Can you show me?
How do you think the sheep will sound when they bleat now?
Shall we practise that together?
Baa, baa! Bleat! Baa, baa! *Sounding scared*

Let's sing and be the big bad wolf together. *Make as if ready to pounce*
Then we'll turn into the sheep for our scared baas at the end.

Hold your hands out like claws, ready to pounce on the word 'wolf'.
Let's sing 'Look! Here comes a big bad wolf!'
Lead the children in pouncing on the word 'wolf' as you sing.

Look! Here comes a big, bad wolf, *Pounce*
a big, bad wolf, *Pounce* **a big, bad wolf!** *Pounce*
Look! Here comes a big, bad wolf! *Pounce*
Baa, baa! Bleat! Baa, baa! *Sounding scared.*

It's all right. Our shepherd will help us . . .
But look! *Point*
Our shepherd's running away! *Shocked*
How are we feeling now with no shepherd? *Shake head*
The wolf can catch us!
We need to get away!!
After three, let's sing: 'The sheep they ran and ran and ran!'

And run on the spot like the sheep!
1, 2, 3 . . . Run!

Lead the children in running on the spot and singing.
The sheep, they ran and ran and ran,
ran and ran, ran and ran!
The sheep, they ran and ran and ran!
Baa, baa! Bleat! Baa, baa!

Let's sit down for a moment.
Oh dear! Poor sheep! That shepherd wasn't very good!

Jesus said, 'Then there was another flock of sheep.'
Let's be the other flock of sheep,
happily chewing our grass.
Now this flock has a GOOD Shepherd.
Our shepherd loves us!
Let's pretend that our hand is our shepherd's hand.
Let's stroke our arm like the shepherd stroking us.
How are you feeling?
Let's practise our baas now . . .

Baa, baa! Bleat! Baa, baa!
Let's sing 'we are all little sheep' and sound like that.

We are a-ll little sheep, *Waggle tails or other sheep action*
little sheep, little sheep!
We are a-ll little sheep!
Baa, baa! Bleat! Baa, baa!

But look! What do you think I can see?!
Hold your hands out like claws, ready to pounce on the word 'wolf'.

Give the children opportunity to respond, then go straight into . . .
Look! Here comes a big, bad wolf, *Pounce*
a big, bad wolf, *Pounce* **a big, bad wolf!** *Pounce*
Look! Here comes a big, bad wolf! *Pounce*
Baa, baa! Bleat! Baa, baa! *Sounding scared*

Oh no! What's the shepherd going to do?
Give the children opportunity to respond.

This shepherd is the Good Shepherd.
He won't run. *Shake head*
He won't leave us.
He'll keep us safe!

Let's stand up and be the Good Shepherd together.
Let's put our feet firmly on the ground: 1, 2 . . .
Lead the children in placing feet.
and fold our arms. *Lead the children in folding arms*
We're NEVER going to leave the sheep.
Let's sing 'I will never, never leave . . .'

I will never, never leave! *Shake head gently*
never leave, never leave!
I will never, never leave! *Shake head gently*
Baa, baa! Bleat! Baa, baa!

This time it was the wolf who ran off!
The sheep were safe!
After three, let's sing 'The wolf, it ran and ran and ran'

and be the wolf, running on the spot as fast as we can.
1, 2, 3 . . .

The wolf, it ran and ran and ran,
ran and ran, ran and ran!
The wolf, it ran and ran and ran! Wait! *Interrupt the singing*
How do you think the sheep will sound now?
The wolf has gone!
The sheep are safe!
Baa, baa! Bleat! Baa, baa!

Lead the children in repeating the joyful, calm, etc. singing of the sheep 2–3 times.

We're safe! The Good Shepherd will never leave us!
Let's sit down for a moment.
Jesus said, 'I am the Good Shepherd!'
You're my little sheep, my little lambs. *Point to the children.*
I love you and I will never leave you. *Shake head.*

Let's close our eyes for a moment.
Let's imagine Jesus coming to us.
Let's sing the Good Shepherd's song quietly:
'I will never, never leave!'
Let's imagine Jesus singing it to us.
Instead of singing our 'baas' at the end,
Let's sing 'thank you, thank you, Je-sus'.

I will never, never leave! *Shake head gently*
never leave, never leave!
I will never, never leave! *Shake head gently*
Thank you, thank you, Je-sus!

Repeat as appropriate.

Week 5: The Loving Stranger/The Good Samaritan

→ Luke 10.29–37
→ Song: 'Help me! Help me! Help me, please!' Words © Sharon Moughtin-Mumby
→ Tune: 'Ring a ring o' roses' (traditional). For a taster, see the Diddy Disciples website.

Tip

The Good Samaritan is an important but fairly complex story for young children, with four characters to keep track of. When you recap the story towards the end of this material, you may find it helpful to have four figures or body templates (see p. 264 or website) ready to represent the traveller and three passers-by as indicated.

If you're using the What's in the Box? option (p. 221), invite one of the children to open the box. Inside will be a heart shape.

What's in the box? *Ask the child to respond.*

All groups:

We've been telling stories about how much Jesus loves us.
Today's story is about how WE can show Jesus' love
to other people.
Can you put your hand up if you have a friend?
Let's close our eyes and imagine one of our friends giving us a hug now.

> *If there are babies and toddlers with parents or carers in your group:*
> Parents and carers, can you give your babies a big hug!

Let's open our eyes.
Can you show me how hugging your friend makes you feel?
EVERYONE knows we should love our friends.
But one day, someone asked Jesus a tricky question.
Can you say this question after me?

Who is my friend? *Hold hands out questioning*
Who is my friend? *Hold hands out questioning*

Let's say that again:
Who is my friend? *Hold hands out questioning*

Note on the translation 'friend':

In Luke 10.25–29 Jesus quotes Leviticus 19.18: 'You shall love your "neighbour" as yourself' (NRSV). The Hebrew word traditionally translated as 'neighbour' can also be translated as 'friend', 'fellow citizen' or 'companion'. We've used 'friend' as a more familiar concept for young children.

To answer the question, Jesus told a story.
Let's tell the story together.

A man went on a long journey, a long trip.
Let's be the man on a journey.

Lead the children in walking on the spot.

On the way some people hurt the man.
Let's sit down on the floor and hold our sore leg.
Lead the children in sitting down on the floor holding your leg.

They took all his money and left him very hurt.
Let's sing a song about feeling hurt.
Let's sing it 'my turn' *point to self* 'your turn' *leader's hands out to group* to start with.

Lead the children in singing line by line as follows:
Ouch! I've hurt my le-eg! *Clutch leg*
Ouch! I've hurt my le-eg! *Clutch leg*
Ouch! I've hurt my ar-m! *Clutch arm*
Ouch! I've hurt my ar-m! *Clutch arm*

Help me! Help me! *Arms held up to beg for help twice*
Help me, please! *Arms held up to beg for help*
Help me! Help me! *Arms held up to beg for help twice*
Help me, please! *Arms held up to beg for help*

Let's try singing it all together.
Ouch! I've hurt my le-eg! *Clutch leg*
Ouch! I've hurt my ar-m! *Clutch arm*

Help me! Help me! *Arms held up to beg for help twice*
Help me, please! *Arms held up to beg for help*

Repeat at least once until the children are singing with feeling.

Look! *Point to the corner of the room*
One of our leaders is coming.
She's a good person. She leads our prayers to God.
I'm sure she'll help us!
Let's sing our song and ask for help.

Ouch! I've hurt my le-eg! *Clutch leg*
Ouch! I've hurt my ar-m! *Clutch arm*
Help me! Help me! *Arms held up to beg for help twice*
Help me, please! *Arms held up to beg for help*

The leader saw the traveller and . . .
what do you think she did?
Let's stand up and be the leader together.
We've got our best clothes on.
Let's stand up straight and look smart.
We've got to be on time!
We're leading prayers this morning.
Let's sing a song to God on our way to prayers.
And walk very fast on the spot while we sing.

Lead the children in singing a song they're very familiar with. This could be the Gathering Song that you've used, a closing song like 'This little light of mine', or another song like 'Allelu! Allelu'. Lead the children in singing very happily and fast while walking on the spot. For example:

This little light of mine, *Walk fast on the spot*
I'm gonna let it shine!
This little . . .

Interrupt the singing . . .

Ssssh!

What's that I can hear? *Hand on ear*
Can you hear that?
Someone's shouting 'Help me! Help me!'
I can't help! I'll be late for prayers.
And the leader rushed on.

Continue singing 'This little light of mine'.
Let it shine, let it shine, let it shine! *Walk fast on the spot*

Let's be the poor man lying on the floor again.
Lead the children in lying on the floor holding your leg or arm.

The leader didn't stop to help you!
How are you feeling?
Accept any responses.
Can you show me?

Never mind. Look! *Point to another corner of the room*
One of our music leaders is coming!
He's a good person.
He leads the music when we pray to God.
I'm sure he'll help us.
Let's sing our help song really loudly so he can hear.

Ouch! I've hurt my le-eg! *Clutch leg*
Ouch! I've hurt my ar-m! *Clutch arm*
Help me! Help me! *Arms held up to beg for help twice*
Help me, please! *Arms held up to beg for help*
You may like to repeat.

What do you think is going to happen next?
Will the music leader help?

Let's stand up and be the music leader together.
We've got our best clothes on, too.
Let's stand up straight and look smart.
We're leading the music this morning.
Let's sing our song to God on our way to prayers.

This little light of mine, *Walk fast on the spot*
I'm gonna let it shine!
This little . . .
Interrupt the singing . . . Ssssh!

What's that I can hear? *Hand on ear*
Can you hear that?
What are they shouting?
'Help me'? Help me'?
I can't help! *Shake head* I'll get dirty!
And the music leader rushed on.

Continue singing 'This little light of mine'.
Let it shine, let it shine, let it shine! *Walk fast on the spot*

Let's be the poor man lying on the floor again.
Lead the children in lying on the floor holding your leg or arm.

The music leader didn't stop to help you!
He was too busy singing songs to God.
How are you feeling?
Can you show me?

Gasp. Look! *Point to another corner of the room*
Oh dear! A stranger is coming! *Look really worried*
Someone who doesn't really belong here.

When Jesus was telling the story,
people thought strangers like that were horrible and dirty
and didn't know how to behave properly.
No one would be friends with the stranger. *Shake head*

Oh dear! I hope the stranger doesn't hurt us even more!
Let's sing our help song again.
But this time let's sing it really quietly.
We're not sure we want the stranger to see us.

Lead the children in singing in a subdued voice . . .
Ouch! I've hurt my le-eg! *Clutch leg.*
Ouch! I've hurt my ar-m! *Clutch arm.*
Help me! Help me! *Arms held up to beg for help twice.*
Help me, please! *Arms held up to beg for help.*

What do you think is going to happen next?
Let's stand up and be the stranger together.

Let's walk along . . .
Lead the children in walking on the spot.

Ssssh! Can you hear that? *Hand over ear*
Someone's shouting . . .
What are they saying?
'Help me'? . . .
We don't know them.
What do you think: shall we help them?

Invite the children to respond and accept their responses.

I think we should help!
The stranger saw that the man was hurt.
The stranger knelt down by the man.
Let's kneel down together.
Lead the children in kneeling down.

The stranger washed the man's sore arm.
Let's wash the man's sore arm together.
Lead the children in miming washing.

The stranger bandaged the man's sore leg.
Let's bandage the man's sore leg.
Lead the children in miming bandaging.

Let's sing together as we bandage the man.
This time let's sing 'I'll help' instead of 'Help me!'

Lead the children gently in changing the words to show the stranger's compassion. Sing quietly and sadly.
Ouch! You've hurt your leg! *Point to leg*
Ouch! You've hurt your arm! *Point to arm*
I'll help! I'll help! *Point to self*
I'll help you! *Point to self*

The stranger put the man on his donkey.
Let's stand up and stroke our donkey's nose.
Now let's put the man on our donkey.
Lead the children in miming helping the man onto the donkey.

And he took the man somewhere safe.
Amazing!

Ask the children to sit quietly for a moment.

Jesus told this story.
If you are using figures or person templates to help young children follow the story, place the first figure lying down at this point.
Here's the hurt traveller lying on the ground.

Then Jesus asked a very important question.
Jesus asked, 'Who do you think showed us how to love our friend?'

Count on your fingers as you list the people. Or, if you are using figures or person templates to represent the passers-by, place them down one by one at this point, facing the children:
The prayer leader?
The music leader?
Or the stranger that everyone was worried about?

Invite the children to respond and give their own opinion.

The STRANGER showed us how to love our friend.
Jesus said, 'Go! *Point* And be like that stranger!'

From that moment the stranger wasn't just called 'the stranger' any more.
He was called 'the loving stranger' or 'the Good Stranger'.
Sometimes we call him 'the Good Samaritan',
because that's where he came from.

Invite the children to close their eyes for a moment of quiet.

God asks us to love EVERYONE.
God wants EVERYONE to be our friend.
Not just our best friends.
Not just the people we think are nice.
But everyone.
I wonder whether in your playing today
you could show love even to the people you don't like so much,
or the people you don't know yet?
Let's open our eyes.
Jesus said:
'Go! *Point at the children around the circle* And be like that stranger!'

Week 6: You Are the Light of the World!

→ **Matthew 5.14–16**
→ **Song: 'This little light of mine' (traditional)**
→ **Tune: Traditional. For a taster, see the Diddy Disciples website.**

If the children are not yet familiar with 'This little light of mine':
Before we tell our story today, we need to learn a song.

Teach the children the first verse and tune.

This little light of mine, I'm gonna let it shine!
This little light of mine, I'm gonna let it shine!
This little light of mine, I'm gonna let it shine!
Let it shine, let it shine, let it shine.

We're ready to begin our story.

If you can, show a picture of a 'first-century Palestine oil lamp' (see the Diddy Disciples website). If you're using the What's in the Box? option (p. 221) you could place this picture in your box and ask a child to open it. If you prefer, you could show a candle and adapt the introduction and Bible storytelling accordingly.

Our story today is about a light.
This is a very old light called an 'oil lamp'.
People used to use lamps to shine light in their house
so they could see.
There was a little wick like a piece of string
that came out of a hole so you could light it. *Show the hole*
Then the lamp would burn.

Let's hold our hand all curled up and imagine it's an oil lamp.
Let's pour some oil into our lamp.
Let's hold our little finger out so it looks like the wick, the string.
Now let's light it . . .

Lead the children in lighting the wick of their oil lamp by striking an imaginary match in the air on a count of three and pretending to light your finger.
1, 2, 3 . . . Tssss!

Lead the children in imagining the flame:
Look at the flame flickering and dancing on our lamp,
like on a candle.

Isn't it beautiful!
Let's wave our bodies like a flame
to show the flame dancing around.

Ask the children to begin curled up on the floor, then to uncurl and to wave their bodies, dipping slightly up and down with the lines of the song, like a flame.

Let's sing as we dance like flames.
Let's sing softly and gently like the gentle light of our oil lamp.

This little light of mine, I'm gonna let it shine!
This little light of mine, I'm gonna let it shine!
This little light of mine, I'm gonna let it shine!
Let it shine, let it shine, let it shine.

How beautiful!
How does that light from the lamp make you feel?

Invite responses.

Can you show me?

But wait a minute!
Look at the imaginary oil lamp in your hand.
Is my lamp lighting up your part of the room as well?
Are you using the light I've made to help you see?
Look a bit cross and fed up.
I didn't say you could share my light, did I! *Shake head*
I don't want to share! *Fold arms*

What shall I do? I know!
I've got a bushel here – like a barrel or box.
Take an imaginary bushel.

Shall I put it over my lamp so no one else can see it?
Great idea!
Let's all put a bushel over our lamp
so no one can share our light.
Lead the children in putting the bushel over their lamp.

Invite the children to sit down.

Wait a minute! Now it's dark!
We can't see the beautiful dancing light any more.
You can't see my light.
But now I can't see my light either! *Shake head*
Let's take the bushel off.
Lead the children in taking the bushel off their lamp.

Oh no! The lamps have gone out!
They didn't like being under the bushel,
They didn't get enough air.
No more flickering dancing light! *Shake head*
How do you feel now the light has gone?
Invite responses.

Jesus said, 'No one puts their lamp under a bushel! *Shake head*
They put it onto a lamp stand so everyone can see!'
Mime putting your lamp up high.

Let's light our lamps again.
Let's dance like a flame.

As before, encourage the children to begin curled up on the floor, then to uncurl and to wave their bodies, dipping slightly up and down with the lines of the song, like a flame.

This little light of mine, I'm gonna let it shine!
This little light of mine, I'm gonna let it shine!
This little light of mine, I'm gonna let it shine!
Let it shine, let it shine, let it shine.

Beautiful!
Jesus doesn't want us to keep our light all to ourselves,
Jesus wants us to share our light.
Let's reach up high and put our lamp up on a lampstand now,
high up so everyone can see its light!

When the children have placed their lamp up high, invite them to sit down with their eyes closed.

Let's imagine our lights, shining high up on the lampstand.
Let's imagine that light shining all the way around this room.
Shining even outside.
Helping lots of people see.
Making lots of people want to dance with the flame.
Ask the children to open their eyes.

Jesus said, 'You. *Point at a child*
And you and you . . . *Point at another child, then another*
and everyone here.
Point around the circle in a sweeping motion, making sure you've pointed to everyone, including any adults.

You are the Light of the World!'
There's a little light, God's love,
shining inside you. *Trace a circle on your heart with your finger.*

Let's show the little light that's inside us now.
Let's make our finger into a candle.
Bring your finger from your heart and hold it out.

Let's be God and light our little light of love together, after three.
Lead the children in lighting their finger candle by striking an imaginary match in the air and pretending to light your finger.
1, 2, 3 . . . Tssss!

Let's look around.
Imagine you can see God's love
shining like little lights in each other.

Jesus said, 'No one puts their lamp under a bushel.
They put it on a lampstand so everyone can see!'

Don't hide the light of love that God has lit in you! *Shake head*
Let everyone see it shining! *Mime holding your light up high*
Share its light – share God's love – with everyone around you.

Let's sing our song one more time.
This time we're going to sing it all the way through.
Let's imagine God's love shining and dancing like light in us.

Wave your finger in front of you as you sing.
This little light of mine, I'm gonna let it shine!
This little light of mine, I'm gonna let it shine!
This little light of mine, I'm gonna let it shine!
Let it shine, let it shine, let it shine!

Blow on your finger as if blowing out a candle on 'puff'. Then hold it up high.
Won't let no one *puff* it out! I'm gonna let it shine!

Won't let no one *puff* it out! I'm gonna let it shine!
Won't let no one *puff* it out! I'm gonna let it shine!
Let it shine, let it shine, let it shine!

Hold your finger behind a cupped hand, then take your cupped hand away to reveal the 'candle' and hold it high.
Hide it under a bushel? No! I'm gonna let it shine!
Hide it under a bushel? No! I'm gonna let it shine!
Hide it under a bushel? No! I'm gonna let it shine!
Let it shine, let it shine, let it shine!

Let's remember to let our little light shine today:
shining bright for everyone to see!

Section 3

Creative Response starter ideas, Jesus' Wonderful Love unit

→ **Guide: p. 228**

These starter ideas are designed to spark imaginations and open up opportunities for the children to respond creatively in their different ways to the worship and storytelling you've taken part in together.

Tip

As outlined in the Guide from p. 228, we've found the following rules of thumb helpful for fostering an environment where children are encouraged to engage personally and openly:

1 Encourage the children to make their own choices.
2 Give the children space to develop their responses as they wish.
3 Create space for 'bridge building'.
4 It's the act of responding that matters, not the final result.
5 These responses are 'holy ground'.

Weekly Starter Ideas relate directly to the Bible storytelling of each session, including a print-and-go option (indicated by the printer icon).

Sensory Starter Ideas are designed for sensory explorers, including babies and toddlers. These can remain the same through the whole unit.

Unit Starter Ideas are designed to remain relevant throughout the whole unit. Keeping these resources available each week gives children the opportunity to deepen and develop their responses, while making preparation more manageable for leaders.

Tip: Free response area

In addition to any other resources you provide, keeping a free response area available every week will give the children the opportunity to create anything they wish in response to the story they've told, building their sense of confidence and personal responsibility. In this area you could simply provide blank paper and crayons, pencils, paints or pastels. If you have them, other interesting media (see p. 256) will provide even more scope for the children to nurture and strengthen their imaginative skills.

Weekly Starter Ideas

Week 1: The Lost Sheep

♡ Invite the children to make their own sheep: as a puppet, part of a picture or collage, a necklace, a card, or anything they like. *Provide sheep template (p. 265 or website), pencils/crayons, etc. If you have cotton wool, lollipop sticks/straws/pipe cleaners, glue, and any other collage materials (p. 255), make these available too.*

♡ Invite the children to reflect on the shepherd in the story by making their own shepherd's crook. Some children may even like to make a 'journey stick', which tells the story of the shepherd's journey (or their journey to church, or another journey that's important to them). Journey sticks have been used for a long time in many cultures around the world. They can help retell the story of a journey through the use of colour, or by means of things collected along the journey (leaves, feathers, seed pods, etc.). Encourage the children to remember moments in the journey from start to finish and add different coloured wool – or tie a symbol to their stick – for each part of that journey. They can use their stick to tell the story of the journey. *Provide real sticks, wool, string, and collage materials (p. 255).*

Week 2: The Lost Coin

♡ Invite the children to reflect on the Lost Coin in the story by creating their own coin that will help them remember how special they, or others, are to God. Encourage the children to imagine what their unique coin will look like. Will it have their face on it or something else that's important to them or someone else? *Provide circle template (p. 266 or website), pencils/crayons, etc. If you have tinfoil and other collage materials (p. 255), make these available too. Alternatively, use a paper plate or even tinfoil circles.*

♡ Give the children the opportunity to create their own precious jewellery in their own way: a necklace or ring, bangles, medals, etc. *Provide materials such as beads, penne pasta, or tinfoil circles, plus wool or pipe cleaners. You could also provide other collage materials (p. 255) for the children to explore. For dyed pasta see p. 257.*

Week 3: The Lost Son

♡ Give the children the opportunity to explore different feelings with their faces and simple face templates. Invite them to work with a partner, practising different expressions and developing the template to show those expressions. See if the children would like to explore using different colours to show different feelings as well as expressions. Our feelings change. How many feelings can they show? *Provide face template (p. 267 or website), plus pencils/crayons/pastels/paints.*

♡ Invite the children to enter into the part of the story where the daddy and his whole house get ready for the party by making party food, decorating (pre-made or bought) fairy cakes or biscuits with icing and sprinkles, making a fruit salad, making chocolate lollipops (fridge required), etc. How would the children like the party food to look? Or you may like to give them the opportunity to make party invitations or party hats.

♡ Hold a party like the daddy's party for his Lost Boy, with favourite food and drink. Perhaps invite the children to help you get ready for the party by each setting their own place at the table. As you enjoy your food and drink, encourage the children to imagine the daddy celebrating finding his Lost Boy. God celebrates when we come back to God, too!

Week 4: The Good Shepherd

♡ Invite the children to make a Good Shepherd puppet. *Provide body templates (p. 264 or website), pencils/crayons, etc. If you have collage materials (p. 255), lollipop sticks/straws/pipe cleaners, glue, make these available too.*

♡ If your group provides a choice of starter ideas, you could repeat the sheep template from Week 1 for children who have not yet made their own sheep, or who would like to make another.

♡ Give the children the opportunity to create their own flock of sheep with fingerpaints and pastels/chalks. Invite them to make the sheep's body from one or more fingerprints, then to add legs and a head with the pastels/chalks. How many sheep will be in their flock? What colours will their sheep be? Black/brown/white or multi-coloured? Or would they like to do something completely different with the finger paints? *Provide fingerpaints (see p. 258 to make your own) and pastels/chalks in all sorts of different colours, including black/white/brown.*

Week 5: The Loving Stranger

♡ Invite the children to make finger puppets so they can retell the story for themselves at home. Encourage the children to develop simple finger puppet templates if they wish. *Provide finger puppet templates (p. 268 or website) plus pencils/crayons. If you can, provide other collage materials (p. 255), plus straws/lollipop sticks/wool to create plenty of options for the children's imagination.*

♡ Give the children the opportunity to enter into the part of the story where the stranger bandages the traveller. Invite them to bandage each other's heads, arms or legs with toilet roll, crepe paper or even real bandages. Or they may prefer to bandage a doll or teddy. *Provide bandaging materials, crepe paper or toilet roll.*

♡ Invite the children to make a 'get well soon' or 'I said a prayer for you' card for someone who's feeling unwell. Encourage them to imagine what their unique card will look like. If appropriate, you could use your church's list of the sick. *Provide card, plus pencils/crayons. If you can, provide other collage materials (p. 255) too.*

♡ Give the children the opportunity to reflect on the traveller's wounds and the stranger's help and love. Invite them to draw bruises and cuts wherever they like on a body, then provide them with plasters to place on the injuries, or strips of paper cut to look like plasters. *Provide: body template (p. 264 or website), red/brown/yellow pencils/crayons, plus pretend or real plasters (check none of the children are allergic to plasters).*

Week 6: You Are the Light of the World!

♡ Invite the children to decorate a simple candle template, making it their own with their own pictures, symbols, or other decorations. Jesus' light shines in us like the light of a candle. *Provide candle template (p. 269 or website) plus pencils/crayons. If you have collage materials (p. 255), you could also make these available, plus red/yellow/orange crepe, tissue, or coloured paper to create flames.*

♡ Invite the children to paint decorations onto a tall wax candle and imagine being a little light for Jesus, sharing Jesus' love. Encourage them to take the candle home and ask an adult to light it as they remember that we are the light of the world. *Provide wax candles and paints. Ready-mixed washable paint works fine on wax candles. Note: glitter or glitter paint may present a fire hazard.*

♡ Invite the children to make an ancient oil lamp or a modern tealight holder – or anything else they might wish to make – from salt dough. If the children make a tealight holder, encourage them to take it home and ask an adult to light it as they remember that we are the Light of the World. *Provide different colours of salt dough (recipe on p. 257). You could also provide tealights and glitter.*

Sensory Starter Ideas

Resources that you might provide for the children (including babies and toddlers) to explore for themselves include:

♡ sheep (plastic, wooden or soft), or different sizes of sheep made from various materials in a cloth bag/box/socks. You could also provide a blanket in case the children wish to play hide and seek with the sheep, or you could place them in a tub with rice, lentils or bits of fabric;

♡ building bricks or other construction toys, e.g. Mega blocks, Duplo, Stickle Bricks, K'Nex, Kapla, Polydron. You could also provide alongside these 'small world' people (small plastic figures such as those from Happyland or Fisher Price, or wooden/knitted figures) or sheep in case the children would like to make an obstacle course or play hide and seek;

♡ fabric for babies and parents to play 'peekaboo' (lost and found);

♡ 'small world' resources: e.g. men, women, children, sheep, pigs, a house, a farm, trees, bushes;

♡ heart-shaped cushions, mats, or other baby-safe heart-shaped items;

♡ sheep and child-safe coins, along with number blocks or symbols to be counted;

♡ musical instruments: these can encourage children to express and explore a range of emotions more openly. Make sure they're at an appropriate noise level for your size of room, bearing in mind the other responses that may be going on;

♡ imaginative aids (like those used for the Gathering Songs from different units). These can encourage sensory explorers to explore movement and feelings more openly;

♡ a range of sparkly jewellery and medals (safe for babies and toddlers) for the children to explore with magnifying glasses, notebooks, and pens;

♡ battery tealights or baby-safe torches to explore light;

♡ board books with pictures inside that show feelings and emotions. You could even make your own from laminated drawings or photographs;

♡ board books of any of the stories from the unit;

♡ dressing-up materials: sheep masks, tea towels and stick (Lost Sheep and Good Shepherd), a purse with child safe coins (Lost Coin), a doctor's bag and bandages (Good Stranger);

♡ child-safe mirrors for the children to explore the way they look as well as facial expressions.

Unit Starter Ideas

Exploring our feelings

The Jesus' Wonderful Love stories open up lots of opportunities to explore different emotions and feelings.

♡ Invite the children to use different coloured pastels, crayons or paint to show different feelings: cross, sad, scared, happy, calm, excited, or other emotions that interest the children. 'What does your anger look like?' 'What does your calm look like?' 'What colour reminds you of "sad"?' 'How will you hold the crayon?' 'How hard will you press?' *Provide paper, crayons, pastels, paint.*

♡ Encourage the children to cut out pictures of faces from newspapers and magazines and create a collage of faces showing one chosen feeling, or a range of different feelings. These may be feelings from the story you've told together, or feelings that the children are experiencing themselves or in those around them. *Provide magazines and newspapers with pictures of faces, paper, glue, scissors, pencils/crayons/pens.*

♡ Give the children the opportunity to explore different feelings using their faces and simple face templates. Invite them to work with a partner, practising different expressions and developing the template to show those expressions. See if the children would like to explore using different colours to show different feelings as well as expressions. Our feelings change. How many feelings can they show? *Provide face template (p. 267 or website), plus pencils/crayons/pastels/paints.*

Sharing Jesus' love

The Jesus' Wonderful Love unit challenges us to wonder how we can be part of sharing God's love for us with others.

♡ Invite the children to reflect on the way God's love spreads and makes our hearts beautiful by dripping paint onto hearts (or other shapes they may like to make) cut from absorbent paper – coffee filters are particularly effective – and watching what happens. *Provide coffee filters and diluted paint in different colours. See heart template (p. 270 or website).*

♡ Invite the children to decorate a heart to make it beautiful in their own unique way, as Jesus makes our hearts uniquely beautiful with love. *Provide heart template (p. 270 or website) plus a range of collage materials (p. 255), glue, wool, straws, masking tape, and colouring/painting materials.*

♡ Invite the children to imagine the colours of Jesus' love in our hearts using paint, pastels or another medium. Encourage the children to explore how they will hold the brush or pastel as they create. How hard will they press? How do they imagine Jesus' love? 'What does Jesus' love look like in your heart?' *Provide: heart template (p. 270 or website), plus paints/pastels/other media.*

♡ Give the children the opportunity to bake or decorate cakes or biscuits for someone in order to show Jesus' love. Encourage them to give (at least one of) their cakes/biscuits away. *Provide cake/biscuit-making ingredients and equipment.*

♡ Invite the children to design a postcard to send to a friend, a relative, or anyone else they choose. They might even like to write a message on it. *Provide: postcard template (online or on p. 271) plus pencils/crayons, etc.*

UNIT 2
GOD THE MAKER (GREEN TIME, HARVEST)

The God the Maker unit aims to nurture and deepen children's natural sense of wonder and thanks for God's beautiful world. There are also opportunities to prepare for a Harvest Festival by telling the story of bread (or other local produce) and to spend one session on an extended activity in which children are encouraged to respond to God's call for us all to become active helpers in caring for God's world.

> **Tip**
>
> If you wish to lengthen this God the Maker unit in future years, you could add Jesus' parable of the Sower from the Let Your Kingdom Come! unit in *Diddy Disciples: January to August*.

Section 1

The Building Blocks, God the Maker unit

Pick and choose from these Building Blocks and their various options to build sessions for your group. Whatever choices you make, we suggest you keep to that pattern for the whole of the unit, as this will open up opportunities for the children to participate fully and confidently during your time together.

> **Build your own Diddy Disciples session** (p. 6) provides an overview of the Building Blocks and a short introduction to fitting them together, along with examples.
>
> **A Guide to the Building Blocks** (p. 217) provides a step-by-step guide to each Building Block.

Welcome

→ **Guide: p. 217**

Welcome your group.

Let's start by going round the circle
And saying our name out loud.
My name's _____.

Go round the circle so that every adult and child has the chance to say his or her name (and introduce any dolls, teddies or toys). If any of the children don't want to say their name or aren't able to, you (or a parent or carer) could say it for them and wave.

It's time to sing our Welcome Song!

Welcome Song: Option 1

→ **Song: 'The Diddy Disciples welcome song'. Words © Sharon Moughtin-Mumby**
→ **Tune: 'Glory, glory, alleluia!' (traditional). For the music see p. 259, or for a taster see the Diddy Disciples website. For tips on teaching songs for the first time, see p. 215.**

Go around the circle the same way as above. See if each of you can remember the others' names and insert them into the song.

Welcome *Name 1* to *St Peter's**
Welcome *Name 2* to *St Peter's**
Welcome *Name 3* to *St Peter's**

You are welcome in the name of the Lord!

* Insert the name of your church or children's group, or sing 'our worship'.

Welcome Song: Option 2

→ **Song: 'You are welcome in the name of the Lord' (traditional)**
→ **Tune: Traditional. For the music see p. 262, or for a taster see the Diddy Disciples website. For tips on teaching songs for the first time, see p. 215.**

Let's wave with one hand. *Lead waving*
Then with our other hand. *Lead waving*
Then let's choose someone and show God's 'glory'!
Move arms up and down in front of you with fingers wiggling, palms facing out, towards one person.
And someone else! *Repeat*
Then let's wave with both hands all around the circle.
Lead waving.

We're ready to sing!

You are welcome in the name of the Lord!
Wave with right hand to one person.
You are welcome in the name of the Lord!
Wave with left hand to another person.
I can see all over you, the glory of the Lord!
Move arms up and down in front of you with fingers wiggling, palms facing out, towards one person and then another.
You are welcome in the name of the Lord!
Wave with both hands all around the circle.

Getting Ready to Worship

→ **Guide: p. 218**

Choose one of the following greetings according to which is familiar in your church. (If your church uses a different greeting, you could use that here instead.)

Getting Ready to Worship: Option 1

→ **Action: The sign of the cross. Words © Sharon Moughtin-Mumby**

Invite the children to make the sign of the cross slowly with you. As the children become more confident, invite a child to lead the action as the whole group says the words and makes the sign of the cross.

In my head, *Touch head*
in my heart, *Touch chest*
and all around me, *Touch shoulders one by one*
Jesus is here. *Open hands in front facing upwards*

Getting Ready to Worship: Option 2

→ **Action: 'The Lord be with you' (open hands)**

Let's start by clenching our hands together tightly.
Lead children in clenching fists against your body to show a defensive posture.

When we close ourselves up like this,
it's hard to let anyone into our heart.
It's hard even to let God into our heart!

When we get ready to worship,
we show that we're open to God and to each other.
Open your hands out, facing up.

Can you show me your open hands?
We're ready to let God and each other in!

The Lord be with you.
Hold hands open to the children.
And also with you.
Invite the children to open their hands towards you.

Introducing the Unit

→ **Guide: p. 218**

Introducing the Unit: Option 1

Week 1
Starting this week, we're going to tell
stories about God the Maker who made the whole world!

Week 2 onwards:
We've been telling stories
about God the Maker who made the whole world!

Introducing the Unit: Option 2 🌳

→ **Focus: the liturgical colour, green**

This introduction is particularly designed for the autumn. If you're using this unit in spring, summer or winter, use Option 2 from the Jesus' Wonderful Love unit instead (see p. 32).

Who can tell us what colour season we're in now?
> *If appropriate:* You may have seen it in church.

Invite a child to respond with the colour.

At the moment, we're in Green Time!
> *If appropriate:* Let's all look out for green when we go back into church.
> *Or:* Let's remember to look and see what colour we're in next time we go into church.

> *Either:*
> In Green Time, the Church grows like a tree or flower.
> We're the Church, so we're going to be growing, too!
> *Or:*
> In Green Time, everything grows, including us!

All around us, flowers and trees have been growing tall.
Can you show me a beautiful tree stretching up to the sun,
waving its branches in the breeze?
Lead the children in being a tree.

Now it's turning to autumn time.
Our leaves are turning brown.
And it's getting more and more windy!
Can you show me the wind
blowing through your branches?
Lead the children in waving arms gently and blowing.

Seeds have been growing on our trees.
Conkers and acorns and pine cones.
Can you wiggle your fingers in the breeze
and show me the little seeds at the ends of your fingers?
Lead the children in wiggling fingers.

Now it's autumn,
it's time for our seeds to drop to the ground.
Let's show our seeds falling gently to the ground.
Lead the children in wiggling fingers down to the ground.
Going down into the soil.
It's time for our seeds to go to sleep!
Let's sleep like the little seeds from the trees.
Lead the children in curling up into a ball.

Sssssssssh!
Let's sleep well so we're ready to wake up
and grow up tall next spring.

Everything that grows plants seeds in Green Time.
I wonder what seeds God is planting inside you?

Today we're going to ask God to plant a seed in us
by telling a story about God the Maker
who made the whole world!

Gathering Song

→ **Guide: p. 219**

Imaginative aids are particularly helpful for this unit's Gathering Songs, encouraging the children to use their whole bodies to explore the weather.

Gathering Song: Option 1

→ **Song: 'It's raining, it's raining!' Words © Sharon Moughtin-Mumby**
→ **Tune: 'A-tisket, A-tasket' (traditional). For a taster see the Diddy Disciples website.**

Our world can have lots of different weather!
Who can tell us what the weather is like today?

Invite a child to respond.

If you're using imaginative aids, ask two or three children to give them out at this point. Then invite the children to warm up their imaginations by exploring actions for different kinds of weather: rainy, snowy, windy, sunny, cloudy, rainbows, chilly, stormy (thunder and lightning), etc.

Introduce each verse of the song by inviting the children to show the kind of weather mentioned with their imaginative aids or their bodies, as exemplified below.

> *When using this song for the first time, you might find it helpful to introduce it by starting with the second half of the song, as these words remain the same every time. For example:*
>
> We have a new song about God the Maker.
> Let's learn some words 'my turn' *both hands to self,* 'your turn' *hands out to group*
>
> God the Maker made the world *both hands to self to show your turn*
> **God the Maker made the world** *hands out to group to show their turn*
> Thank you, God the Maker! *both hands to self to show your turn*
> **Thank you, God the Maker!** *both hands to self to show your turn*
>
> Now let's add the tune 'my turn' *both hands to self,* 'your turn' again *hands out to group*
>
> *Sing the second half of the song, line by line.*
> God the Maker made the world *both hands to self to show your turn*
> **God the Maker made the world** *hands out to group to show their turn*
> Thank you, God the Maker! *both hands to self to show your turn*
> **Thank you, God the Maker!** *hands out to group to show their turn*
>
> Let's try that all together. *Lead the group in singing.*
> **God the Maker made the world.**
> **Thank you, God the Maker!**
>
> We're ready to add some weather!
>
> Who can show me rain?!
> *Follow the children's actions for rain.*
>
> Let's say 'It's raining, it's raining, outside it is raining!'
> **It's raining, it's raining, outside it is raining!**

Now let's try singing that and let's add the rest of our song to the end.
Let's show rain the whole time we're singing.

Lead the children in their rain action as you sing:
It's raining, it's raining, outside it is raining!
God the Maker made the world
Thank you, God the Maker!
Continue from 'Now let's imagine it's sunny outside' below.

Let's start off by imagining it's raining outside!
Can you show me rain?
Let's sing 'It's raining, it's raining'.

Continue with the action as you sing:
It's *raining*, it's *raining*!
Outside it is *raining*!
God the Maker made the world.
Thank you, God the Maker!

Now let's imagine it's sunny outside!
Can you show me sunny?

Continue with the action as you sing:
It's *sunny*, it's *sunny*!
Outside it is *sunny*!
God the Maker made the world.
Thank you, God the Maker!

Look! I can see a rainbow!
Can you show me a rainbow?
These actions will become the 'rainbow action' for the song.

Let's sing 'a rainbow, a rainbow!
Outside there's a rainbow!'

Continue with the action as you sing:
A rainbow, a rainbow!
Outside there's a rainbow!
God the Maker made the world.
Thank you, God the Maker!

Oh my goodness, now there's thunder!
Can you show me thunder with your feet?
And lightning! Can you show me lightning?
It's stormy!

Continue with the action as you sing:
It's *stormy*, it's *stormy*!
Outside it is *stormy*!
God the Maker made the world.
Thank you, God the Maker!

Wow! Now there's snow,
Soft, beautiful snow, falling all around.
Can you show me snow?

Continue with the action as you sing:
It's *snowing*, it's *snowing*!
Outside it is *snowing*!
God the Maker made the world.
Thank you, God the Maker!

And now listen. *Put your hand over your ear.*
Lead the children in blowing to imitate wind.
Can you hear that?
Lead the children in blowing louder and louder.
It's windy outside! Can you show me wind?

Continue with the action as you sing:
It's *windy*, it's *windy*!
Outside it is *windy*!
God the Maker made the world.
Thank you, God the Maker!

Yawn. Who's feeling tired after all that weather?
Let's sit back in our place and go to sleep . . .
Lead the children in being sleepy.

Look! *Point up.* Outside the stars are twinkling. *Twinkle hands*
Can you show me the twinkling stars?

Lead the children in twinkling with hands as you sing quietly and sleepily.
It's starry, it's starry,
outside it is starry.
God the Maker made the world.
Thank you, God the Maker!

End by falling asleep quietly and peacefully.

Gathering Song: Option 2

→ **Song: 'God the Maker made the world!' Words © Sharon Moughtin-Mumby**
→ **Tune: 'Aiken Drum' (traditional). For a taster see the Diddy Disciples website.**

God the Ma-ker made the world, so beau-ti-ful, so beau-ti-ful! God the Ma-ker

made the world. Thank you, God the Ma-ker! And to-day, it's rain-ing, it's

rain-ing, it's rain-ing! And to-day, it's rain-ing! Thank you, God the Ma-ker!

Our world can have lots of different weather!
Who can tell us what the weather is like today?

Invite a child to respond.

If you're using imaginative aids, ask two or three children to give them out at this point. Then invite the children to warm up their imaginations by exploring actions for different kinds of weather: rainy, snowy, windy, sunny, cloudy, rainbows, chilly, stormy (thunder and lightning), etc.

God the Maker made the weather!
Let's thank God for every kind of weather
with our God the Maker song.

> *If your group is singing this song for the first time, you may find the following introduction helpful.*
>
> Let's learn the words to a new song
> 'my turn' *both hands to self*, 'your turn' *hands out to group*

God the Maker made the world *both hands to self to show your turn*
God the Maker made the world *hands out to group to show their turn*
so beautiful, so beautiful! *both hands to self to show your turn*
so beautiful, so beautiful! *hands out to group to show their turn*
God the Maker made the world *both hands to self to show your turn*
God the Maker made the world *hands out to group to show their turn*
thank you, God the Maker! *both hands to self to show your turn*
thank you, God the Maker! *hands out to group to show their turn*

Now let's add the tune 'my turn' *both hands to self*, 'your turn' *hands out to group*
God the Maker made the world *both hands to self to show your turn*
so beautiful, so beautiful!
God the Maker made the world *hands out to group to show their turn*
so beautiful, so beautiful!
God the Maker made the world *both hands to self to show your turn*
thank you, God the Maker!
God the Maker made the world *hands out to group to show their turn*
thank you, God the Maker!

Continue as below.

Don't worry about teaching the words for each of the weather verses. These are very repetitive, so that the children will pick them up as they go, and the tune is the same as the refrain.

Who can show us an action for 'beautiful'?
Choose one of the actions and imitate it.
And 'thank you God the Maker'?
Choose one of the actions and imitate it.
We're ready to sing our song!

Lead the group in singing the song with the actions.
God the Maker made the world, *Circle or other action*
so beautiful! So beautiful! *'Beautiful' action*
God the Maker made the world, *Circle or other action*
thank you, God the Maker! *'Thank you' action*

Introduce each verse by inviting the children to show the kind of weather mentioned with their imaginative aids, or with their bodies as exemplified below. You may like to find your own order and introductions.

For instance:
Let's start off by imagining it's raining outside!
Can you show me rain?

Continue with the action as you sing:
And today it's *raining*! *Children's rain action*
It's *raining*! It's *raining*!
And today it's *raining*!
Thank you, God the Maker! *Thank you action*

You can either repeat the God the Maker refrain each time as indicated below, or you could move through the different weather verses without the refrain. At St Peter's we tend to sing the refrain after each of the first two verses, then to sing a few weather verses in a row without the refrain. We sing the refrain to end the song.

Example
God the Maker made the world, *Circle or other action*
so beautiful! So beautiful! *Beautiful action*
God the Maker made the world, *Circle or other action*
thank you, God the Maker! *Thank you action*

Now listen. *Hand over your ear.*
Lead the children in blowing to imitate wind.

Can you hear that?
Lead the children in blowing louder and louder.

It's windy outside! Can you show me wind?

Continue with the action as you sing:
And today it's *windy*!
It's *windy*, it's *windy*!
And today it's *windy*!
Thank you, God the Maker! *Thank you action*

Refrain

Now let's imagine it's sunny outside!
Can you show me sunny?

Continue with the action as you sing:
And today it's *sunny*!
It's *sunny*, it's *sunny*!
And today it's *sunny*!
Thank you, God the Maker! *Thank you action*

Refrain (if you choose).

Look! Now there's snow,
Soft, beautiful snow, falling all around.
Can you show me snow?

Continue with the action as you sing:
And today it's *snowing*!
It's *snowing*! It's *snowing*!
And today it's *snowing*!
Thank you, God the Maker! *Thank you action*

Refrain (if you choose).

Oh my goodness, now there's thunder!
Can you show me thunder with your feet?
And lightning! Can you show me lightning?
It's stormy!

Continue with the action as you sing:
And today it's *stormy*!
It's *stormy*! It's *stormy*!
And today it's *stormy*!
Thank you, God the Maker! *Thank you action*

Refrain (if you choose).

Listen! The thunderstorm's stopped!
Look! *Point.* I can see a rainbow!
Can you show me a rainbow?
Let's sing 'today, there's a rainbow!'

Continue with the action as you sing:
And today there's a rainbow!
A rainbow! a rainbow!
And today there's a rainbow!
Thank you, God the Maker! *Thank you action*

Refrain (if you choose).

Last of all, what did we say the weather was like today?
Can anyone tell me?
Can you show me *rain* ?
Let's sing one more time.
Let's thank God the Maker for our weather today.

Continue with the action as you sing:
And today it's _____!
It's _____! It's_____!
And today it's _____!
Thank you, God the Maker! *Thank you action*

God the Maker made the world. *Circle or other action*
So beautiful! So beautiful! *Beautiful action*
God the Maker made the world. *Circle or other action*
Thank you, God the Maker! *Thank you action*

Getting Ready for Bible Storytelling

→ **Guide: p. 221**

Getting Ready for Bible Storytelling: Option 1

→ **Action: opening your group's box and naming this week's object**

See the beginning of the weekly storytelling material for ideas of items to place in your box.

Invite one of the children to open the box.

What's in the box? *Ask the child to respond.*

Getting Ready for Bible Storytelling: Option 2

→ **Song: 'Jesus, open up my eyes'. Words © Sharon Moughtin-Mumby**
→ **Tune: 'Michael, row the boat ashore' (traditional). For the music, see p. 262, or for a taster see the Diddy Disciples website. For tips on teaching songs for the first time, see p. 215.**

It's time to open the Bible.
Let's get ready!
Let's take our thumb *Lead children in showing thumb*
And draw our cross on our eyes, *Draw cross*
and our lips, *Draw cross*
and our heart. *Draw cross*
Let's ask Jesus to help us get ready to listen out for God!

Jesus, open up my eyes. Alleluia!
Trace a cross between your eyes.
Jesus, open up my lips. Alleluia!
Trace a cross on your lips.
Jesus, open up my heart. Alleluia!
Trace a cross on your heart.
Jesus, help me hear your voice. Alleluia!
Cup your hands behind your ears.

Interactive Bible Storytelling

→ **Guide: p. 221**

See the Bible Storytelling material in Section 2 of this chapter.

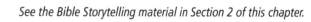

Saying Sorry to God

→ **Guide: p. 223**

Invite the children to sit in a circle for a moment of quiet.

God the Maker made this world.
God asks us to take care of the world
and to take care of each other.
But we don't always take good care. *Shake head*
It's time for us to say sorry to God.
Let's sing our Sorry Song together.

Option 1

→ **Song: 'The Diddy Disciples sorry song'. Words © Sharon Moughtin-Mumby**
→ **Tune: © Sharon Moughtin-Mumby. For the music see p. 259, or for a taster see the Diddy Disciples website. For tips on teaching songs for the first time, see p. 215. For a description of the 'I'm Sorry' and 'New Start' signs, see p. 225 or the website.**

Let's put our hands on our head.
I wonder if there's anything we've thought this week
that we wish we hadn't thought?

Lead the children in placing your hands on head, singing.
With my hands on my head,
I remember the things I've thought today,
I remember the things I wish I'd thought a different way.

I'm sorry, I'm sorry, *Diddy Disciples 'I'm Sorry' sign (see p. 225).*
I wish I could start again. *Diddy Disciples 'New Start' sign (see p. 225).*
I'm sorry, I'm sorry, *'I'm Sorry' sign.*
I wish I could start again. *Repeat 'New Start' sign.*

Let's put our hands by our mouths.
I wonder if there's anything we've said this week
that we wish we hadn't said?

With hands by mouth, singing . . .
With my hands on my mouth,
I remember the things I've said today,
I remember the things I wish I'd said a different way.

Repeat 'I'm Sorry' and 'New Start' signs as above.
I'm sorry, I'm sorry,
I wish I could start again.
I'm sorry, I'm sorry,
I wish I could start again.

Let's cross our hands on our chest.
I wonder if there's anything we've done this week
that we wish we hadn't done.

With hands crossed on chest, singing . . .
With my hands on my chest,
I remember the things I've done today,
I remember the things I wish I'd done a different way.

Repeat 'I'm Sorry' and 'New Start' signs as above.
I'm sorry, I'm sorry,
I wish I could start again.

I'm sorry, I'm sorry,
I wish I could start again.

Continue with a Saying Sorry Action or move straight to God Gives Us a New Start below.

Option 2

→ **Song: 'We need a new start'. Words © Sharon Moughtin-Mumby**
→ **Tune: Molly Malone (traditional). For the music see p. 259, or for a taster see the Diddy Disciples website. For tips on teaching songs for the first time, see p. 215. For a description of the 'I'm Sorry' and 'New Start' signs, see p. 225 or the website.**

> ### Tip
>
> This song can be sung using 'we're sorry' as indicated, or as 'I'm sorry', adapting the material accordingly.

Let's put our hands on our head.
I wonder if there's anything we've thought this week
that we wish we hadn't thought?

Lead the children in placing your hands on head, singing.
For the things we have thou-ght
that we wish we'd not thou-ght,
we're sor-ry, we're sor-ry, *Diddy Disciples 'I'm Sorry' sign twice (see p. 225).*
we need a new start. *Diddy Disciples 'New Start' sign (see p. 225).*

Let's put our hands by our mouths.
I wonder if there's anything we've said this week
that we wish we hadn't said?

With hands by mouth, singing . . .
For the things we have sa-id
that we wish we'd not sa-id,
we're sor-ry, we're sor-ry, *'I'm Sorry' sign twice.*
we need a new start. *'New Start' sign.*

Let's cross our hands on our chest.
I wonder if there's anything we've done this week
that we wish we hadn't done.

With hands crossed on chest, singing . . .
For the things we have do-ne
that we wish we'd not do-ne,
we're sor-ry, we're sor-ry, *'I'm Sorry' sign twice.*
we need a new start. *'New Start' sign.*

Continue with a Saying Sorry Action or move straight to God Gives Us a New Start below.

Saying Sorry Action

→ **Guide: p. 223**

For alternative actions that can be used during any unit at any time of year, see Saying Sorry Actions options 2, 3, and 4 on p. 40–43. For more Green Time options themed around growing and summer time, see Special Options for Green Time in Diddy Disciples: January to August.

Saying Sorry Action: Option 1

→ **Action: remove paper weeds from a 'garden' filled with paper flowers**

> ## Tip
>
> At St Peter's, Walworth, we use a tray filled with soil or with a brown cloth folded onto it for our 'garden'. We scatter this with paper flowers, then cover the flowers with strips of green paper that are cut to look like long green leaves or 'weeds'.

In Green Time, everything grows!
Flowers grow, trees grow

> *Either:* and the Church grows.
> We're part of the Church, so we're growing too!
> *Or:* and we grow.

> *If appropriate:* What do gardens need to grow?
> *Accept the children's responses. You might like to add/repeat:*
> Gardens need sun, rain, etc., to grow.

To help gardens grow, we also need to pull the weeds out.

Place your 'garden' in the centre of the circle.

Let's imagine that our heart's like this garden,
covered with weeds.
When we say sorry to God,
it's like we're weeding our heart.
We're pulling all the bad things out
and making space for the beautiful flowers.
Let's go round the circle
and pull one weed out of the garden each
so we can see the beautiful flowers growing beneath.

While all the children and adults who wish to weed the garden do so, lead the group in either:

> *Option 1: singing the 'I'm sorry' refrain, or*
> *Option 2: humming the first two lines of the 'We need a new start' song followed by singing the refrain 'We're sorry, we're sorry, we need a new start'*

Ask the last child to remove any remaining weeds on behalf of the group. If your group has a large number of children, you may wish to carry two 'gardens' around the circle in opposite directions. When the group is ready:

Look at our beautiful garden!
Now we can see all the flowers growing.
The Good News is that when we say sorry,
God will always give us a new start!
We can grow beautifully again
Just like our beautiful garden.

After three, let's say 'God gives us a new start!'
1, 2, 3: God gives us a new start!

Let's use our new start to share God's love this week!

Saying Sorry Action: Option 2

→ **Action: growing from a seed**

The Good News is:
God always wants to give us a new start!
God wants to plant a little seed, *Show imaginary seed between fingers*
the seed of love, in all of us.
Let's close our eyes for a moment.

Let's imagine Jesus coming to us now.
Let's ask Jesus to make our hearts ready.
Now let's imagine Jesus planting
that seed in our hearts.
Let's open our eyes again.

Let's imagine we're the little seed
that Jesus has planted in us.
Let's curl up into a ball.
Lead the children in curling up into a ball.

Let's show our roots with our fingers.
Lead the children in wiggling fingers.

We need to let our roots grow down deep.
Lead the children in wiggling fingers down.

Then after three, let a little shoot pop up.
1, 2, 3 . . . Pop!
Poke your hands up over your head like a little shoot.

Then start to grow up tall.
Gradually stand up, swaying like a growing stalk.
Taller and taller onto our tiptoes . . .
Reach up with pointy hands and on tiptoes.

Let's turn our faces up towards the sun!
Then let our leaves or branches spread out wide.
Arms stretch slowly outwards.

After three, let's say 'God gives me a new start!'
1, 2, 3 . . . God gives me a new start!

What beautiful plants!
Let's ask for Jesus' love
to grow inside us today.
And let's remember to share Jesus' love
by caring for each other and for God's beautiful world.

God Gives Us a New Start

→ **Guide: p. 225**

Every time of Saying Sorry should end by assuring the children that God gives them a new start. Most Diddy Disciples Saying Sorry Actions already include this promise of a new start. If they don't – or if you have created your own Saying Sorry Action – you should choose one from the following New Start options, or create your own assurance of forgiveness. You could also choose to move straight from the Sorry Song to God's promise of a new start, without any Saying Sorry Action.

New Start Action: Option 1

→ **Action: tracing a cross or smile on each other's forehead**

The Good News is:
God always wants to give us a new start!
Let's turn to the person next to us
and show that God gives them a new start.
Let's take our thumb/finger *Show thumb/finger*
and draw a cross/smile on their forehead *Draw a cross/smile in the air*

> *If your group is drawing a smile, add:*
> to show that God is very happy with them!

Let's say 'God gives you a new start!'
Then let them give you a new start, too!

When the group has finished drawing a cross/smile to show each other God's new starts:

Let's use our new start to share God's love this week!

New Start Action: Option 2

→ **Action: standing up and hugging each other**

The Good News is:
God always wants to give us a new start!
Let's help someone next to us stand up from the floor.
Then let them help you stand up too!

Lead the children in helping each other stand up.

Then let's give each other a hug and say:
'God gives you a new start!'

When the group has finished helping each other up to show each other God's new starts:

Let's use our new start to share God's love this week!

New Start Action: Option 3

→ **Song: 'God loves to give me a new start!' Words © Sharon Moughtin-Mumby**
→ **Tune: 'Give me oil in my lamp' (traditional). For the music see p. 260, or for a taster see the Diddy Disciples website. For tips on teaching songs for the first time, see p. 215.**

The Good News is:
God always wants to give us a new start!
Let's sing our New Start song together.

[Yes, my] God loves to give me a new start! *Trace a smile/cross on your own forehead*
How amazing God's love for me! *Cross hands on your chest*
[Yes, my] God loves to give me a new start! *Trace a smile/cross on your own forehead*
How amazing is God's love for me!

Sing hosanna! Sing hosanna! *Wave hands in the air*
Sing hosanna to the King of kings!
Wave hands in the air followed by the placing of an imaginary crown on your head.
Sing hosanna! Sing hosanna! *Wave hands in the air*
Sing hosanna to the King!
Wave hands in the air followed by placing of crown on head.

Introduction to Prayers

It's time for us to bring our prayers to God the Maker,
who made the whole world and everything in it.

Prayers for Other People

→ **Guide: pp. 223 and 225**

Invite the children to sit in a circle for a moment of quiet.

Let's imagine holding our prayer gently,
hands together gently in traditional prayer gesture, but cupped so you can imagine a prayer inside
and then let it go up to God,
hands opened upwards to God

> *If you're using Option 1 (below):*
> Jesus, *Hands together, cupped*
> hear our prayer. *Hands opened upwards to God*
> Let's pray . . .

Prayers for Other People: Option 1

→ **Song: 'Jesus, hear our prayer!' Words © Sharon Moughtin-Mumby**
→ **Tune: 'Brown girl in the ring' (traditional). For the music see p. 260, or for a taster see the Diddy Disciples website. For tips on teaching songs for the first time, see p. 215. For similar words designed to fit with the alternative tune 'He's got the whole world in his hands', see p. 260.**

For the world:	**Jesus, hear our prayer!**
Make a circle shape	*Open hands upwards to God*
For the Church:	**Jesus, hear our prayer!**
Praying hands	*Open hands upwards to God*
For our place, *Walworth**:	**Jesus, hear our prayer!**
Hands down, moving out in	*Open hands upwards to God*
a semi-circle to show	
the area around us	

Lord Jesus, hear our prayer. Amen.
Open hands upwards to God

* *Insert your local area/school/church/community/parish.*

For the sick and lonely:	**Jesus, hear our prayer!**
Fingers imitating tears falling	*Open hands upwards to God*
down cheeks	
For our friends and family:	**Jesus, hear our prayer!**
Arms around yourself	*Open hands upwards to God*
For ourselves:	**Jesus, hear our prayer!**
Both hands on heart	*Open hands upwards to God*

Lord Jesus, hear our prayer. Amen.
Open hands upwards to God

Let's close our eyes for a moment.
I wonder if there's someone special
you'd like to pray for?
Let's imagine that person now.

Now, let's imagine Jesus coming to that person.
Does Jesus say anything?
Does Jesus do anything?

Let's open our eyes.

Continue with one of the Prayer Action options outlined below. Once the Prayer Action has been completed, you may like to use the following verse to close this time of prayer.

Take our prayers:	**Jesus, hear our prayer!**
Hands together gently	*Open hands upwards to God*
Make them holy:	**Jesus, hear our prayer!**
Hands together gently	*Open hands upwards to God*
Make them beautiful:	**Jesus, hear our prayer!**
Hands together gently	*Open hands upwards to God*
Lord Jesus, hear our prayer! Amen.	

Hands together gently, then open hands upwards to God

Prayers for Other People: Option 2

→ **Song: 'The Diddy Disciples little prayers song'. Words © Sharon Moughtin-Mumby**
→ **Tune: 'Frère Jacques' (traditional). For the music see p. 258, or for a taster see the Diddy Disciples website. For tips on teaching songs for the first time, see p. 215.**

These prayers are especially suited to churches that prefer less traditional prayer forms.

> *Either: choose what you'd like the group to pray for before the session.*
> *Or: ask the children at this point if there is anything or anyone that they'd like to pray for.*

Ask them or others to suggest actions for their prayer request. You will need two different 'thank you' suggestions and two different 'hear our prayer' suggestions. Try to encourage the offering of at least one prayer for people outside the group.

Invite the children to sing after you, repeating your words and their actions. Sometimes it might be almost impossible to fit the child's own words in! But it's really valuable to do so where possible, resisting the urge to try and 'tidy up' their suggestions. For examples, see Unit 1, 'Jesus' wonderful love', p. 47:

Having sung your prayers, you could insert a Prayer Action, repeat the process, or move straight on to close with the following (or other words that remain the same each week).

For today,	*Point hands down for 'now'*
For today,	*Point hands down for 'now'*
Thank you, God!	*Open hands upwards to God or hands together in prayer*
Thank you, God!	*Open hands upwards to God or hands together in prayer*
Fo-r your love,	*Cross hands on chest*
Fo-r your love,	*Cross hands on chest*
Thank you, God!	*Open hands upwards to God or hands together in prayer*
Thank you, God!	*Open hands upwards to God or hands together in prayer*

Prayer Actions

→ **Guide: p. 225**

Prayer Action: Option 1

→ **Action: placing paper, fabric, wooden, or real flowers in a 'garden'**

> ### Tip
>
> At St Peter's, Walworth, we use a tray filled with soil or a with brown cloth folded onto it for our 'garden'. We use daisies that we pick on the way to church as our flowers. We recommend that all the flowers look the same so the children don't become distracted by having to choose.

Either: It's Green Time!

Or: It's spring/summer/autumn/harvest time!
We can see flowers and trees
growing beautifully all around us.
The world's full of so many different colours!
When we pray, we can be part of bringing God's life
to the world around us.
We can be part of helping other people to grow.

Ask the children to take round baskets filled with the flowers.

Name and *Name* are going to bring round these baskets of flowers.
If you like, you can take a flower.
Let's ask God to see these flowers as a prayer for a special person.

Hum the tune together, with the words 'Jesus, hear our prayer!' as a refrain, until all the children and adults who wish to take a flower have done so. Place your 'garden' in the centre of the circle.

If you like, you can place your flower in our garden as a prayer.
This Green Time, let's watch beautiful things
growing in our garden and in our lives as we pray.

Hum the tune together again while the group place their flowers. Larger groups may like to invite two children to carry the 'garden' around the circle to collect the children's flowers. This garden can then be placed in the centre of the circle.

End this time of prayer with the final verse of the Prayer Song you've chosen.

Prayer Action: Option 2

→ **Action: growing from a seed**

Either: It's Green Time!

Or: It's spring/summer/autumn/harvest time!

We can see flowers and trees
growing beautifully all around us.
When we pray, it can be like planting a little seed:
a seed that will grow into something beautiful.
Let's imagine that the prayer we've just prayed
for a special person is a seed.
Let's be that seed now.

Let's curl up into a ball.
Lead the children in curling up into a ball.
Let's show our roots with our fingers.
Lead the children in wiggling fingers.
We need to let our roots grow down deep.
Lead the children in wiggling fingers down.
Then after three, let a little shoot pop up.
1, 2, 3 . . . Pop!
Poke your hands up over your head like a little shoot.

Then start to grow up tall.
Gradually stand up, swaying like a growing stalk.
Taller and taller onto our tiptoes . . .
Reach up with pointy hands and on tiptoes.

Let's turn our faces up towards the sun!
Then let our leaves or branches spread out wide.
Arms stretch slowly outwards.

What beautiful plants!
When we pray, it can be like planting little seeds of love
all around us.

End this time of prayer with the final verse of the Prayer Song you've chosen.

Thank You, God

→ **Guide: p. 227**

Thank You, God: Option 1

→ **Song: 'My hands were made for love'. Words © Sharon Moughtin-Mumby**
→ **Tune: 'Hickory, dickory, dock' (traditional). For the music, see p. 262, or for a taster see the Diddy Disciples website. For tips on teaching songs for the first time, see p. 215.**

Invite the children to sit in a circle for a moment of quiet.

It's time to remember all the things we've done this week.
It's time to say 'thank you' to God
for when we've been part of showing God's love.

Let's wiggle our fingers!
I wonder when you've shown love
with your hands this week?

Wiggle fingers as you sing.
My hands were made for love!
My hands were made for love!
Thank you for the love they've shown.
My hands were made for love!

Let's wiggle our feet!
I wonder when you've shown love
with your feet this week?

Wiggle feet as you sing.
My feet were made for love!
My feet were made for love!
Thank you for the love they've shown.
My feet were made for love!

Let's put our hands gently on our neck.
Let's sing 'Ahhh!'
Ahhhhh!
Can you feel your throat vibrating and dancing?
I wonder when you've shown love
with your voice this week?

Hold neck and feel your voice 'dancing' as you sing.
My voice was made for love!
My voice was made for love!
Thank you for the love it's shown.
My voice was made for love!

Thank You, God: Option 2

→ **Song: 'For the love we've shown'. Words © Sharon Moughtin-Mumby**
→ **Tune: 'All through the night' (traditional). For the music see p. 259, or for a taster see the Diddy Disciples website. For tips on teaching songs for the first time, see p. 215.**

Most suitable for use with children over the age of four.

Invite the children to sit in a circle for a moment of quiet.

It's time to remember all the things we've done this week.
It's time to say 'thank you' to God
for when we've been part of showing God's love.

> *Either:* Let's wiggle our fingers.
> *Or:* Let's hold up our hands.

I wonder when you've shown love
with your hands this week?

> *Either:* Let's wiggle our feet.
> *Or:* Let's show our feet.

I wonder when you've shown love
with your feet this week?

Let's put our hands gently on our neck.
Let's sing 'Ahhh!'
Ahhhhh!

Can you feel your neck vibrating and dancing with your voice?
I wonder when you've shown love
with your voice this week?

Let's sing our 'thank you' song to God
for the times we've been part of sharing God's love.

For the love we've shown with our hands, *Hold hands up or wiggle fingers*
thank you, God!
For the love we've shown with our feet, *Point to feet or wiggle feet*
thank you, God!
When we love all those around us, *Cross hands on chest*
it's the same as loving Jesus!
For the love we've shown with our voice, *Hands on neck or point to singing mouth*
thank you, God!

Creative Response

→ **Guide: p. 228**

See the Creative Response starter ideas in Section 3 of this chapter (p. 122).

Sharing God's Peace

→ **Guide: p. 231**

This Building Block is particularly designed for children's groups that join the adult congregation to share communion, but it can also be used to end any session or Service of the Word.

Sharing God's Peace: Option 1

→ **Song: 'I've got peace like a river' (traditional). Isaiah 66.12,** NIV
→ **Tune: Traditional. For a taster, see the Diddy Disciples website. For tips on teaching songs for the first time, see p. 215.**

> *Either: Hold one end of the peace cloth (see Guide, p. 231) and ask one of the older children or an adult to hold the other end. Start singing the Peace Song. As the children begin to gather, invite them to join in holding a small section of the cloth, raising and lowering it so it 'flows' like a river as you sing together.*

> *Or: Invite the children to sit in a circle in the worship space. Start singing the Peace Song. As the children begin to gather, invite them to join in raising and lowering their hands like the waters of a flowing river.*

I've got peace like a river,
I've got peace like a river,
I've got peace like a river in my soul.
I've got peace like a river,
I've got peace like a river,
I've got peace like a river in my soul.

If your group is about to rejoin the adults for communion: when all the children are gathered, continue with the words of the Peace following Option 3 below.

Sharing God's Peace: Option 2

→ **Song: 'Peace is flowing like a river' (traditional). Isaiah 66.12, NIV**
→ **Tune: Traditional. For a taster, see the Diddy Disciples website. For tips on teaching songs for the first time, see p. 215.**

> *Either: Hold one end of the peace cloth (see Guide, p. 231) and ask one of the older children or an adult to hold the other end. Start singing the Peace Song. As the children begin to gather, invite them to join in holding a small section of the cloth, raising and lowering it so it 'flows' like a river as you sing together.*

> *Or: Invite the children to sit in a circle in the worship space. Start singing the Peace Song. As the children begin to gather, invite them to join in raising and lowering their hands like the waters of a flowing river.*

Peace is flowing like a river,
flowing out through you and me.
Spreading out into the desert,
setting all the captives free.

If your group is about to rejoin the adults for communion, when all the children are gathered, continue with the words of the Peace following Option 3 below:

Sharing God's Peace: Option 3

→ **Song: 'I've got peace in my fingers' © 1995 Susan Salidor ASCAP**
→ **Tune: © 1995 Susan Salidor ASCAP**
→ **The words and music can be found on the album** *Little Voices in My Head* **by Susan Salidor © 2003 Peach Head. They can also be found on iTunes, YouTube, or at www.susansalidor.com**

Invite the children to sit in a circle in the worship space. Start singing the Peace Song. As the children begin to gather, invite them to join in with the song and actions. If your group is about to rejoin the adults for communion, when all the children are gathered, continue with the words of the Peace below:

The Peace

→ **2 Thessalonians 3.16; 1 Peter 5.14**

Once you've finished singing . . .

The peace of the Lord be always with you.
Hold hands open to the children.

And also with you.
Invite the children to open their hands towards you.

Let's shake hands or hug each other
and say 'Peace be with you' *or whatever is said on sharing the Peace in your church* as a sign of God's peace.

Lead the children in giving and receiving the Peace. Immediately following this, at St Peter's, Walworth, we lead the children back to join the rest of the congregation to continue our worship with the Eucharistic Prayer.

Taking God's Love into the World

→ Song: 'This little light of mine' (traditional)
→ Tune: Traditional. For a taster, see the Diddy Disciples website. For tips on teaching songs for the first time, see p. 215.
→ Guide: p. 232

This Building Block is particularly designed for standalone groups or groups that are held during a Service of the Word. Alternatively, you could use one of the Peace Songs above to end your worship.

Our time together is coming to an end.

Invite the children to sit in a circle for a moment of quiet.

God has lit a little light of love inside all of us.
Trace a circle on your heart with your finger.
Let's make our finger into a candle.
Bring your finger from your heart and hold it out.
Let's be God and light our little light of love together, after three.
Lead the children in lighting their finger candle by striking an imaginary match in the air on a count of three and pretending to light your finger.
1, 2, 3 . . . Tssss!

Let's imagine God's love shining and dancing like light in us.

Wave your finger in front of you as you sing.
This little light of mine, I'm gonna let it shine!
This little light of mine, I'm gonna let it shine!
This little light of mine, I'm gonna let it shine!
Let it shine, let it shine, let it shine!

Blow on your finger as if blowing out a candle on 'puff'. Then hold it up high.
Won't let no one *puff* it out! I'm gonna let it shine!
Won't let no one *puff* it out! I'm gonna let it shine!
Won't let no one *puff* it out! I'm gonna let it shine!
Let it shine, let it shine, let it shine!

Hold your finger behind a cupped hand, then take your cupped hand away to reveal the 'candle' and hold it high!
Hide it under a bushel? No! I'm gonna let it shine!
Hide it under a bushel? No! I'm gonna let it shine!
Hide it under a bushel? No! I'm gonna let it shine!
Let it shine, let it shine, let it shine!

Lead the children in placing your finger back on your heart.
Now let's put our little light of love
back in our hearts, where it belongs.
Let's remember to let our little light shine
in all our playing and working today . . .

If you're building a Service of the Word and this is your final Building Block, you may like to close with a familiar blessing, the Peace, and/or one of the following. If you're introducing one of these call-and-responses to your group for the first time, see p. 53 for an introduction.

> *Either:* Praise the Lord! *Both hands to self*
> **Alleluia!** *Both arms upwards in 'V' shape*
>
> *Or:* Let us bless the Lord. *Both hands to self*
> **Thanks be to God.** *Both arms upwards in 'V' shape*
>
> *Or:* And all the people said . . . *Both hands to self*
> **Amen!** *Both arms upwards in 'V' shape*

Section 2

The Bible Storytelling material, God the Maker unit

Week 1: God the Maker

→ Genesis 1.1—2.3
→ Song: 'And it was good!' Words © Sharon Moughtin-Mumby
→ Tune: 'Here we go round the mulberry bush' (traditional). For a taster, see the Diddy Disciples website.

'Let there be light!' And there was light! There was light! There was light!

'Let there be light!' And there was light! And it was good!

You may like to use real numbers to tell this story, either printed on separate pieces of A4 paper or – if you have the facilities – projected onto a screen or smartboard. If you're using the What's in the Box? option (p. 221), you could place the numbers inside the box.

> **Tip**
>
> At St Peter's, Walworth, we use numbers decorated with illustrations of the days of creation, which are available freely on the internet. A link can be found on the Diddy Disciples website. If you choose to use these illustrated numbers, you could point out the drawing inside as you put each number up during the storytelling. For example, as you put up Number 2: 'Look! On Day Two, God made the sky!'

Either: If you're using numbers, show them to the children at this point.
Can anyone tell us what these are?

Or: What's in the box?
Ask a child to respond.

In our story today, God makes the world in seven days.
Let's count to seven together:
1, 2, 3, 4, 5, 6, 7.
We're ready to tell our story . . .

Let's imagine we're going right back
to the very beginning.

Before there was anything at all.
Not even any light.
Let's close our eyes.
In the beginning all was dark.
Let's feel the dark.
Let's sing quietly, in a whisper,
with our eyes closed.

In the beginning all was dark,
all was dark, all was dark.
In the beginning all was dark.
Ssssh! Ssssh! Ssssh!

In the dark, a wind was blowing.
It was God's wind! The Spirit's here!
With your eyes closed, can you sing quietly
and blow like a gentle wind?

In the beginning *Blow! Blow! Blow!*
In the beginning *Blow! Blow! Blow!*

Then God said, 'Let there be light!' *Throw arms out*
And there was light!
Let's open our eyes!

Let there be light, and there was light, *Throw arms out*
there was light, there was light. *Throw arms out*
Let there be light, and there was light. *Throw arms out*
[And] it was good! *Thumbs up action*

Let's put our thumbs up to show 'And it was good!'
And sing that last line again:

[And] it was good! *Thumbs up action*

That was the first day!

> *If you're using numbers:*
> What number do we need to put up for the first day?
> *Ask a child to respond.*

Can you show me one finger?
That was Day One!
What comes after one? *Invite responses*

If you're using numbers, put number 2 up at this point.

On Day 2, God said, 'Let there be sky!'
And there was sky!

Invite the children to make up an action for sky and use this action as you sing.
Let there be sky, and there was sky.
There was sky, there was sky.
Let there be sky, and there was sky.
[And] it was good! *Thumbs up action*

That was Day Two!
Let's count the days we've had so far on our fingers.
1, 2 . . .
What's next? What comes after two?
1, 2, 3! Day Three!

If you're using numbers, put number 3 up.

On Day Three, God said, 'Let there be plants
and flowers and trees.'
Let's be a flower or tree growing from the ground.
Let's curl up into a little ball like a seed.
Lead the children in curling up into a ball.

First, we need to put our roots down.
Let's show our roots with our fingers.
Lead the children in wiggling fingers.

We need to let our roots grow down deep.
Lead the children in wiggling fingers down.

Then after three, let a little shoot pop up.
1, 2, 3 . . . Pop!
Poke your hands up over your head like a little shoot.

Then start to grow up tall.
Gradually stand up, swaying like a growing stalk.
Taller and taller onto our tiptoes . . .
Reach up with pointy hands and on tiptoes.

Let's turn our faces up towards the sun!
Then let our leaves or branches spread out wide.
Arms stretch slowly outwards. When the children have grown up like a plant once:

Let's do that again as we sing.

Lead the children in curling up on the ground again and growing up as you sing.
Let there be plants, and there were plants.
There were plants, there were plants.
Let there be plants, and there were plants.
[And] it was good! *Thumbs up action*

Look at all those beautiful flowers and trees!
All those beautiful colours!

That was Day Three.
Let's count the days we've had so far . . .
Can you show me your fingers? 1, 2, 3!
What's next? What comes after three?
Day Four!

If you're using numbers, put number 4 up.

On Day Four, God said, 'Let there be sun, moon and stars.'

Choose actions for sun, moon or stars and use them as you sing.
Let there be sun and moon and stars.
Moon and stars, moon and stars.
Let there be sun and moon and stars.
[And] it was good! *Thumbs up action*

That was Day Four.
Let's count the days we've had so far . . .
Can you show me your fingers? 1, 2, 3, 4 . . .
What's next? What comes after four?
Day Five!

If you're using numbers, put number 5 up.

On Day Five, God said 'Let there be fish!'
And there were fish!

Ask the children for an action for fish and use it as you sing.
Let there be fish and there were fish!
There were fish! There were fish!
Let there be fish and there were fish!
[And] it was good! *Thumbs up action*

And God said, 'Let there be birds!'
And there were birds!

Ask the children for an action for birds and use it as you sing.
Let there be birds and there were birds!
There were birds! There were birds!
Let there be birds and there were birds!
[And] it was good! *Thumbs up action*

That was Day Five.
Let's count the days we've had so far . . .
Can you show me your fingers? 1, 2, 3, 4, 5 . . .
What's next? What comes after five?
Day Six!

If you're using numbers, put number 6 up.

On Day Six, God said, 'Let there be animals!'
I wonder what your favourite animal is?

Invite the children to name different animals and show actions.
Invite the children to be any animal they like as you sing.
Change between different animals as you lead them.

Let there be animals and there were animals!
There were animals! There were animals!
Let there be animals and there were animals!
[And] it was good! *Thumbs up action*

But wait! God isn't finished yet today!
God said, 'Let us make people to be like us!' Men and women!
Let's sing 'Let there be people and there were people!'

Ask the children to choose an action for people and use it as you sing.
Let there be people and there were people!
There were people, there were people!
Let there be people and there were people!
[And] it was good! *Thumbs up action*

But wait! This time it wasn't good.
This time, God saw that it was VERY good.
Let's sing the end again, but this time let's sing
(sing) 'And it was very good!' *Thumbs up high*
[And] it was VERY good! *Thumbs up high*

That was Day Six.
Let's count the days we've had so far . . .
Can you show me your fingers? 1, 2, 3, 4, 5, 6 . . .
What's next? What comes after six?
Day Seven! The seventh day. The last day!

If you're using numbers, put number 7 up.

On Day Seven, God said, 'Time to rest now! Ssssh! Ssssh!'
It's always important to take time to rest like God.

Ask the children to choose an action for 'rest' and use it as you sing.
Time to rest now. Ssssh! Ssssh!
Ssssh! Ssssh! Ssssh! Ssssh!
Time to rest now. Ssssh! Ssssh!
It was VERY GOOD! *Thumbs up above head*

So that's the story about God the Maker
making the world in seven days.
Let's count to seven together again:
1, 2, 3, 4, 5, 6, 7!

God the Maker made the world in seven days.
And it was VERY GOOD. *Thumbs up above head*
Let's finish by singing a 'thank you' to God.
Let's sing 'God the Maker made the world'.
What action could we use for the world?

Choose from the actions suggested by the children.

At the end let's sing 'And it was VERY GOOD!' *Thumbs up high above head*
as loud as we can to say 'thank you' to God the Maker
for this beautiful world.

God the Maker made the world, *Children's action for the world*
made the world, made the world.
God the Maker made the world,
and it was VERY GOOD! *Thumbs up high above head*

Week 2: God Plants a Garden

→ **Genesis 2.4–15**
→ **Song: 'There was a garden long ago'. Words © Sharon Moughtin-Mumby**
→ **Tune: 'There was a princess long ago' (traditional). For a taster, see the Diddy Disciples website. If your group aren't familiar with the song, you could also sing it to 'Have you seen the muffin man?'**

If you're using the What's in the Box? option (p. 221), invite one of the children to open the box. Inside will be a trowel, or a watering can, and a tray or bowl of mud/soil to represent the garden.

What's in the box? *Ask the child to respond.*

In our story today, God plants the world
like we plant a garden or park.
Let's tell our story together.

In the beginning there was a garden.
Let's look around our garden!
Lead the children in looking right and left around an imaginary garden.

There were no trees, no plants, no grass!
Just mud! Let's squelch our feet in the mud.
Lead the children in squelching feet in imaginary mud.

Freeze!
The garden was called Eden,
which means 'misty place' because it was full of mist!
Can you show me misty?
Lead the children in waving hands in the air.

Misty means there's lots of tiny bits of water in the air.
The water is making the mud very, very muddy!

Shall we sing a song about our garden of Eden?
Let's squelch in the mud as we sing.

There was a garden long ago,
long ago, long ago.
There was a garden long ago.
Long ago! *Both thumbs pointing behind shoulder*

In this story, we're going to be God the Maker.

Let's stand up tall and be God!
When all the children are standing up tall . . .

God bent down.
Lead the children in kneeling down . . .

God took a handful of mud.
Lead the children in miming taking a handful of mud . . .

And God made it into a shape.
Let's make our mud into a shape.
God made the mud into a man!
Shall we make our mud into a man as well?

Lead the children in miming shaping the mud as you sing.
God took some mud and made a man,
made a man, made a man.
God took some mud and made a man,
made a man.

Then God, very gently, held the man.
Lead the children in holding an imaginary tiny man in your cupped hands.
And puffed wind into the man's nose.
After three, shall we blow wind very gently into our man's nose?
1, 2, 3 . . . *Blow.*

The mud man got up!
Lead the children in showing the mud man's legs with their fingers.
And walked around!

Walk the 'finger man' around on your other arm, up over your shoulders and head and down your body as you sing.
The man got up and walked around,
walked around, walked around!
The man got up and walked around,
walked around!

Next, God did some planting.
God dug. Let's dig together like God.
And God planted plants.

Let's kneel down and plant like God.
I wonder what colours and flowers and trees will be in your garden?
Let's be a flower or tree growing from the ground.

Let's curl up into a little ball like a seed.
Lead the children in curling up into a ball.

First, we need to put our roots down.
Let's show our roots with our fingers.
Lead the children in wiggling fingers.

We need to let our roots grow down deep.
Lead the children in wiggling fingers down.

Then after three, let a little shoot pop up.
1, 2, 3 . . . Pop!
Poke your hands up over your head like a little shoot.

Then start to grow up tall.
Gradually stand up, swaying like a growing stalk.
Taller and taller onto our tiptoes . . .
Reach up with pointy hands and on tiptoes.

Let's turn our faces up towards the sun!
Then let our leaves or branches spread out wide.
Arms stretch slowly outwards.

Let's do that again as we sing.

Lead the children in miming the movements from seed to plant as you sing.
Then God planted the trees and flowers,
trees and flowers, trees and flowers.
Then God planted the trees and flowers.
Trees and flowers.

Look at our beautiful garden!
Look at all those beautiful colours!
And smell! *Breathe in deeply*
Smell those beautiful flowers!

God put the man in the garden
to look after it.

Let's be God again!
Let's hold the garden in one of our hands
with the little man in it.
Let's sing to the man and point to our garden.

'This is my garden! Care for it!
Care for it! Care for it!'
'This is my garden! Care for it!
Care for it!'

Sit down together for a moment of quiet.

That story from long ago is in the Bible.
When we're telling the story the garden looks tiny.
Point to your cupped hand.

And the man looks tiny. *Show the little finger man standing in your cupped hand*
But that's because we're being God!
Everything looks tiny to God!

But let me tell you a secret.
Whisper: The garden in our song is the whole world!
Move arms upwards and outwards.

Normal voice: The tiny man *Show the little finger man*
is as tall as me! *Stand up as leader*
Much taller than you!
Sit down again.

God made the whole world!
In our song, who did God ask
to look after the world, the garden?
Accept responses from the children.

God still asks people to look after our world.
That means it's our job, too!

If appropriate, give a short example that would be relevant to your group. For example:

> *Either:* How can we care for our world?
> We can grow things!
> Has anyone here grown a plant?
> That's helping to take care of God's world.
> Who'd like to do some planting like God?
> We can do that after *our Sorry Song/our Prayers/we finish our story, etc.*

> *Or:* How can we care for our world?
> We can 'recycle' things.
> That means use things again
> instead of throwing them away.
> Let's not fill God's world with lots of rubbish!
> Let's 'recycle' and use things for something different.
> *Show a box of recyclable materials that look interesting.*
> Like these!
> Who'd like to make something new out of these?

> *If you will be providing recyclable materials as a Creative Response:*
> We can do that after *example:* our Sorry Song.

Let's sing 'This is my world! Care for it!' again.
This time, let's sing it to each other.
As we sing, let's show our world. *Hands out*
Then point to each other. *Point to three children, one by one*
And let's not forget to point to ourselves too! *Point to self*
What will we do to look after our world?

This is my wor-ld! *Hands out.* **Care for it!** *Point at three children*
Care for it! *Point at three children.* **Care for it!** *Point at three children*
This is my wor-ld! *Hands out.* **Care for it!** *Point at yourself three times*
Care for it! *Point round the circle at everyone*

Repeat

Week 3: Everything in All the World Sings 'Alleluia!'

→ **Psalm 148**
→ **Song: 'Everything in all the world sings "Alleluia!"' Words © Sharon Moughtin-Mumby**
→ **Tune: 'Old Macdonald had a farm' (public domain). For a taster, see the Diddy Disciples website.**

This week's song is based on Psalm 148 and can be used to sing about the weather (Option 1: Psalm 148.8), or birds and animals (Option 2: Psalm 148.10), or both. Groups that are exploring the weather in the Gathering Song may like the opportunity to explore animals and birds here. However, if your group has not yet explored the wonderful weather that God has created, the weather version may be useful for preparing the children for the story of Jesus calming the storm in Week 4.

In the Bible, there's a song where everything sings 'Alleluia!'
Alleluia is a special 'thank you' word
that means 'Praise God!'
After three, let's shout 'Alleluia' together.

1, 2, 3 . . . Alleluia!

In our song, it's not just people who sing 'Alleluia!'
but everything in the whole world.

Option 1: Weather

→ **Psalm 148.8**

With younger children, you might like to use pictures of the weather to support their understanding where indicated. These can become the items for the What's in the Box? option (p. 221) where appropriate.

> *If you're using the What's in the Box? option, invite one of the children to open the box.*

> What's in the box? *Ask the child to respond.*

> *Invite the children to name the different kinds of weather on the pictures.*

Our world has lots of different kinds of weather.
Let's sing a song about how
all the different weathers sing 'Alleluia' to God the Maker!

Let's start with thunder. *Show thunder symbol*
What noise does thunder make?

Invite the children to respond and accept their responses.
Encourage them to make up a full body action, too.

That's how thunder sings 'Alleluia!' *Lead the children in making their sound and action*
Let's sing our 'Alleluia' song together:

Everything in all the world *Circle to show the globe*
sings 'Alleluia!' *Arms raised in 'V' shape*
[The] *thunder* always loves to sing 'Alleluia!' *Arms raised in 'V' shape*
With a ____! ____! here! *Add the children's sound and action*
And a ____! ____! there!
Here a ____! There a ____!
Everywhere a ____! ____!
Everything in all the world *Circle to show the globe*
sings 'Alleluia!' *Arms raised in 'V' shape*

Continue by inviting the children to choose the weather for each verse, or, if you prefer, use the following order. Use the weather symbols to support the children as appropriate. Before singing each verse, invite the children to make up a noise and a full body action for the weather, as in the example above. Examples of sounds are given below in case your group needs a starter idea for any of them, but encourage the children to develop their own sounds.

- *thunder (clap, or stamp on the floor)*
- *rain (drum fingers on the floor to make the sound of rain on the ground and rooftops)*
- *snow (a swishing sound)*
- *sun (our children loved making silent star jumps to show the sun blazing)*
- *wind (Wooooo!)*
- *lightning (Ptchooo, ptchoo!)*

> *To end, either:*
> What weather is it today?
> Let's sing about our weather for today.
> Then when you go outside later,
> and feel or hear or see the weather,
> remember, it's singing 'Alleluia!' to God.
> *Sing appropriate words for today's weather.*
>
> *Or:*
> *Yawn.* Who's feeling really tired after all that weather!
> It's time for bed . . .
> *Lead the children in lying down to sleep on the floor.*
>
> Look at the stars! *Twinkle hands in the air*
> The stars are singing 'Alleluia!' to God, too!
> Sssssh! Let's sing in a whisper
> about how the stars sing 'Alleluia!' with their twinkle . . .
>
> *Sing in a hushed voice, lying on the floor to sleep, with one hand raised making a twinkle sign for the stars in the sky.*
> **Everything in all the world** *Sleeping action*
> **sings 'Alleluia!'** *Arms raised in 'V' shape*
> **[The] *stars* always love to sing 'Alleluia!'** *Arms raised in 'V' shape*
> **With a *twinkle, twinkle* here!** *Add the children's sound and action*
> **And a *twinkle, twinkle* there!**
> **Here a *twinkle*! There a *twinkle*!**
> **Everywhere a *twinkle, twinkle*.**
> **Everything in all the world** *Sleeping action*
> **sings 'Alleluia!'** *Slow down and end in sleepiness*

Option 2: Animals and birds

→ Psalm 148.10

With younger children, you might like to use pictures of animals or birds, figures, or soft toys to support their understanding. These can become the items for the What's in the Box? option (p. 221) where appropriate.

If you're using the What's in the Box? option, invite one of the children to open the box.

What's in the box? *Ask the child to respond.*

Invite the children to name the different kinds of animals and birds on the pictures/figures.

Our world has lots of animals and birds.
Let's sing a song about how
all the different birds and animals sing 'Alleluia'
to God the Maker!

Let's start with a duck!
Who can tell us what noise a duck makes?
Invite the children to respond and accept their responses. Encourage them to show an action, too.

That's how a duck sings 'Alleluia!' *Children's sound and action*

Everything in all the world *Circle* **sings 'Alleluia!'** *Arms raised in 'V' shape*
[The] *ducks* **always love to sing 'Alleluia!'** *Arms raised in 'V' shape*
With a ____! ____! here! *Add the children's sound and action*
And a ____! ____! there!
Here a ____! There a ____!
Everywhere a ____! ____!
Everything in all the world *Circle* **sings 'Alleluia!'** *Arms raised in 'V' shape*

Continue by inviting the children to choose a different animal with a noise and action for each verse. You may wish to limit the children to a certain group of animals that you have symbols or figures for – e.g. farm animals, jungle animals – or you may be happy to let them go wild! Before singing each verse, invite the children to make up an action and noise for the animal as in the example above.

To end:
In our song from the Bible,
everything sings 'Alleluia! Praise God!'
When you go out and about today,
whenever you see an animal,
remember, it's singing 'Alleluia!' to God.
Maybe you could listen out *Hand over ear*
and see if you can hear it singing 'Alleluia!'

I think all of us will be able to see or hear a bird today!
How do birds sing 'Alleluia'?

You may like to encourage the children to focus on a common, local bird.
Invite the children to respond and accept their responses. Encourage them to show an action, too.

That's how *birds* sing 'Alleluia!' *Children's sound and action*

Everything in all the world *Circle* **sings 'Alleluia!'** *Arms raised in 'V' shape*
The *birds* **always love to sing 'Alleluia!'** *Arms raised in 'V' shape*
With a ____! ____! here! *Add the children's sound and action*
And a ____! ____! there!
Here a ____! There a ____!
Everywhere a ____! ____!
Everything in all the world *Circle* **sings 'Alleluia!'** *Arms raised in 'V' shape*

Let's listen out for the birds
and all the other animals we see
singing 'Alleluia!' to God the Maker today.

Week 4: Jesus the Maker (The Calming of the Storm)

→ Luke 8.22–25 (also Matthew 8.23–27 and Mark 4.35–41)
→ Song: 'On the Sea of Galilee'. Words © Sharon Moughtin-Mumby
→ Tune: 'The big ship sails on the Ally, Ally-O' (traditional). For a taster, see the Diddy Disciples website.

If you're using the What's in the Box? option (p. 221), invite one of the children to open the box. Inside will be a boat.

What's in the box? *Ask the child to respond.*

Today we're going to tell a story
about a boat and a HUGE storm!
It's the story of when Jesus stopped the storm
and Jesus' friends, the disciples, saw that
Jesus was God the Maker.

We're going to be the disciples,
So let's get into our boat.
Let's put our legs out in front of us so we can row.
Let's pick up our oar and row.

Lead the children in rowing as in 'Row, row, row your boat', but singing to the tune of 'The big ship sails on the Ally, Ally-O'.
[Let's] row, row, row on the Sea of Galilee,
the Sea of Galilee, the Sea of Galilee!
[Let's] row, row, row on the Sea of Galilee,
on the Sea of Galilee!

But look! *Point in shock*
There's a storm coming!
And the wind goes 'Whoosh!' *Fling arms outwards*
and the waves go 'Crash!' *Bring arms down quickly, palms downwards to show waves crashing*

Lead the children in singing.
And the wind goes 'Whoosh!' *Fling arms outwards*
and the waves go 'Crash!', *Waves crashing action*
the waves go 'Crash!', the waves go 'Crash!'
The wind goes 'Whoosh!' *Fling arms outwards*
and the waves go 'Crash!' *Waves crashing action*
on the Sea of Galilee.

How do you think Jesus' friends felt in the storm?
Can you show me?

You may like to lead the children in singing again as they show the feelings they've identified with their faces, as well as showing the actions of the sea with their bodies.

And the wind goes 'Whoosh!' *Fling arms outwards*
and the waves go 'Crash!', *Waves crashing action*
the waves go 'Crash!', the waves go 'Crash!'
The wind goes 'Whoosh!' *Fling arms outwards*
and the waves go 'Crash!' *Waves crashing action*
on the Sea of Galilee.

Help! Where's Jesus?
Lead the children in looking around with hand shielding eyes.

Look! *Point* Jesus is sleeping *Sleeping action*
at the bottom of the boat!

Lead the children in singing, with the sleeping action throughout.
Jesus is sleeping at the bottom of the boat,
the bottom of the boat, the bottom of the boat!
Jesus is sleeping at the bottom of the boat,
on the Sea of Galilee.

And the wind goes 'Whoosh!' *Fling arms outwards*
and the waves go 'Crash!', *Waves crashing action*
the waves go 'Crash!', the waves go 'Crash!'
The wind goes 'Whoosh!' *Fling arms outwards*
and the waves go 'Crash!' *Waves crashing action*
on the Sea of Galilee.

Jesus' friends were terrified!
Let's wave our hands in the air to show we're scared!
Let's shout to Jesus:
'Come on Jesus! Help! Wake up!'

Lead the children in waving their hands in the air in panic and sing together:
'Come on Jesus! Help! Wake up!
'Help! Wake up! Help! Wake up!
'Come on Jesus! Help! Wake up!'
on the Sea of Galilee.

And the wind goes 'Whoosh!' *Fling arms outwards*
and the waves go 'Crash!', *Waves crashing action*
the waves go 'Crash!', the waves go 'Crash!'
The wind goes 'Whoosh!' *Fling arms outwards*
and the waves go 'Crash!' *Waves crashing action*
on the Sea of Galilee.

But Jesus didn't panic. *Shake head*
Let's be Jesus and sit up calmly.
Jesus spoke to the storm. Jesus said:
'Be calm!' *Palms outwards* 'Be still!' *Palms downwards*
Let's say: 'Be calm!' *Palms outwards* 'Be still!' *Palms downwards*

'Be calm!' *Palms outwards* **'Be still!'** *Palms downwards*

Lead the children in singing.
Jesus says, 'Be calm! *Palms outwards* **Be still!'** *Palms downwards*
'Be calm! *Palms outwards* **Be still!'** *Palms downwards*
'Be calm! *Palms outwards* **Be still!'** *Palms downwards*
Jesus says, 'Be calm! *Palms outwards* **Be still!'** *Palms downwards*
on the Sea of Galilee.

And guess what happened!
The winds were calm! *Palms outwards*
And the waves were still! *Palms downwards*

Lead the children in singing.
And the winds are calm! *Palms outwards*
And the waves are still, *Palms downwards*
the waves are still! the waves are still! *Palms downwards*
And the winds are calm, *Palms outwards*
and the waves are still, *Palms downwards*
on the Sea of Galilee.

How do you think Jesus' friends felt
when they saw that the storm did what Jesus said?
Can you show me?
Jesus' friends looked at each other, amazed!
And they asked a very important question:
'Who is Jesus?' *Hands upwards in question, the disciples showing their feelings with their faces*
Shall we ask that together?

Who is Jesus? *Hands upwards in question, showing your feelings with your face*

'Who is Jesus? *Hands upwards in question, the children showing their feelings with their face*
Look! The winds and waves have stopped!' *Make a* stop sign *with palm of hand*

Lead the children in singing:
Who is Jesus? *Questioning action*
Look! The winds and waves have stopped! *Stop sign*
The winds and waves have stopped! *Stop sign*
The winds and waves have stopped! *Stop sign*
Who is Jesus? *Questioning action*

Look! The winds and waves have stopped *Stop sign*
on the Sea of Galilee.

It was then that Jesus' friends knew that
Jesus was the God the Maker.
Jesus was God who made the wind,
and the waves:
all the weather,
the whole world!
I wonder how they felt?
Can you show me?

Invite the children to sit quietly for a moment, and to close their eyes.

Sometimes, when we're cross or scared,
it can feel like there's a storm inside us.
It can feel a bit scary.
Next time you feel stormy inside,
maybe you could ask Jesus to say,
'Be calm! Be still!'

Let's open our eyes.
Let's sing about the storms we can sometimes feel inside ourselves.
Instead of 'on the Sea of Galilee',
let's sing 'inside me'. *Both hands on stomach*

And the wind goes 'Whoosh!' *Fling arms outwards*
and the waves go 'Crash!', *Waves crashing action*
the waves go 'Crash!', the waves go 'Crash!'
The wind goes 'Whoosh!' *Fling arms outwards*
and the waves go 'Crash!' *Waves crashing action*
inside me. *Both hands on stomach*

Now let's imagine Jesus there,
calming the storm inside us.

Lead the children in singing.
Jesus says, 'Be calm! *Palms outwards* **Be still!'** *Palms downwards*
'**Be calm!** *Palms outwards* **Be still!'** *Palms downwards*
'**Be calm!** *Palms outwards* **Be still!'** *Palms downwards*
Jesus says, 'Be calm!' *Palms outwards* **'Be still!'** *Palms downwards*
inside me. *Both hands on stomach*

And now let's imagine our storm calming inside us. Sssssh!

And the winds are calm! *Palms outwards*
And the waves are still, *Palms downwards*
the waves are still! the waves are still! *Palms downwards*
And the winds are calm! *Palms outwards*
And the waves are still, *Palms downwards*
inside me. *Both hands on stomach*

Week 5: Harvest: Thank You, God the Maker!

→ **Song: 'This is the way we sow the seed'. Words © Sharon Moughtin-Mumby**
→ **Tune: 'Here we go round the mulberry bush' (traditional). For a taster, see the Diddy Disciples website.**

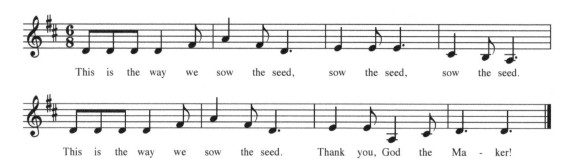

This is the way we sow the seed, sow the seed, sow the seed.

This is the way we sow the seed. Thank you, God the Ma - ker!

This session works well towards the end of the God the Maker unit. However, if you have a Harvest Festival or Thanksgiving, it may make sense to rearrange the weeks so that you tell this story together the week beforehand, or on the day itself.

The session material tells the story of how bread is made. Wheat is the most common crop in the UK and bread is a staple in many households. If there are other crops or produce local to your area, however (or if your group includes children who cannot eat gluten), you could adapt the material appropriately to tell the story of another crop or item of produce (or a food containing it that the children will readily recognize) – for example fruit, corn, vegetables, rape, barley, oats, sugar beet, dairy, wool, fish. Telling the story of meat would need to be handled sensitively but may be appropriate in some areas.

This Green Time we've been telling stories about God the Maker.
We've been thanking God for this beautiful world.
Today, we're not going to tell a story from the Bible.
We're going to tell a story from our life.
Did you know everything we eat has a story?

> *If you're using the What's in the Box? option (p. 221), invite one of the children to open the box at this point, with bread inside.*

> What's in the box? *Ask the child to respond.*

Today, we're going to tell the story of this bread.
Then we're going to thank God for bread.
So let's stand up and get ready.
For this story, we need to go to a field [in the countryside].

For groups that aren't located in the countryside:

> After three, we're going to close our eyes and
> *Either:* turn around three times *or* count to three.
> When we open our eyes again, we'll be in the countryside.
> Let's go . . .
> **1, 2, 3.** *Turning around or counting on fingers*
> Open your eyes!
> We're here!
> We're in an empty field in the countryside.

Our story begins in autumn time.
We're going to plant some wheat seeds in this field.
We've got too many seeds to plant with our hands,
so let's jump into our tractor and start it up.

Lead the children in miming getting in and turning on the engine.

What sound does it make?
Let's bounce up and down in our tractor
as our tractor goes up and down the field,
'sowing' – that means 'planting' – our wheat seeds.

Encourage the children to bounce up and down in a rhythm.

Let's sing together:

This is the way we sow the seed,
sow the seed, sow the seed.
This is the way we sow the seed.
Thank you, God the Maker!

All done! Let's get out of our tractor.

Lead the children in miming turning off the engine and getting out.

Winter time is coming.
It's cold! How do you look when it's cold?
Lead the children in shivering etc.

The wheat seeds go to sleep in the winter.
They 'hibernate'.
Can you show me the wheat seeds sleeping?
Lead the children in curling up on the ground like a seed, sleeping.

Ssssh! The field is silent . . . sing quietly in a whisper

This is the way the wheat seed sleeps,
the wheat seed sleeps, the wheat seed sleeps.
This is the way the wheat seed sleeps.
Thank you, God the Maker!

It's spring time!
The world is waking up! Listen!
Invite the children still lying on the ground 'asleep' to follow you in making sounds and actions.

We can hear the birds singing . . .
'Twitter, twitter, twitter!'
Show the birds' beaks opening and closing with your hands.

The seeds begin to wake up.
Let's uncurl now, and begin to stretch up, like the seed
waking up and growing and stretching up into the lovely warm sun.

Lead the children in standing and stretching upwards as you sing.
This is the way the wheat seed grows,
the wheat seed grows, the wheat seed grows.
This is the way the wheat seed grows.
Thank you, God the Maker!

Now it's late spring.
The spring rains begin to fall giving the seed all the water they need.
Can you hear the sound of rain falling? Let's make the sound together.

Drum fingers on floor.

Now can you show me rain falling?

Lead the children in their chosen rain action as you sing.
This is the way the spring rain falls,
the spring rain falls, the spring rain falls.
This is the way the spring rain falls.
Thank you, God the Maker!

The wheat grows and grows through the summer
until it stretches as tall as it can up to the sun.
Can you show me?

And it sways gently in the summer breeze.
Can you sway gently like the wheat?

It's autumn time again.
At last it's time to harvest our wheat.
Let's get into our combine harvesters:
big tractors that will harvest our wheat for us.

Lead the children in miming getting into the harvesters.

Let's turn them on. What noise can you hear? *Children's harvester noise*
Now let's harvest our wheat.

This is the way we harvest the wheat,
harvest the wheat, harvest the wheat.
This is the way we harvest the wheat.
Thank you, God the Maker!

Good work!
So we have our wheat but even then, this isn't bread.
There's still lots to do!
We need to grind our grain into tiny pieces – into flour.

Show the children how to mime grinding grain in a bowl.

Let's grind our grain together.

This is the way we grind the grain,
grind the grain, grind the grain.
This is the way we grind the grain.
Thank you, God the Maker!

At last! We have some flour.
Time to make the bread!

Lead the children in acting out the following actions.
Let's pour some warm water in a bowl . . .
Add two spoons of yeast to make the bread rise: 1, 2 . . .
Two spoons of sugar to wake the yeast up: 1, 2 . . .
Now let's pour in some oil.
And three cups of our flour.
1, 2, 3.
Time to mix it up!

This is the way we mix it up,
mix it up, mix it up.
This is the way we mix it up.
Thank you, God the Maker!

And the baker ends up with dough.
A bit like playdough, but this time real dough:
bread dough.
We knead the dough. *Show the children how to pretend to knead imaginary dough*
And shape it. *Lead the children in shaping the dough*
And put our bread in the oven.
Lead the children in being careful opening an imaginary oven door and putting the bread in the oven.

Let's close the door and wait for the bread to bake.

Invite the children to sit down for a moment of quiet.

What a lot of work!
Who's feeling tired?

Show the bread that you showed at the beginning.

When we see food,
let's remember that every food has a story.
That's why we thank God before we eat.
We thank God for the soil and sun and rain
that helped the seed grow.
We thank God for the people who worked hard
to plant and harvest and make the food.

Let's see if our bread is ready.
Let's open our oven and take our bread out.

Lead the children in taking out their imaginary bread.

Smell that bread! Mmmmm!
Shall we say 'thank you' to God now for our bread?
    Either: Let's hold our hands up to God to show 'thank you'.
    Or: Let's put our hands together and close our eyes and sing 'thank you'.
    Or: Let's put our hands out and sing 'thank you'.

As we sing, *Name* and *Name* are going to come round
and share our bread.
If you'd like some bread,
can you hold your hands out like this? *Model to the children*

Name and *Name* will give you a piece.
Keep the bread in your hands 'til everyone has some.
Don't eat it yet!
We're going to sing 'thank you' to God first!

This is the way we say 'Thank you' to God,
'Thank you' to God, 'Thank you' to God.
This is the way we say 'Thank you' to God,
Thank you, God the Maker!

If you have shared the bread, invite the children to eat their bread slowly, really tasting and enjoying it.

Week 6: Let's Take Care of God's World

→ **Extended activity, Genesis 2.15**

This week, in the place of the Bible Storytelling, your group could do an extended project to help to care for God's world, as God asks of us in Genesis 2.15. Choose from the various activities available under 'Taking care of God's world' in the unit starter ideas on p. 128 below, or your group may have its own ideas.

Section 3

Creative Response starter ideas, God the Maker unit

→ **Guide: p. 228**

These starter ideas are designed to spark imaginations and open up opportunities for the children to respond creatively in their different ways to the worship and storytelling you've taken part in together.

Tip

As outlined in the Guide from p. 228, we've found the following rules of thumb helpful for fostering an environment where children are encouraged to engage personally and openly.

1. Encourage the children to make their own choices.
2. Give the children space to develop their response as they wish.
3. Create space for 'bridge building'.
4. It's the act of responding that matters, not the final result.
5. These responses are 'holy ground'.

Weekly Starter Ideas relate directly to the Bible storytelling of each session, including a print-and-go option (indicated by the printer icon).

Sensory Starter Ideas are designed for sensory explorers, including babies and toddlers. These can remain the same through the whole unit.

Unit Starter Ideas are designed to remain relevant throughout the whole unit. Keeping these resources available each week gives children the opportunity to deepen and develop their responses, while making preparation more manageable for leaders.

Tip: Free response area

In addition to any other resources you provide, keeping a free response area available every week will give the children the opportunity to create anything they wish in response to the story they've told, building their sense of confidence and personal responsibility. In this area you could simply provide blank paper and crayons, pencils, paints, or pastels. If you have them, other interesting media (see p. 256) will offer even more scope for the children to nurture and strengthen their imaginative skills.

Weekly Starter Ideas

Week 1: God the Maker

🌳 Invite the children to make their own magnifying glass to explore God's wonderful world for themselves. Alternatively, they could make themselves a telescope or binoculars from rolled card secured with masking tape. Encourage the children to make these instruments 'their own' by decorating them. *Provide magnifying glass templates (p. 272 or website), card, masking tape and scissors, plus pencils and crayons. If you have glue and collage materials (p. 255), make these available too, or even cellophane (clear or coloured) or another transparent material (e.g. an old wipe-clean tablecloth).*

🌳 Invite the children to decorate a person or face template to look like themselves. Encourage them to think about the colour of their hair and eyes and skin, and all the things that make them unique. Some children may choose to make the body template look like someone else. *Provide body templates or face templates (pp. 264, 267 or website), plus pencils and crayons or other interesting media (see p. 256). If you have them available, you could also provide glue and collage materials in case the children would like to use them to collage clothes for themselves. If you have child-safe mirrors, you could leave these available for the children to use.*

🌳 Give the children the opportunity to enter into the part of the story where God's wind, the Spirit, blows over the face of the waters. Provide blue/green diluted paint and straws and invite the children to blow the paint gently across a piece of paper. What will their waters of creation look like? *Provide diluted blue/green paint, straws, thick paper/card.*

🌳 Give older children an opportunity to explore what it means to be made 'in God's image'. Provide them with thick paper or card that has been folded in half lengthways then opened out again. On one half, ask them to draw a picture of themselves (or someone else) in pencil. Then invite them to use watercolours or paints to paint themselves. Encourage them to have a go at using colours to show how they feel rather than to describe how they look. If they then press the two halves together and open them out again, the side that is now full of colours (but without a pencil outline) may give us a glimpse of what God looks like! We're made in God's image so when people look at us, they can see a little bit what God is like.

🌳 Invite the children to create their own real or imaginary animals – or anything else they'd like to make – from whatever you have to hand. *Provide recycling materials, shells/stones/pine cones, etc. You may also like to provide salt dough (recipe on p. 257) as a base, plus pipe cleaners/straws and stick-on googly eyes.*

🌳 Give the children the opportunity to create their own animals from inflated balloons and felt tips. Invite them to draw on the balloons gently. (It might help to explain that they might burst if we press too hard, but that's OK.) *Provide balloons, felt tips.*

🌳 Invite the children to explore Matisse's collage work *The Snail*, then provide coloured paper for them to create their own animal pictures. The children may like to use scissors for some of their paper and to tear other pieces, like Matisse. *Provide a copy of Matisse's* The Snail, *coloured paper, scissors, glue.*

DIDDY DISCIPLES • **PART 2**

UNIT 2 • GOD THE MAKER

Section 3: Creative Response starter ideas

Week 2: God Plants a Garden

🌳 Invite the children to design their own garden or park, providing simple flower templates as a starting point. Encourage the children to go wild with their imagination: what will their unique garden or park look like? *Provide flower templates (p. 273 or website), paper, scissors, glue, pencils, crayons. If you have some to hand, you could provide catalogues and magazines containing pictures of flowers and trees for the children to use as collage.* Alternatively, see the second print-and-go option from week 1.

🌳 Invite the children to create mud men and women – or other creations. *Provide mud, clay, playdough or salt dough (see p. 257).*

🌳 Give the children an opportunity to plant their own mini garden. *Provide jar lids and cotton wool or kitchen roll or soil, as well as cress/grass seeds and pebbles.* The children may even like to make a little animal from a pebble or shell, etc., to live in their garden, or a little woman or man made from a pipe cleaner or paper to look after it.

🌳 Give the children an opportunity to create a nature garden. *Provide recycled tubs (margarine, ice-cream, etc.) plus soil, conkers, pine cones, moss, twigs, dead leaves, etc. for the children to choose from.*

🌳 See also the 'Taking care of God's world' starter ideas below.

Week 3: Everything in All the World Sings 'Alleluia!'

🌳 Give the children the opportunity to make their own weather wheel to take home. Encourage the children to use it to thank God for the weather. *Provide wheel template with arrow (p. 274 or website), paper fasteners, plus pencils or crayons. If you like, you could also provide magazines, newspapers, or printed sheets with pictures of weather or weather symbols in case the children would like to cut them out and use them on their wheel, instead of drawing their own symbols.*

🌳 Invite the children to draw their favourite animal in a picture frame. They may even like to create their own imaginary animal. How does that animal sing 'Alleluia!'? *Provide: picture frame template (p. 275 or website), pencils/crayons, scissors. You could also provide a range of interesting media (p. 256) if you have some to hand.*

🌳 See 'Wonderful weather' below for more weather-based starter ideas. See week 1 above for more animal-based ideas.

Week 4: Jesus the Maker

🌱 Invite the children to make a puppet. It could be a puppet representing themselves when they're feeling 'stormy' or of Jesus calming the storm. It could be a puppet of one of the disciples, or of someone else the child knows. Encourage the children to explore stormy feelings in the way they hold their pencil/crayon/pastel and in how hard they press, or in the colours they use. What does your 'feeling angry' look like? What does your 'feeling scared' look like? *Provide body templates (p. 264 or website) plus pencils/crayons, scissors. If you have them, you could also provide straws/lollipop sticks and masking tape or sticky tape.*

🌱 Give the children an opportunity to design and make their own model of a boat from recycling materials. *Provide a range of recycling materials, glue, masking tape.*

🌱 Invite the children to explore the different colours and textures of rough or calm water by looking at a photograph or painting of the sea. Encourage them to create their own picture of the sea: will it be stormy, calm, or something else? *Provide a photograph or painting of the sea, for instance Turner's* Rough Sea and Wreckage *or* The Shipwreck, *or Henry Moore's* A Calm Sea *(these can be found online), plus paper and watercolours/pastels/ paints.*

🌱 Invite the children to collage a storm. *Provide a range of different textured collage materials (p. 255), glue and paper.*

🌱 Give a small group of children the opportunity to work together to make a boat to sit in from whatever you have to hand. They may like to create a sea around themselves. Encourage them first to imagine they're on a stormy sea and then Jesus calming the storm. Alternatively, allow them to get caught up in the act of creating. *Provide a range of open-ended materials: chairs, tables, rugs, blue/white sheets and pillowcases, brush handles, etc.*

🌱 Invite the children to explore making water pictures with different coloured cooked spaghetti, or uncooked dyed fusilli pasta. *Provide dyed cooked spaghetti (p. 257) or dyed fusilli pasta (p. 257).*

🌱 Invite the children to explore making sea pictures with string. Encourage them to dip the string/wool into glue and explore the shapes and colours of water with their creation. Will they make the sea rough, or calm, or somewhere in between? *Provide: either lots of different lengths and shades of blue/green wool and white PVA glue; or white string and pots of blue/green dyed PVA glue.*

🌱 Invite the children to create fingerprint pictures of the sea or a lake. Encourage them to explore the different colours of water. Will they create rough or calm waters? Or would they like to try both? *Provide white paper/ card, a range of blue and green shades of paints (mix them accordingly) in tubs. Optional: edible cornflour paint (p. 258).*

Week 5: Harvest: Thank you, God the Maker!

🌱 Invite the children to make a 'thank you' card for God the Maker. *Provide blank card and pencils/crayons/ paints or other interesting media (p. 256). If you have collage materials (p. 255) and glue, you could also make these available.*

🌱 Invite the children to draw or collage on a plate what they had for breakfast or lunch, or they may like to draw a favourite meal or food. When they've finished, lead them in saying (or even support them in writing) 'thank you' to God the Maker. *Provide circle template (p. 266 or website) or paper plate, plus pencils/ pens. If you have collage materials (p. 255) and glue, or food magazines, you could also make these available.*

🌱 Give the children an opportunity to make their own jam or cheese sandwiches (it's easier without butter or margarine), fruit kebabs or another snack together and enjoy eating. 'Thank you, God the Maker!' *Provide cooking materials.*

🌱 You could make bread together, or provide the children with (pre-made or bought) bread dough and encourage them to shape it into a roll, loaf, or whatever shape they wish. *Provide bread ingredients or bread dough. See the recipe on p. 258, use your own recipe, or buy a ready-made bread mix. Either bake the bread on your premises, or wrap it in cling film dusted with flour and send it home with the children along with instructions for baking.*

🌱 If you can get hold of some wheat, you could give the children the opportunity to grind wheat grains into flour.

Sensory Starter Ideas

Resources that you could provide for the children (including babies and toddlers) to explore for themselves include:

- 'small world' resources (small plastic figures and models such as those from Happyland or Fisher Price, or wooden or knitted figures, etc.) including farm animals, farm buildings, tractors, farmers, etc.;

- a range of natural objects on a tray (or in a cloth bag, a box or socks) for the children to touch and feel. Can the children guess what they are by touch? Can they guess what they are by smell? Ideas include different kinds of vegetables and fruit, herbs, conkers, seed pods, leaves, twigs, bark, pine cones, 'helicopter seeds', bulbs, clean feathers. You may even like to place the objects in a large container filled with sand/rice and invite the children to pull them out. Make sure nothing is a safety hazard;

- plastic, soft, or finger-puppet animals or fish for the children to explore;

- dressing-up materials: watering cans, clean wellies, plant pots, plastic gardening equipment like trowels, animal/bird/fish masks, or animal dressing-up outfits from home;

- child-safe mirrors for the children to explore the way they look;

- lots of different kinds of laminated leaves to explore;

- leaf shapes or laminated real leaves with holes punched in them, plus shoelaces for the children to use as sewing cards;

- Octonauts vehicles with 'small world' people (small plastic figures such as those from Happyland or Fisher Price, or wooden or knitted figures) instead of the Octonauts characters. We can explore God's wonderful world like the BBC CBeebies characters the Octonauts;

- board books of any of the stories from the unit, or about animals or animal noises;

- rain makers, thunder boards, or other objects that make a sound like different kinds of weather;

- edible cornflour finger paints (p. 258) to allow children to make and create like God;

- seed catalogues and gardening magazines to explore and from which to cut out pictures;

- dry autumn leaves and a large piece of fabric. Encourage the children to wave the fabric with the leaves on top, and send the leaves up into the air. Collect and repeat.

Unit Starter Ideas

Exploring God's wonderful world

🌳 Encourage the children to explore and discover the natural world for themselves by providing discovery equipment, such as magnifying glasses, sand timers, torches, children's tweezers, rulers, weighing scales, notebooks and pencils, books on growing things – even a children's microscope, if you have one. Provide a range of natural objects for the children to explore, depending on what's readily available near you. Ideas include different kinds of plants and flowers, soil, seeds, leaves, tree branches with leaves on, fruit or vegetables. If you like you could provide bowls in case the children would like to sort the items into different groups. *In addition to your chosen equipment and natural objects, you may like to provide copies of the 'God the Maker made this' template (p. 276 or website) in case the children would like to use them to record their discoveries.*

🌳 Invite the children to make an observational drawing of something that God the Maker has made. *Provide a range of natural objects (see above for ideas), plus paper and pencils or other interesting media (p. 256). You may also like to provide copies of the 'God the Maker made this' template (p. 276 or website) in case the children would like to use them for their drawings.*

🌳 Invite the children to explore a range of autumn leaves. They may like to draw them, feel the different textures, sort them by shape (e.g. pointed, round, wide, narrow) onto different plates, etc. *Provide autumn leaves, plates, pencils, paper.*

🌳 Invite the children to make a shell or rock showcase in an old chocolate box. *Provide shells/rocks and old chocolate boxes with compartments, or similar.*

🌳 Give the children the opportunity to learn how to press leaves or daisies, fallen petals, etc. *Provide your chosen leaves or flowers to press, absorbent paper or kitchen roll, heavy books or other equipment to press them in.*

🌳 Invite the children to make bark rubbings, either inside or outside. *Provide bark, paper, wax crayons (these work best when you use them on their side).*

🌳 Go on a nature walk together. As you walk, encourage the children to explore their different senses: what can you see, smell, hear, feel? Or you might like to give the children paper bags in which to collect autumn treasure to take home with them and explore. Alternatively, go on a scavenger hunt. Create a sheet in advance with ten things to collect that are readily available where your hunt will take place; for instance a conker, a yellow leaf, a curved stick, a pebble, a feather, a pointed leaf, a straight stick.

Making with God the Maker

🌳 Give the children the opportunity to make their own paint from crushed berries and/or mud. Make completely sure the berries are edible. *Provide sticks, mud or berries to crush. You could also provide paper or cardboard in case the children would like to create artwork with their paint, using their sticks as 'brushes'.*

🌳 Invite the children to print pictures using pine cones, bark, leaves or twigs, halved fruit or vegetables (oranges, lemons, carrots, onions, potatoes). *Provide paper, paints, your chosen objects for printing.*

🌳 Give the children the opportunity to create their own patterns with seeds, pressed flowers or leaves. *Provide seeds/flowers/leaves. The patterns can be created on the table or on paper as 'ephemeral' or 'transient' art (p. 256). Alternatively, you might like to provide PVA glue for the children to make more permanent patterns.*

🌳 Invite the children to paint pine cones with autumn colours. *Provide pine cones and red/yellow/orange/green/brown paint. You could even provide glitter in case the children would like to add some sparkle.*

🌳 Give the children the opportunity to add their own fingerprint leaves to a picture of a bare tree. *Provide bare tree templates (p. 277 or website) and red/yellow/orange/brown finger paints. You could even provide edible cornflour finger paints (p. 258).*

🌳 Invite the children to create their own twig sculptures by winding coloured wool around forked branches with two or three prongs. *Provide twigs with at least three branches coming off them, different coloured wool. You might also like to provide seed pods, conker husks, or long grasses in case the children would like to weave them into their design.*

Taking care of God's world

🌳 Give the children the opportunity to plant a sunflower or other flower/vegetable to take home and grow. *Provide paper cups or plant pots, compost, seeds. You might also like to provide some pebbles for the bottom of the pot and/or a lollipop stick with which to label the plant. At St Peter's, Walworth, we use plain white compostable paper cups; these can be decorated with crayons or pencils before the compost is added.*

🌳 Invite the children to design their own wildflower seed packet. Encourage them to give the packet to someone with a garden, yard or window box. *Provide plain envelopes suitable for turning into seed packets, wildflower seeds, pencils/crayons. You may even like to provide glue and collage materials (p. 255) for younger children.*

🌳 Go outside as a group and take part in some gardening in your church or school, or a local garden.

🌳 Give the children the opportunity to make their own bird food (recipes can be found online). *Provide bird food ingredients and containers to take the bird food home in.*

🌳 Invite the children to make their own bug house (instructions can be found online).

🌳 Give the children the opportunity to learn how to sort recyclable materials according to how recycling is sorted in your local area, and challenge them to help with recycling at home. *Provide rags (e.g. worn-out clothes that are unsuitable for giving to charity), clean plastic (no bags), metal (without sharp edges), paper. Where appropriate, you could use the rags for your own collaging. Many charity shops will accept clean 'rags' and can sell them for recycling.*

Wonderful weather

🌳 Invite the children to make a 'wind stick' by taping ribbons etc. to a stick. Encourage them to watch it wave in the wind. *Provide ribbons, wool, crepe or cellophane strips and a straw/lollipop stick or real stick, plus masking tape or sticky tape.*

🌳 Give older children the opportunity to make a wind chime and listen to the wind. *Provide a metal hanger (or twigs fastened in a cross shape), plus string and metal items such as old keys, large screws, old Allan keys from self-assembly furniture, or large paperclips. Make sure that none of these present a safety hazard.*

🌳 Invite the children to make and decorate a thunder board and then explore its thundery sounds. *Provide thick, bendable card (check what sound it makes when you bend it), glue and collage materials (p. 255), plus pencils/crayons to decorate.*

UNIT 3
IN NOVEMBER, WE REMEMBER! (GREEN TIME OR KINGDOM SEASON)

The *In November, We Remember* unit gives young children the opportunity to take part in the 'remembering' that goes on at this time of year. It's particularly appropriate for groups from churches holding services for Remembrance Sunday, All Saints and Christ the King, but other groups may also find the material helpful.

In week 3, children are gently invited to explore death and dying as a natural part of life, first through the beauty of dying autumn leaves, and then through a leader remembering someone who has died. It can be hugely beneficial to young children to witness an adult talking in a healthy way and in a safe environment about their memories of someone they love who has died. More guidance on how to go about this in your group is given in the introduction to that week's session.

This unit also contains an extra week (it can replace any of the other weeks or be added to the week prior to November), which invites young children to take part in raising money for those in need. Your group may like to choose a local or overseas project for which to raise money. Alternatively, if your church or school is already getting involved in a Children in Need project this November, you might like to contribute to that.

Section 1

The Building Blocks, In November, We Remember unit

Pick and choose from these Building Blocks and their various options to build sessions for your group. Whatever choices you make, we suggest you keep to that pattern for the whole of the unit as this will open up opportunities for the children to participate fully and confidently during your time together.

> **Build your own Diddy Disciples session** (p. 6) provides an overview of the Building Blocks and a short introduction to fitting them together, along with examples.
>
> **A Guide to the Building Blocks** (p. 215) provides a step-by-step guide to each Building Block.

Welcome

→ **Guide: p. 218**

Welcome your group.

Let's start by going round the circle
and saying our name out loud.
My name's _____.

Go round the circle so that every adult and child has the chance to say his or her name (and introduce any dolls, teddies or toys). If any of the children don't want to say their name or aren't able to, you (or a parent or carer) could say it for them and wave.

It's time to sing our Welcome Song!

Welcome Song: Option 1

→ **Song: 'The Diddy Disciples welcome song'. Words © Sharon Moughtin-Mumby**
→ **Tune: 'Glory, glory, alleluia!' (traditional). For the music see p. 259, or for a taster see the Diddy Disciples website. For tips on teaching songs for the first time, see p. 215.**

Go around the circle the same way as above. See if each of you can remember the others' names and insert them into the song.

Welcome *Name 1* to *St Peter's**
Welcome *Name 2* to *St Peter's**
Welcome *Name 3* to *St Peter's**
You are welcome in the name of the Lord!

* Insert the name of your church or children's group, or sing 'our worship'.

Welcome Song: Option 2

→ **Song: 'You are welcome in the name of the Lord' (traditional)**
→ **Tune: Traditional. For the music see p. 262, or for a taster see the Diddy Disciples website. For tips on teaching songs for the first time, see p. 215.**

Let's wave with one hand. *Lead waving*
Then with our other hand. *Lead waving*
Then let's choose someone and show them God's 'glory'!
Move arms up and down in front of you with fingers wiggling, palms facing out, towards one person.

And someone else! *Repeat*
Then let's wave with both hands all around the circle.
Lead waving.

We're ready to sing!

You are welcome in the name of the Lord!
Wave with right hand to one person.
You are welcome in the name of the Lord!
Wave with left hand to another person.
I can see all over you the glory of the Lord,
Move arms up and down in front of you with fingers wiggling, palms facing out, towards one person and then another.
You are welcome in the name of the Lord!
Wave with both hands all around the circle.

Getting Ready to Worship

→ **Guide: p. 218**

Choose one of the following greetings according to which is familiar in your church. (If your church uses a different greeting, you could use that here instead.)

Getting Ready to Worship: Option 1

→ **Action: The sign of the cross. Words © Sharon Moughtin-Mumby**

Invite the children to make the sign of the cross slowly with you. As the children become more confident, invite a child to lead the action as the whole group says the words and makes the sign of the cross with that child.

In my head,	*Touch head*
in my heart,	*Touch chest*
and all around me,	*Touch shoulders one by one*
Jesus is here.	*Open hands in front facing upwards*

Getting Ready to Worship: Option 2

→ **Action: 'The Lord be with you' (open hands)**

Let's start by clenching our hands together tightly.
Lead children in clenching fists against your body to show a defensive posture.

When we close ourselves up like this,
it's hard to let anyone into our heart.
It's hard even to let God into our heart!

When we get ready to worship,
we show that we're open to God and to each other.

Open your hands out, facing up.

Can you show me your open hands?
We're ready to let God and each other in!

The Lord be with you.
Hold hands open to the children.

And also with you.
Invite the children to open their hands towards you.

Introducing the Unit

→ **Guide: p. 218**

Who can tell us which month
we're in at the moment? *Accept the children's responses*
In November, we remember!
We remember all sorts of things.

Gathering Song

→ **Guide: p. 219**
→ **Song: 'In November, we remember'. Words © Sharon Moughtin-Mumby**
→ **Tune: The refrain of 'O my darling, Clementine' (traditional). For a taster see the Diddy Disciples website.**

If you're using imaginative aids, ask 2–3 children to give them out. Encourage the children to warm up their imaginations by exploring making different shapes with their aids. Invite some children, one at a time, to lead the group in making a shape or action. See p. 220 for examples of actions for scarves or ribbons, but don't limit the children's imagination to these:

What else could these be?

Once the children have finished warming up:
We need to make up some actions for our November song.
Who can show me an action for:
Sing: 'In November, we remember'?
Choose an action.

Let's sing that together:
In November, we remember *Action 1*

Now, who can show me an action for:
Sing: 'all the good things our God gives'?
Choose an action.

Let's sing that together:
all the good things our God gives *Action 2*

Now let's hide our scarves/ribbons/streamers/hands behind our back
and sing 'so that nothing is forgotten'.
So that nothing is forgotten *Hide hands behind back*

Last of all, who's seen or heard fireworks this week?
In November there are lots of fireworks in the sky!
So our song for November ends with a fireworks action.
Who can show me fireworks?!
For instance, waving scarves/ribbons/hands above your head quickly.

Let's sing 'and our special memories live!' and show our fireworks.
And our special memories live! *Fireworks action*

Let's try and sing that all together:

In November, we remember *Action 1*
all the good things our God gives. *Action 2*
So that nothing is forgotten, *Hide hands behind back*
and our special memories live! *Fireworks!*

Repeat

Getting Ready for Bible Storytelling

→ **Guide: p. 220**

Getting Ready for Bible Storytelling: Option 1

→ **Action: opening your group's box and naming this week's object**

See the beginning of the weekly storytelling material for ideas of items to place in your box. Invite one of the children to open the box.

What's in the box? *Ask the child to respond.*

Getting Ready for Bible Storytelling: Option 2

→ **Song: 'Jesus, open up my eyes'. Words © Sharon Moughtin-Mumby**
→ **Tune: 'Michael, row the boat ashore' (traditional). For the music, see p. 262, or for a taster see the Diddy Disciples website.**

It's time to open the Bible.

Let's get ready!
Let's take our thumb *Lead children in showing thumb*
And draw our cross on our eyes, *Draw cross*
and our lips, *Draw cross*
and our heart. *Draw cross*
Let's ask Jesus to help us get ready to listen out for God!

Jesus, open up my eyes. Alleluia!
Trace a cross between your eyes.
Jesus, open up my lips. Alleluia!
Trace a cross on your lips.
Jesus, open up my heart. Alleluia!
Trace a cross on your heart.
Jesus, help me hear your voice. Alleluia!
Cup your hands behind your ears.

Interactive Bible Storytelling

→ **Guide: p. 221**

See the Bible Storytelling material in Section 2 of this chapter.

Saying Sorry to God

As November is filled with remembrance for other people, we recommend that you use one of the options from Prayers for Other People in this month. Alternatively, use one of the Saying Sorry Actions on pp. 40–43 (options 2, 3, and 4) that can be used during any unit.

Introduction to Prayers

In November, we remember!
It's time to remember other people in our prayers.

Prayers for Other People

→ **Guide: p. 223 and p. 225**

Invite the children to sit in a circle for a moment of quiet.

Let's imagine holding our prayer gently,

Hands together gently in traditional prayer gesture, but cupped so you can imagine a prayer inside
and then let it go up in prayer to God,
Hands opened upwards to God

If you're using Option 1:
Jesus *Hands together, cupped*
hear our prayer *Hands opened upwards to God*
Let's pray . . .

Prayers for Other People: Option 1

→ **Song: 'Jesus, hear our prayer!' Words © Sharon Moughtin-Mumby**
→ **Tune: 'Brown girl in the ring' (traditional). For the music see p. 260, or for a taster see the Diddy Disciples website. For tips on teaching songs for the first time, see p. 215. For similar words designed to fit with the alternative tune 'He's got the whole world in his hands' (traditional), see p. 260.**

For the world:	**Jesus, hear our prayer.**
Make a circle shape	*Open hands upwards to God*
For the Church:	**Jesus, hear our prayer.**
Praying hands	*Open hands upwards to God*
For our place, *Walworth**:	**Jesus, hear our prayer.**
Hands down moving out in	*Open hands upwards to God*
a semi-circle to show the area around us	
Lord Jesus, hear our prayer, Amen.	
Open hands upwards to God	

* Insert local area/school/church/community/parish.

For the sick and lonely:	**Jesus, hear our prayer.**
Fingers showing tears falling	*Open hands upwards to God*
down cheeks	
For our friends and family:	**Jesus, hear our prayer.**
Arms around yourself	*Open hands upwards to God*
For ourselves:	**Jesus, hear our prayer.**
Both hands on heart	*Open hands upwards to God*
Lord Jesus, hear our prayer, Amen.	
Open hands upwards to God.	

Let's close our eyes for a moment.
I wonder if there's someone special
you'd like to pray for?
Let's imagine them now.

Now, let's imagine Jesus coming to them.
Does Jesus say anything?
Does Jesus do anything?
Let's open our eyes.

Continue with one of the Prayer Action options outlined below. Once the Prayer Action has been completed, you may like to use the following verse to close this time of prayer.

Take our prayers:	**Jesus, hear our prayer.**
Hands together gently	*Open hands upwards to God*
Make them holy:	**Jesus, hear our prayer.**
Hands together gently	*Open hands upwards to God*
Make them beautiful:	**Jesus, hear our prayer.**
Hands together gently	*Open hands upwards to God*
Lord Jesus, hear our prayer, Amen.	
Hands together gently, then open hands upwards to God.	

Prayers for Other People: Option 2

→ Song: 'The Diddy Disciples little prayers song'. Words © Sharon Moughtin-Mumby
→ Tune: 'Frère Jacques' (traditional). For tips on teaching songs for the first time, see p. 215. For the music see p. 258, or for a taster see the Diddy Disciples website.

These prayers are especially suited to churches that prefer less traditional prayer forms.

> *Either: choose what you'd like the group to pray for before the session.*
> *Or: ask the children at this point if there is anything or anyone that they'd like to pray for.*

Ask the children or others to suggest actions. You will need two different 'thank you' suggestions and two different 'hear our prayer' suggestions. Try to encourage the offering of at least one prayer for other people outside the group.

Invite the children to sing after you, repeating your words and their actions. Sometimes it might be almost impossible to fit the child's own words in! But it's really valuable to do so where possible, resisting the urge to try and 'tidy up' their suggestions. For examples, see Unit 1, Jesus' Wonderful Love, p. 47.

Having sung your prayers, you could insert a Prayer Action, repeat the process, or move straight on to close with the following (or other words that remain the same each week).

For toda-ay,	*Point hands down for 'now'*
For toda-ay,	*Point hands down for 'now'*
thank you, God!	*Open hands upwards to God or hands together in prayer*
thank you, God!	*Open hands upwards to God or hands together in prayer*
Fo-r yo-ur lo-ve,	*Cross hands on chest*
Fo-r yo-ur lo-ve,	*Cross hands on chest*
thank you, God!	*Open hands upwards to God or hands together in prayer*
thank you, God!	*Open hands upwards to God or hands together in prayer*

Prayer Actions

→ Guide: p. 226

Continue with one of the Prayer Action options outlined below, or you can use the Prayer Action options 2 and 3 on p. 48 at any time of year.

Prayer Action, week 1: All the saints

→ Action: placing battery tealights or paper stars on a cross/heart or dark or white/gold piece of fabric.

> ## Tip
>
> We ask an adult to light the battery tealights in advance as we've found younger children can be distracted by attempts to light the tealights themselves.

Place one or more baskets/trays with lit battery tealights or paper stars in front of you.

> *If using battery tealights:*
> Now as we pray, we're going to turn the lights off
> for a moment and look at these candles.

> *Ask an adult or child to turn off the lights.*

The saints are like lights in the world!
God calls us to be little lights in the world too.
In a moment,
Name and *Name* are going to bring around these candles/stars.
If you like, you could take a candle/star
and hold it up like this.

Model to the children holding their tealight/star up.

Let's sing as we wait in the dark to be given our little light.

Hum the tune together, with the words 'Jesus, hear our prayer!' as a refrain, until all the children and adults who wish to take tealights or stars have done so. Continue holding up your tealight/star throughout as a model.

Let's pray that we can be little lights in the world for God.
Let's give our light prayers to God as we sing.

Hum the tune together, with the words 'Jesus, hear our prayer!' as a refrain, as you lead the children in placing the candles in the centre of the circle on a cross/heart or on a dark or white/gold piece of fabric. Some groups may like to invite two children to go around the circle with a cross or piece of fabric on a tray to collect the candles. This can then be placed in the centre. End this time of prayer with the final verse of the Prayer Song you've chosen.

Prayer Action, week 2: Remembrance Sunday

→ **Action: placing poppies on a piece of brown fabric (used in the Bible Storytelling)**

Show the children one or more baskets/trays containing poppies.

In a moment, *Name* and *Name*
are going to bring round these poppies.
If you like, you could take one and hold it up like this.

Model to the children holding up their poppy.

Let's ask God to see our poppy as a prayer for peace.

Lead the children in humming the tune together, with the words 'Jesus, hear our prayer!' as a refrain, until all the children and adults who wish to take a poppy have done so.

Let's give our poppy prayers for peace to God as we sing.
You can put your poppy anywhere you like on our cloth.

Indicate the cloth that was laid over the 'small world' people in Bible Storytelling (see p. 151).

Let's ask God to hear our poppy as a prayer
that we – and all our leaders – will use our words instead of fighting.

Hum the tune together, with the words 'Jesus, hear our prayer!' as a refrain, as you lead the children in placing their poppies. Some groups may like to invite two children to go around the circle in opposite directions with trays to collect the poppies. The poppies can then be laid on the cloth by one or two of the children. End this time of prayer with the final verse of the Prayer Song you've chosen.

Prayer Action, week 3: All who have died

→ **Action: placing candles (battery tealights) or flowers on a cross, paper heart or piece of fabric**

> **Tip**
>
> We ask an adult to light the battery tealights in advance as we've found younger children can be distracted by attempts to light the tealights themselves.

I wonder whether you know someone who's died?
Or maybe you've heard an adult talking
about someone special who has died,
like my *Nanny Ken*.

> *Either:* If you don't know anyone who's died,
> you could join me in remembering my *Nanny Ken*.

> *Or, if appropriate:*
> If you don't know anyone who's died,
> you could join *our church* in remembering

Name, Name, and *Name.*
List the first names of 1–4 people who've died and are being remembered in your church or other group at the moment.

Let's close our eyes for a moment.
Let's remember someone who's died now.
Let's remember something that they did
that makes us smile . . .

Let's open our eyes.

Place your cross, heart or fabric in the centre of the circle.

> *If using battery tealights:*

> Now as we pray, we're going to turn the lights off
> for a moment and look at these candles.

> *Ask an adult or child to turn off the lights.*

In a moment, *Name* and *Name* are going to bring around
these *candles/flowers.*
If you like, you could take one and hold it up like this.

Model to the children holding their flower/candle up.

Let's ask God to see our flower/candle
as a 'thank you' prayer for our special person who's died.

Hum the tune together, with the words 'Jesus, hear our prayer!' as a refrain, until all the children and adults who wish to take a flower/candle have done so.

Let's give our flower/candle prayers to God
as we sing.
You can put your flower/candle
anywhere you like on this *heart/cross/fabric.*

Hum the tune together, with the words 'Jesus, hear our prayer!' as a refrain, as you lead the children in placing their flowers/candles. Some groups may like to invite two children to go around the circle in opposite directions with trays to collect the flowers/candles. The trays can then be placed in the centre. End this time of prayer with the final verse of the Prayer Song you've chosen.

Prayer Action, week 4: Christ the King

→ **Action: placing a paper crown, a tealight or another object on a piece of fabric, a cross or another symbol of Jesus (for instance a drawing or painting, an icon, a manger, a throne)**

Place your cross, fabric or other symbol of Jesus in the centre of the circle. Show the children one or more baskets of paper crowns or pictures of crowns, or other object you've chosen.

In a moment, *Name* and *Name* are going to bring around these crowns.
If you like, you can take a crown and hold it up to God.
Model holding a crown in the air to the children.

Hum the tune together, with the words 'Jesus, hear our prayer!' as a refrain, until all the children and adults who wish to take a crown have done so.

Let's ask God to see these *crowns* as 'thank you' prayers.
In a moment, if you like, you can put yours
anywhere you like on this *cross.*
Let's say 'thank you' to Jesus, our King.
Let's give King Jesus the crown he deserves!

Hum the tune together again while the group place their crowns. Larger groups may like to invite two children to carry the cross on a tray around the circle to collect the children's crowns. This crown can then be placed in the centre of the circle. End this time of prayer with the final verse of the Prayer Song you've chosen.

Extra: Remembering people in need

If you still wish to keep a time of prayer during this week's session, hold it at the end of the extended activity.

Place a tray of whatever you have made in the centre of the circle.

We've made these beautiful _____
to help people who need God's help.
Let's hold our hands out towards them
and show what we've made to God.

Lead the children in holding their hands out with palms up towards the tray.

Let's ask God to see them as a prayer
for the people we want to help.
For _____.
Let's sing together.

Sing the last verse of the Prayers for Other People song as you hold your hands out towards whatever you've made.

Thank You, God

→ **Guide: p. 227**

Thank You, God: Option 1

→ **Song: 'My hands were made for love'. Words © Sharon Moughtin-Mumby**
→ **Tune: 'Hickory, dickory, dock' (traditional). For the music, see p. 262, or for a taster see the Diddy Disciples website. For tips on teaching songs for the first time, see p. 215.**

Invite the children to sit in a circle for a moment of quiet.

It's time to remember all the things we've done this week.
It's time to say 'thank you' to God
for when we've been part of showing God's love.
Let's wiggle our fingers!
I wonder when you've shown love
with your hands this week?

Wiggle fingers as you sing.
My hands were made for love!
My hands were made for love!
Thank you for the love they've shown.
My hands were made for love!

Let's wiggle our feet!
I wonder when you've shown love
with your feet this week?

Wiggle feet as you sing.
My feet were made for love!
My feet were made for love!
Thank you for the love they've shown.
My feet were made for love!

Let's put our hands gently on our neck.
Let's sing 'Ahhh!'
Ahhhhh!

Can you feel your throat vibrating and dancing?
I wonder when you've shown love
with your voice this week?

Hold neck and feel your voice 'dancing' as you sing.

My voice was made for love!
My voice was made for love!
Thank you for the love it's shown.
My voice was made for love!

Thank You, God: Option 2

→ Song: 'For the love we've shown'. Words © Sharon Moughtin-Mumby
→ Tune: 'All through the night' (traditional). For the music see p. 259, or for a taster see the Diddy Disciples website. For tips on teaching songs for the first time, see p. 215.

Most suitable for use with children over the age of four.

Invite the children to sit in a circle for a moment of quiet.

It's time to remember all the things we've done this week.
It's time to say 'thank you' to God
for when we've been part of showing God's love.

> *Either:* Let's wiggle our fingers.
> *Or:* Let's hold up our hands.

I wonder when you've shown love
with your hands this week?

> *Either:* Let's wiggle our feet.
> *Or:* Let's show our feet.

I wonder when you've shown love
with your feet this week?

Let's put our hands gently on our neck.
Let's sing 'Ahhh!'
Ahhhhh!

Can you feel your neck vibrating and dancing with your voice?
I wonder when you've shown love
with your voice this week?

Let's sing our 'thank you' song to God
For the times we've been part of sharing God's love.

For the love we've shown with our hands, *Hold hands up or wiggle fingers*
Thank you, God!
For the love we've shown with our feet, *Point to feet or wiggle feet*
Thank you, God!
When we love all those around us, *Cross hands on chest*
It's the same as loving Jesus!
For the love we've shown with our voice, *Hands on neck or point to singing mouth*
Thank you, God!

Creative Response

→ **Guide: p. 228**

See the Creative Response starter ideas in Section 3 of this chapter.

Sharing God's Peace

→ Guide: p. 231

Sharing God's Peace is a particularly important theme during the In November, We Remember unit. Option 3, Susan Salidor's 'I've Got Peace in my Fingers', © 1995 Susan Salidor ASCAP, can be especially meaningful at this time, with its focus on our part in bringing about God's peace in the world.

Sharing God's Peace: Option 1

→ **Song: 'I've got peace like a river' (traditional). Isaiah 66.12,** NIV
→ **Tune: Traditional. For a taster, see the Diddy Disciples website. For tips on teaching songs for the first time, see p. 215.**

Either: Hold one end of the peace cloth (see Guide, p. 231) and ask one of the older children or an adult to hold the other end. Start singing the Peace Song. As the children begin to gather, invite them to join in holding a small section of the cloth, raising and lowering it so it 'flows' like a river as you sing together.

Or: Invite the children to sit in a circle in the worship space. Start singing the Peace Song. As the children begin to gather, invite them to join in raising and lowering their hands like the waters of a flowing river.

I've got peace like a river,
I've got peace like a river,
I've got peace like a river in my soul.
I've got peace like a river,
I've got peace like a river,
I've got peace like a river in my soul.

If your group is about to rejoin the adults for communion, when all the children are gathered, continue with the words of the Peace following Option 3 below.

Sharing God's Peace: Option 2

→ **Song: 'Peace is flowing like a river' (traditional). Isaiah 66.12,** NIV
→ **Tune: Traditional. For a taster, see the Diddy Disciples website. For tips on teaching songs for the first time, see p. 215.**

Either: Hold one end of the peace cloth (see Guide, p. 231) and ask one of the older children or an adult to hold the other end. Start singing the Peace Song. As the children begin to gather, invite them to join in holding a small section of the cloth, raising and lowering it so it 'flows' like a river as you sing together.

Or: Invite the children to sit in a circle in the worship space. Start singing the Peace Song. As the children begin to gather, invite them to join in raising and lowering their hands like the waters of a flowing river.

Peace is flowing like a river,
flowing out through you and me.
Spreading out into the desert,
setting all the captives free.

If your group is about to rejoin the adults for communion: when all the children are gathered, continue with the words of the Peace following Option 3 below:

Sharing God's Peace: Option 3

→ **Song: 'I've got peace in my fingers' © 1995 Susan Salidor ASCAP**
→ **Tune: © 1995 Susan Salidor ASCAP**
→ **The words and music can be found on the album *Little Voices in My Head* by Susan Salidor © 2003 Peach Head. They can also be found on iTunes, YouTube, or at www.susansalidor.com**

Invite the children to sit in a circle in the worship space. Start singing the Peace Song. As the children begin to gather, invite them to join in with the song and actions. If your group is about to rejoin the adults for communion: when all the children are gathered, continue with the words of the Peace below.

The Peace

→ 2 Thessalonians 3.16; 1 Peter 5.14

Once you've finished singing:

The peace of the Lord be always with you.
Hold hands open to the children.

And also with you.
Invite the children to open their hands towards you.

Let's shake hands or hug each other
and say 'Peace be with you' as a sign of God's peace.
or whatever is said on sharing the Peace in your church.

Lead the children in giving and receiving the Peace. Immediately following this, at St Peter's, Walworth, we lead the children back to join the rest of the congregation to continue our worship with the Eucharistic Prayer.

Taking God's Love into the World

→ **Song: 'This little light of mine' (traditional)**
→ **Tune: Traditional. For a taster, see the Diddy Disciples website. For tips on teaching songs for the first time, see p. 215.**
→ **Guide: p. 232**

This Building Block is particularly designed for standalone groups or groups that are held during a Service of the Word. Alternatively, you could use one of the Peace Songs above to end your worship.

Our time together is coming to an end.

Invite the children to sit in a circle for a moment of quiet.

God has lit a little light of love inside all of us.
Trace a circle on your heart with a finger.
Let's make our finger into a candle.
Bring your finger from your heart and hold it out.
Let's be God and light our little light of love together, after three.
Lead the children in lighting their finger candle by striking an imaginary match in the air on three and pretending to light your finger.
1, 2, 3 . . . Tssss!

Let's imagine God's love shining and dancing like light in us.

Wave your finger in front of you as you sing.
This little light of mine, I'm gonna let it shine!
This little light of mine, I'm gonna let it shine!
This little light of mine, I'm gonna let it shine!
Let it shine, let it shine, let it shine!

Blow on your finger as if blowing out a candle on 'puff'. Then hold it up high.
Won't let no one *puff* it out! I'm gonna let it shine!
Won't let no one *puff* it out! I'm gonna let it shine!
Won't let no one *puff* it out! I'm gonna let it shine!
Let it shine, let it shine, let it shine!

Hold your finger behind a cupped hand, then take your cupped hand away to reveal the 'candle' and hold it high!
Hide it under a bushel? No! I'm gonna let it shine!
Hide it under a bushel? No! I'm gonna let it shine!
Hide it under a bushel? No! I'm gonna let it shine!
Let it shine, let it shine, let it shine!

Lead the children in placing your finger back on your heart.
Now let's put our little light of love
back in our hearts, where it belongs.

Let's remember to let our little light shine
in all our playing and working today . . .

If you're building a Service of the Word and this is your final Building Block, you may like to close with a familiar blessing, the Peace, and/or one of the following. If you're introducing one of these call-and-responses to your group for the first time, see p. 53 for an introduction.

Either: Praise the Lord! *Both hands to self*
            Alleluia! *Both arms upwards in 'V' shape*

Or: Let us bless the Lord. *Both hands to self*
            Thanks be to God. *Both arms upwards in 'V' shape*

Or: And all the people said . . . *Both hands to self*
            Amen! *Both arms upwards in V shape*

Section 2

The Bible Storytelling material, In November, We Remember unit

Week 1: We Remember: All the Saints!

→ **(1 Corinthians 1.2 and Ephesians 4.11–12)**
→ **Song: 'O when the saints!' (traditional); additional verses © Sharon Moughtin-Mumby**
→ **Tune: Traditional. For a taster, see the Diddy Disciples website.**

Note: this storytelling material for All Saints could also be adapted for patronal festivals or specific saints' days.

> *If you're using the What's in the Box? option (p. 221), invite one of the children to open the box. Inside will be a picture of a saint, for instance the saint after whom your church is named, or a well-known saint like Peter or Mary.*

> What's in the box? *Ask the child to respond.*

In November, we remember all sorts of things.
One of the things we remember is 'saints'.

'Saints' are normal people like you and me.
But they gave the things they were good at to Jesus.
They became special, holy.
They became saints.
We're going to tell the story of some of the saints today.

> *If your group includes children who are unsettled by loud noises, you could teach the children how to 'air stamp', bringing your foot down as if to stamp, but stopping just short of the floor.*

Let's stand up together and march on the spot!

1, 2, 3, 4, 1, 2, 3, 4 . . .
There's a well-known song about the saints,
Where the saints march into heaven to meet God!
Let's sing it together and see if you can march in time . . .

Lead the children in singing until they seem confident.
O, when the saints go marching in!
O, when the saints go marching in!
I want to be in that number, *March on the spot*
when the saints go marching in!

There are lots and lots of saints.

Show the children a picture of a saint that they may have heard of. If you've chosen the What's in the Box option, use the box for this picture. We start with St Peter because our church and school are called St Peter's. Your group can adapt the material accordingly.

This is Saint Peter.

If the picture shows a halo, you might like to point it out and explain that the halo shows that Peter is a saint, especially if you're planning to provide halo materials as a starter idea for your time of Creative Response later.

Before Peter met Jesus, Peter was a fisherman!
What does a fisherman do?
Accept the children's responses.

Let's stand up and be fishermen!
Can you show me how we catch fish?
Lead the children in catching fish by net.

When Peter met Jesus,
Jesus asked Peter to help God fish.
Not to fish for fish,
but to fish for people!
To help God catch people!

Let's be Saint Peter together.
Let's stand up tall and look strong like a fisherman.
Let's fish together!
Let's throw our net out.
Lead the children in throwing an imaginary fishing net out to sea.

And drag it back in.
Lead the children in dragging the net back in.

And out . . . *Throw the net out*
And in . . . *Drag the net in*
Can you sing with me . . . ?

O, yes, I'll fish, I'll fish for God! *Fishing action*
O, yes, I'll fish, I'll fish for God!
I want to be in that number, *March on the spot*
when the saints go marching in!
Repeat

Peter was good at fishing!
Peter gave his fishing to God.
Now we call Peter 'Saint Peter'!

Here's another saint.
Show a picture of Mary.
If your group is exploring another saint, introduce that saint briefly and choose appropriate words and an action for the song.

Who can tell us who this is?
Accept the children's responses.
What did *Mary* do?
Accept the children's responses.

Mary was Jesus' mummy!
Mary did something very special.
She gave her love to Jesus!

Shall we be Mary together?
Let's hold Baby Jesus in our arms,
very gently.
Let's rock Baby Jesus
and sing 'O, yes, I'll love! I'll love for God!'
Ssssh! We don't want to wake Baby Jesus!

Continue rocking the baby as you sing quietly.
O, yes, I'll love, I'll love for God!
O, yes, I'll love, I'll love for God!
I want to be in that number, *March on the spot*
when the saints go marching in!

And don't forget Peter!

Loudly.
O, yes, I'll fish, I'll fish for God! *Fishing action*
O, yes, I'll fish, I'll fish for God!
I want to be in that number, *March on the spot*
when the saints go marching in!

Show picture of St Paul.

Here's another saint.
This is Saint Paul!

Paul was very good at writing!
Can you show me writing?
Lead the children in writing in the air or on the palm of their hand.

Jesus met Paul and asked Paul to write for God.
So Paul gave his writing to God.
Let's sit up straight at our desk
and be St Paul writing together!

Lead the children in writing in the air. Continue writing as you sing.
O, yes, I'll write, I'll write for God!
O, yes, I'll write, I'll write for God!
I want to be in that number, *March on the spot*
when the saints go marching in!

And Mary. Ssssh! *Quietly*
O, yes, I'll love, I'll love for God! *Rock baby in arms*
O, yes, I'll love, I'll love for God!
I want to be in that number, *March on the spot*
when the saints go marching in!

And don't forget Peter! *Loudly*
O, yes, I'll fish, I'll fish for God! *Fishing action*
O, yes, I'll fish, I'll fish for God!
I want to be in that number, *March on the spot*
when the saints go marching in!

Peter and Mary and Paul are all saints.
They were all good at different things.
Peter was good at fishing. *Fishing action*
Mary was good at loving. *Rock Baby Jesus*
Paul was good at writing. *Writing action*
They gave the things they were good at to God.
So they became special, holy!

There are lots and lots and lots more saints!
They were all good at different things.
Now, let me show you this . . .

Show the children a mirror.
Hold it up around the circle so that the children, one by one, can see themselves in it.

Who's this?
Accept the children's responses.

It's you!
In November, we remember all the saints.
And we remember that God calls US to be saints too!
God asks US to give what WE'RE good at to God!

> *Either: go around the circle and sing about what each child and adult is good at and could give to God, with accompanying actions.*

> *Or: choose from the following material. Note: using all this material would be far too much, so choose verses as appropriate for your group, or make up your own.*

I wonder what you're good at?
What you really like doing.
Let's see . . .
Who's good at using their bodies?
Who's good at dancing?
Show me your groovy moves!
Or who's good at wriggling and jiggling?
Show me your wriggles!
Maybe you have a gift for moving with your body.
You could give your clever body to God!
Let's sing 'O, yes, I'll move . . .' and give our bodies to God.

Lead children in moving and dancing as you sing together.
O, yes, I'll move, I'll move for God!
O, yes, I'll move, I'll move for God!
I want to be in that number, *March on the spot*
when the saints go marching in!

Who's good at counting here?
Let's count to ten together. *Count on your fingers*
1, 2, 3, 4, 5, 6, 7, 8, 9, 10.
What brilliant counting!
Let's sing 'O, yes, I'll count . . .'
and give our counting to God.

Lead children in counting on fingers as you sing together.
O, yes, I'll count, I'll count for God!
O, yes, I'll count, I'll count for God!
I want to be in that number, *March on the spot*
when the saints go marching in!

And who here is good at playing?
Can you show me an action for playing?
God loves playing!
We can all give our playing to God.
Let's sing 'O, yes, I'll play . . .'
and give our playing to God.

Lead children in their chosen 'playing' action as you sing together.
O, yes, I'll play, I'll play for God!
O, yes, I'll play, I'll play for God!
I want to be in that number, *March on the spot*
when the saints go marching in!

Is there anyone here who's good at asking 'why?'
I bet there is!
Can you show me an action for 'why?'
Asking 'why?' for God is such an important gift!
There are lots of saints who asked 'why?' for God.
Let's give our asking 'why?' to God.
Let's sing, 'O I'll ask "why?", ask "why?" for God . . .'

O, I'll ask 'why?', ask 'why?' for God!
O, I'll ask 'why?', ask 'why?' for God!
I want to be in that number, *March on the spot*
when the saints go marching in!

Is there anyone here that likes cooking? Hands up!
Let's take a bowl, put in some flour . . .
Lead the children in miming putting the ingredients into the bowl and then stirring.
Some sugar . . .
Some butter . . .
And let's crack an egg . . .
And stir! What great cooks!
You could give your cooking to God!
Let's sing 'O, yes, I'll cook . . .'
and give our cooking to God.

Lead the children in stirring a bowl as you sing together.
O, yes, I'll cook, I'll cook for God!
O, yes, I'll cook, I'll cook for God!
I want to be in that number, *March on the spot*
when the saints go marching in!

Who's good at discovering things?
Finding things out?
Can you show me an action for discovering?
Discovering new things for God is a great gift!
Let's sing 'O, I'll discover!' to God.

Lead the children in their 'discovering' action as you sing together.
O, I'll discover, discover for God!
O, I'll discover, discover for God!
I want to be in that number, *March on the spot*
when the saints go marching in!

Who here is good at helping people?
Hands up!
You could give your helping to God!
Who can show me an action for helping?

If they find this challenging, you could suggest you all hold hands in a circle.

O, yes, I'll help, I'll help for God!
O, yes, I'll help, I'll help for God!
I want to be in that number, *March on the spot*
when the saints go marching in!

All groups:
There's one gift that God has given all of us:
the gift of love.
Like Mary we can give our love to God.

Let's imagine we're holding Baby Jesus
in our own arms.
We're not being Mary this time.
We're being ourselves.
Jesus said when we love other people,
it's the same as loving Jesus.
Let's rock Baby Jesus gently and sing
'O, yes, I'll love . . .'

O, yes, I'll love, I'll love for God!
O, yes, I'll love, I'll love for God!
I want to be in that number, *March on the spot*
when the saints go marching in!

So today we remember all the saints,
all the people who give their gifts to God,
including us!
After three, let's shout together
'We're all saints!'
1, 2, 3 . . . We're all saints!
Let's march with all the saints
and sing one last time as we march.

O when the saints go marching in!
O when the saints go marching in!
I want to be in that number, *March on the spot*
when the saints go marching in!

Week 2: We Remember: Remembrance Sunday

→ Song: 'The Diddy Disciples poppy song'. Words © Sharon Moughtin-Mumby
→ Tune: 'Lavender's blue' (traditional). For a taster, see the Diddy Disciples website.

See in the fields, blos-som, blos-som, red pop-pies grow. Signs of new

life, blos-som, blos-som, let-ting us know... Time to fall quiet, blos-som, blos-som, for all who

died. Time now for hope, blos-som, blos-som, time now for life. See in the

fields, blos - som, blos - som, red pop - pies grow.

Signs of new life, blos - som, blos - som. Now let peace flow!

This week's storytelling involves using 'small world' people (such as Happyland or Fisher Price plastic figures, or wooden or knitted figures) and two brown pieces of fabric or tissue/crepe paper large enough to cover the figures when they are lain down.

> **Tip**
>
> At St Peter's, Walworth, we use the Happyland set my children used to play with at home. You could borrow 'small world' figures for the week from a family or your local school, or you may like to buy some for your group, as they're useful to provide during the Creative Response sessions across the different units.

Invite the children to sit in a circle so they can all see.

In November, we remember.
Today's a very special day for remembering.
It's called 'Remembrance Sunday/Day'.
It's the day when we remember the World Wars.

Show a poppy. If you're using the What's in the Box? option (p. 221), invite one of the children to open the box at this point, with a poppy inside.

Has anyone seen one of these around?
What is it?
Accept the children's responses.

We use these poppies to help us remember.
We have a song about the poppies.
Let's learn it together now.
It has the words 'blossom, blossom' in it.
Let's say that 'my turn' *point to self,* 'your turn' *leader's hands out to group*
'blossom, blossom' *point to self*
'blossom, blossom' *leader's hands out to group*
We're ready to learn the whole song.

Ask the children first to say the words after you while performing the actions. Then add the tune. Very young children may choose only to join in with the actions and the 'blossom, blossom' words.

See in the fields (blossom, blossom),
Hand shading eyes, looking
red poppies grow.
Twist hands upwards like a snake/poppy stem growing.
Signs of new life (blossom, blossom),
Open palms while keeping wrists together to form a cup shape.
letting us know . . .
Hand to chest.

Time to fall quiet (blossom, blossom)
Finger to mouth.
for all who died.
Hands crossed on chest.
Time now for hope (blossom, blossom),
Twist hands upwards like a snake/poppy stem growing.
time now for life.
Open palms while keeping wrists together to form a cup shape.

See in the fields (blossom, blossom),
Hand shading eyes, looking.
red poppies grow.
Twist hands upwards like a snake/poppy stem growing.
Signs of new life (blossom, blossom),
Open palms while keeping wrists together to form a cup shape.
now let peace flow! *Hands flowing like a river*

These poppies tell a story.
We're going to listen to that story now.
This story is different from any other story
that we tell together.
Normally we all join in.
But this is a special story.
It's a story to be quiet for.
Who can show me quiet?
This is a story that we listen to using our ears. *Hold ears*
Not our mouths. *Finger on lips*
Or our hands or our feet.

> *If appropriate:*

> In the main building the adults are stopping
> everything and being completely quiet
> for two whole minutes,
> standing still.

> This is the story that everyone will be thinking about.
> So we're going to sit still here
> and be quiet for two minutes as well.

We're going to place our hands on our chest like this.
Show the children how to fold their arms in a cross on their chest.

And while we're quiet,
I'm going to tell you the poppies' story.
Are you ready?

When the children are ready:

About one hundred years ago people started fighting.

Place three 'small world' men down.

They started fighting for lots of reasons.
But once they started, they couldn't stop.
More people joined in

Place more men down, including farmers, shopkeeper, horses, etc.

and then more
until almost the whole world was fighting.
Not just soldiers,
but farmers and policemen,
teachers and artists.

Even people who didn't like fighting had to fight.
Even horses.
Lots of people got very badly hurt;
lots of people died.

Lay down the people on the floor in silence and lay a brown cloth over the fallen figures.

Everyone was very sad.
Then something surprising happened.
In the fields where the fighting had happened, red poppies grew!

Lay the poppies down on the brown cloth.

People looked at the beautiful poppies
and remembered how beautiful life can be.
They shook their heads and said,
'We must never fight like this again! *Shake head*
We must remember this, so it never happens again!
These poppies will remind us!'
That was the First World War.

But just a few years later,
the fighting began again.
This time, there were some bullies.

Place men down next to the last brown cloth.

They began to hurt people.

Place women and children down and lay them down.

'What can we do?' everyone asked.
The bullying got worse and worse.
'We have to stop them.
We will have to fight!' they said.
So the fighting began again.

Place men down.

Like last time, not only soldiers had to fight,
but firefighters and shopkeepers,
bus drivers and dancers.

Place women, children, older people, pets, etc. down.

But this time, the fighting spread
so it even hurt people at home.
Children and old people, animals and pets.

Lots of people were badly hurt.
Lots of people died.

Lay the people and animals down.

But the bullies were stopped.
That was the Second World War.

Place the second brown cloth over the people.

When the fighting finished,
everyone shook their heads and said,
'We must never fight like this again!
We must remember these World Wars
so they never happen again!
We must learn not to fight when we're cross or scared,
but to use our words instead.
The beautiful poppies will remind us!'

Indicate the red poppies on the first brown cloth.

That's why we wear poppies in November.
To remember the World Wars.
To remember all the people who died.

Today, there's still fighting
all around the world.
We remember the people who have died.
We remember the soldiers who try to keep us safe.
And we promise to try to learn to use our words
and not fight,
from the very littlest of us.

I wonder when we forget to use our words
and hurt people instead?

We have a song about the poppies.
Can you remember the words, 'blossom, blossom'?
Let's sing our song now
and maybe you can help me with the actions.

See in the fields (blossom, blossom), *Hand shading eyes, looking*
red poppies grow. *Twist hands upwards like a snake/poppy stem growing*
Signs of new life (blossom, blossom), *Open palms while keeping wrists together to form a cup shape*
letting us know . . . *Hand to chest*

Time to fall quiet (blossom, blossom) *Finger to mouth*
for all who died. *Hands crossed on chest*
Time now for hope (blossom, blossom), *Twist hands upwards like a snake/poppy stem growing*
time now for life. *Open palms while keeping wrists together to form a cup shape*

See in the fields (blossom, blossom), *Hand shading eyes, looking*
red poppies grow. *Twist hands upwards like a snake/poppy stem growing*
Signs of new life (blossom, blossom), *Open palms while keeping wrists together to form a cup shape*
now let peace flow! *Hands flowing like a river*

> *Either: lead into the Prayers for Other People, using the special option for Remembrance Sunday.*

> *Or: show the children one or more baskets/trays with poppies.*

> In a moment, *Name* and *Name*
> are going to bring round these poppies.

If you like, you could take one and hold it up like this.
Model to the children holding up their poppy.

Let's ask God to see our poppy as a prayer for peace.

Sing the 'Diddy Disciples poppy song' until all the children and adults who wish to take a poppy have done so.

Let's give our poppy prayers for peace to God as we sing.
You can put your poppy anywhere you like on our cloth.
Indicate the cloth that was laid over the 'small world' people in the storytelling.

Let's ask God to hear our poppy as a prayer
that we – and all our leaders – will use our words instead of fighting.

Sing the 'Diddy Disciples poppy song' again as you lead the children and adults in placing their poppies. Some groups may like to invite two children to go around the circle in opposite directions with trays to collect the poppies. The poppies can then be laid on the cloth by one or two of the children. You may like to end by saying the last verse of the song as a closing prayer.

See in the fields (blossom, blossom),
red poppies grow.
Signs of new life (blossom, blossom),
now let peace flow!

Week 3: We Remember: All Who've Died

→ **(Revelation 21.3–4, 23–25)**
→ **Song 1: 'Thank you, God, for Nanny Ken'. Words © Sharon Moughtin-Mumby**
→ **Tune 1: 'O my darling Clementine' (traditional) like the 'In November, We Remember' Gathering Song.**
→ **Song 2: 'The Diddy Disciples heaven song', Words © Sharon Moughtin-Mumby**
→ **Tune 2: 'London's burning' (traditional).**
→ **For a taster of either song, see the Diddy Disciples website.**

For this week's storytelling you will need: (1) some dry, crinkly autumn leaves; (2) a flower or battery tealight for every person in the group (including any adults). These could be real, imitation, or paper flowers. At St Peter's, Walworth, we have used daisies picked on the way to church; (3) a memory box filled with 3–4 items that remind you of someone who has died. See the storytelling for examples. If your group has chosen the 'What's in the Box' option, this memory box and its items can serve as your 'What's in the Box' material this week.

Song 1

Thank you, God, thank you, God, thank you, God, for Nan-ny Ken.

Thank you, God, thank you, God, thank you, God, for Nan-ny Ken.

Song 2

No more hurt-ing, no more hurt-ing. No more cry-ing, no more

cry-ing. No dark, no dark. God is with me, God is with me.

Who can tell us what season we're in
in the world at the moment?
Accept the children's responses.

153

What happens in the autumn?
Give a child chance to talk about the autumn in her or his own way.

Autumn is a time when seeds fall from the trees
ready to grow next spring.
Wiggle fingers and show seeds falling.

It's also a time when things around us die.
We see leaves falling from the trees like these leaves.

Show dry, crinkly, brown leaves.

These leaves have died.
Has anyone here seen leaves like this around?
Some autumn leaves are beautiful.
Look at these beautiful leaves that have died.
In November, we remember all sorts of things.
One of the things we remember
is people who've died.

At this point, you have the opportunity to talk about someone you know who has died. We change the person that we talk about every year. As this may be the first time some of the children have spoken about death, we recommend that you choose someone:

- *you are very comfortable talking about*
- *whose death you feel very much at peace about*
- *who died some time ago*
- *who died in old age.*

For example:

I know someone who's died:
my Nanny Ken.
Her name was Olive, but I called her Nanny Ken.
She died about ten years ago.
I feel sad because I can't see my nanny any more.
But when I remember her, I feel happy as well.
I have so many lovely things to remember
about my nan
and those memories are beautiful.

> *Either: ask a child to take one object out of the memory box and tell the story of that object, before letting another child choose the next object, etc.*

> *Or: take the objects out yourself so you can choose their order.*

I have some of these memories in this box.
Let's have a look together.

I take out a photograph of my nan.

This is my Nanny Ken with her lovely smile!
Who can smile like my nan?
Lovely!
I love remembering my nanny's smile.
Let's sing 'Thank you, God for Nanny Ken'
and draw a smile on our face with our finger
as we sing to remember my nan's lovely smile.

Lead the children in singing the following song, or another 'thank you' song they're already familiar with.

Thank you, Go-d, thank you, Go-d, *Draw a smile*
thank you, God, for *Nanny Ken*. Draw a smile

Thank you, Go-d, thank you, Go-d, *Draw a smile*
thank you, God, for *Nanny Ken*. *Draw a smile*

I take out some toy giraffes that belonged to my nan.

Nanny Ken used to collect giraffes.
I started her collection
when I gave her this giraffe when she wasn't well.
Then everyone started giving her giraffes!
Now, whenever I see a giraffe, I think of my nan.
I even got a new one myself last week.
Shall we all be giraffes with long necks together?

Lead the children in stretching your arm up in the air to be a long neck and making your hand into the giraffe's head. You could even make horns with your first and fourth fingers.

Nan would have loved that!

Let's sing 'Thank you, God for Nanny Ken'.
Our giraffes can sing with us too!

Open and close your giraffe's mouth as you sing.
Thank you Go-d, thank you, Go-d,
thank you, God, for *Nanny Ken*.
Thank you, Go-d, thank you, Go-d,
thank you, God, for *Nanny Ken*.

I take out a pack of playing cards.

When I stayed at Nan's house
she used to play cards with me.
She always used to let me win!
Now when I play cards I remember my nan
and playing cards at her house with her.
Let's sing 'Thank you, God for Nanny Ken'
and 'deal' some cards as we sing.

Show children how to act dealing cards.
Then lead the children in singing.
Thank you, Go-d, thank you Go-d, *Deal cards*
thank you, God, for *Nanny Ken*. *Deal cards*
Thank you, Go-d, thank you Go-d, *Deal cards*
thank you, God, for *Nanny Ken*. *Deal cards*

I loved my nan.
Ten years ago she died, which is sad.
But I like remembering her.
She showed me lots of love and life and laughter.

When we follow Jesus, we believe that when we die,
we go to be in heaven with God.
We don't know where heaven is,
but there's a poem in the Bible
that tells us about heaven.
Let's sing the poem together:
'my turn' *point to self*, 'your turn' *leader's hands out to group*

No more hurting, *Shake head and hold sore tummy*
No more hurting. *Shake head and hold sore tummy*
No more crying, *Shake head and run fingers down face to show tears*
No more crying. *Shake head and run fingers down face to show tears*

No dark, *Place hands over eyes*
No dark. *Place hands over eyes*
God is with me. *Cross hands on chest*
God is with me. *Cross hands on chest*
Repeat

In November, we remember all sorts of things.
One of the things we remember
is people who've died.
It can make us feel sad and happy all at the same time
and that's all right.
We can remember people
by looking at things that remind us of them,
like the things in my box.

> *Either: show a battery tealight.*
> In the Church, sometimes we use candles
> to remember people who've died.
> We're going to do that together now.

> *Or: show a flower.*
> In our country, sometimes we use flowers
> to remember people who've died.
> We're going to do that together now.

Option 1: lead into the Prayer Actions, using the special option for 'We remember: all those who've died' (week 3).

Option 2:
I wonder whether you know someone who's died?
Or maybe you've heard an adult talking
about someone special who has died,
like my *Nanny Ken*?

> *Either:*
> If you don't know anyone who's died,
> you could join me in remembering my Nanny Ken.

> *Or, if appropriate:*
> If you don't know anyone who's died,
> you could join *our church* in remembering
> *Name*, *Name* and *Name*.
> *List the first names of 1–4 people who've died and are being remembered in your church or other group at the moment.*

Let's close our eyes for a moment.
Let's remember that person now.
Let's remember something that they did
that makes us smile . . .

Let's open our eyes.
We're going to sing our 'Thank you, God' song again.
This time we're going to sing different words.
Can you say after me?

Thank you, God for all who've died.
Thank you, God for all who've died.

If you're using battery tealights you may like to turn the lights down or off at this point.

As we sing quietly,
I'm going to pass around these candles/flowers.
If you like you can take one and hold it up like this.
Let's ask God to see our flower/candle as a 'thank you' prayer for our special people who've died.

Lead the children in singing repeatedly until everyone who would like one has a flower/candle.

Place a heart/cross shape or a piece of fabric in the centre of the circle. We use gold placemats in a cross shape.

Now let's place our candles/flowers on this _____.
Let's say 'thank you' to God for our special person.

Lead the children in singing repeatedly until all the flowers/candles have been placed. Some groups may like to invite two children to go around the circle in opposite directions with trays to collect the flowers/candles. The trays can then be placed in the centre.

Thank you, Go-d, thank you, Go-d,
thank you, God for all who've died.
Thank you, Go-d, thank you, Go-d,
thank you, God, for all who've died.

Having brought up the subject of death, it's appropriate to offer some space for other children or adults to talk about their own experiences and loved ones. This could be done during the time for Creative Response, or immediately after your session. You could use the following words, or you could ask an appropriate and familiar member of the lay or clergy team to be available.

In November, we remember people who've died.
It's good to remember them.
It can make us feel happy and sad all at the same time.
We're going to *move to our tables* now
but if you'd like to come and talk
about someone who's died
I *or Name* will be sitting over here.

Be very clear when the leader or other person is going to be available.

Week 4: We Remember: Christ the King

Option 1: Do This to Remember Me

→ **The Last Supper, Matthew 26.26–28 (also Mark 14.22–24)**
→ **Poem: 'Do this to remember me'. Words © Sharon Moughtin-Mumby**

This option is particularly appropriate for groups which meet during a communion service. To tell the story of Jesus' Last Supper, you'll need to have ready two or more trays: one set holding a piece of bread for each child and adult; the other set holding a cup with a small amount of grape juice at the bottom for each child and adult.

> **Tip**
>
> You could use matzo (unleavened) bread, pitta bread or everyday bread for this action. We cut the bread into small squares beforehand with scissors.
>
> There are benefits in making connections both with the kind of bread that you use in your church's communion service, and with the kind that your children will be familiar with from home, school or nursery. As this story is told at Lent and Easter time as well as to remember Christ the King, you could move between the different kinds of bread to support the children in making these connections.

In November, we remember all sorts of things.
This is our last Sunday in November.
It's our last Sunday of remembering

> *If appropriate:*
> before the Church begins a whole new year
> next week.

Today we remember the most important thing of all:
we remember Jesus is King: 'Christ the King'. *Show a crown*

If you're using the What's in the Box? option (p. 221):

How will we remember Jesus?

Invite one of the children to open the box. Inside will be bread and a cup or chalice.

What's in the box? *Ask the child to respond.*

We're going to remember Jesus the King
with the story of Jesus sharing bread and wine. *Show cup and bread*
Jesus said, 'Do this to remember me'.

If appropriate:
We remember this story every week in church.

Let's tell the story together now.
Jesus and his friends were getting ready
for a very special party called the Passover.
When it was dark, they sat down to eat together,
like we're sitting here.
Then Jesus did something new.

Invite two children to take around small pieces of bread in two baskets for everyone who wants to receive them.

Name and *Name* are going to
bring round some bread now.
If you'd like some bread,
can you hold your hands out like this? *Model to the children*
Name and *Name* will give you a piece.
Keep the bread in your hands 'til everyone has some.
Don't eat it yet!

You may like to sing 'In November, We Remember' as you wait for your bread.

When the group is ready:
After dinner, Jesus did something new.
Can you say these words after me and copy my actions?
My turn *point to self*, your turn *leader's hands out to group*

Jesus took the bread.	*Take bread in one hand*
Jesus took the bread.	*Take bread in one hand*
He said, 'Thank you, God!'	*Hold bread up if this is in your tradition*
He said, 'Thank you, God!'	*Hold bread up if this is in your tradition*
Jesus broke the bread.	*Break bread*
Jesus broke the bread.	*Break bread*
Then he shared it.	*Mime handing bread out in a circle*
Then he shared it.	*Mime handing bread out in a circle*
This is my body,	*Hold bread or point to it*
This is my body,	*Hold bread or point to it*
broken for you.	*Hold bread back together then separate it again*
Broken for you.	*Hold bread back together then separate it again*
Do this to remember me!	*Hold bread up if this is in your tradition*
Do this to remember me!	*Hold bread up if this is in your tradition*

Invite the children to eat their bread slowly, really tasting and enjoying it. Once the children's hands are empty, distribute cups with just 1–2 cm of grape juice at the bottom. These cups are best distributed by adults or responsible, older children.

While you finish eating,
we're going to bring around cups.
If you'd like a cup,
can you hold your hands out like this? *Model to the children*

Keep the cup in your hands 'til everyone has one.
Don't drink from it yet!

You may like to sing 'In November, We Remember' as you wait for your cup. Once all the children and adults who wish to receive a cup have done so:

When they'd finished eating,
Jesus took the cup.
Can you say these words after me and copy my actions?
'My turn' *point to self*, 'your turn' *leader's hands out to group*

Jesus took the cup.	*Take cup in both hands*
Jesus took the cup.	*Take cup in both hands*
He said, 'Thank you, God!'	*Hold cup up if this is in your tradition*
He said, 'Thank you, God!'	*Hold cup up if this is in your tradition*
Jesus poured the wine.	*Mime pouring wine*
Jesus poured the wine.	*Mime pouring wine*
Then he shared it.	*Mime handing cup out in a circle*
Then he shared it.	*Mime handing cup out in a circle*
This is my blood,	*Lift cup or point to it*
This is my blood,	*Lift cup or point to it*
poured out for you.	*Mime pouring wine*
Poured out for you.	*Mime pouring wine*
Do this to remember me!	*Hold cup up if this is in your tradition*
Do this to remember me!	*Hold cup up if this is in your tradition*

Invite the children to drink the grape juice slowly and to really taste and enjoy it. When they've finished, ask for a moment of quiet.

I wonder how you feel when you eat the bread
and drink from your cup?
Can you show me?

The children may respond silently, inside themselves, or they may offer a facial expression, or a single word or more. Accept all of their responses.

In November, we remember.
On our last remembering day, we remember Jesus.
We remember that Jesus is King.
And we remember Jesus in the way
he asked us to remember him:
with broken bread and a cup.

Option 2: The Humble King

→ **(Luke 2.1–20; Philippians 2.6–11)**

In November, we remember all sorts of things.
This is our last Sunday in November.
It's our last Sunday of remembering

> *If appropriate:*
> before the Church begins a whole new year
> next week.
>
> *If you're using the What's in the Box? option (p. 221):*
>
> How will we remember Jesus?
>
> *Invite one of the children to open the box. Inside will be a crown.*
>
> What's in the box? *Ask the child to respond.*

Today we remember Jesus is King: 'Christ the King'.
Let's imagine we're going to be king!
Let's stand up tall!
Imagine: you can have anything you want!
Anything at all!
How does that make you feel?
Can you show me?

Today, we're going to be king!
We're going to do some choosing!
We're going to choose all the amazing things
we want as king.

> *At this point, you can stay in your circle, or move to a table.*
> Let's find a place at our table and listen.

Give out the first Christ the King sheet (see website) and a crayon/pencil/pen. With older children, you could lay all four sheets out beforehand, but this is likely to confuse younger children.

So you're the king.
Look at all these lovely homes!

Point to all the homes on the sheet and describe them. Example: there's a treehouse, a castle, etc.

You can choose any home you like!
You have the power to have any home at all!
You could even design your own home in this box later.
Which home will you choose?
Put a big circle round it . . .

Tip

While the children are choosing each time, you might like to play a short excerpt of a hymn or song related to Christ the King. If your group is meeting during a church service, you might like to choose a hymn that will be sung in your service later.

In smaller groups, invite each child to tell the group what their choice is. In larger groups you might like to choose 3–4 children each time, trying to aim for all the children to have one chance in the session (there will be four opportunities). If your group is too big for this, then they could show the person next to them. At St Peter's we've found that parents or carers with babies quite enjoy trying to guess what their baby might choose and why.

Give out the second Christ the King sheet.

So remember, you're the king.
Look at all these lovely beds!

Point to all the beds on the sheet and describe them.

You can choose any bed you like!
You have the power to have any bed at all!
You could even design your own bed in this box later.
Which bed will you choose?
Put a big circle round it . . .

Offer the children a second opportunity to share their choices.

Give out the third Christ the King sheet.

Look at all these lovely clothes!

Point to all the clothes on the sheet and describe them.

You're the king!
You can choose any clothes you like!
You have the power to have any clothes at all!
You could even design your own clothes
in this box later.
Which clothes will you choose?
Put a big circle round them . . .

Offer the children a further opportunity to share their choices.

Give out the fourth Christ the King sheet.

Last choice as king!
Look at all these special people.
You're the king and people want to visit you!

Point to all the people on the sheet and describe them.

You can choose any visitors you like!
You have the power to have any visitors at all!
You could even draw your own visitors in this box later.
Which visitors will you choose?
Put a big circle round them . . .

Offer the children a final opportunity to share their choices.

Who enjoyed being king?
Who would like to be able to choose anything they like!
Hands up . . .

In November, we remember.
We remember Jesus the King.
Jesus was King, but Jesus was a very different kind of king.
Jesus was God!

Jesus could have chosen anything at all
when he was born.
He could have had a palace and servants
and beautiful clothes.
But Jesus didn't choose those things.

Jesus – God – wanted to be with us so much
that God came as a tiny baby:
with no house, *Shake head*
with no bed, *Shake head*
with no clothes. *Shake head*

Being born, being with us, was special enough for God.
So God came to us as a tiny baby, Jesus.

At this point, you could show the children a relevant nativity picture, pointing out the stable, manger and swaddling bands.

Jesus was born in a stable where animals live.
Jesus slept in a bed made from an animal's food bowl.
Jesus had no special clothes,
just some white bands like any baby.

Today [*if appropriate:* is 'Christ the King':]
we remember all the things Jesus chose.
We remember God wanted to be with us so much
that Jesus was happy to come with nothing at all.
We say 'thank you' to Jesus.

If appropriate:
And we give Jesus the crown and the presents we think he deserves.
We have the chance to make a crown or a present for Jesus now.

Extra Week: We Remember People in Need

→ **Acts 20.35**

This week, in place of the Bible storytelling, your group could work together on an extended project to remember and raise money for people in need. Your group may like to choose a local or overseas project to raise money for. Alternatively, if your church or school are getting involved in a Children in Need project this November, you might like to contribute to that.

Section 3

Creative Response starter ideas, In November, We Remember unit

→ Guide: p. 228

These starter ideas are designed to spark imaginations and open up opportunities for the children to respond creatively in their different ways to the worship and storytelling you've taken part in together.

> **Tip**
>
> As outlined in the Guide (from p. 228), we've found the following rules of thumb helpful for fostering an environment where children are encouraged to engage personally and openly:
>
> 1 Encourage the children to make their own choices.
> 2 Give the children space to develop their response as they wish.
> 3 Create space for 'bridge building'.
> 4 It's the act of responding that matters, not the final result.
> 5 These responses are 'holy ground'.

Weekly Starter Ideas relate directly to the Bible storytelling of each session, including a print-and-go option (indicated by the printer icon).

Sensory Starter Ideas are designed for sensory explorers, including babies and toddlers. These can remain the same through the whole unit.

Unit Starter Ideas are designed to remain relevant throughout the whole unit. Keeping these resources available each week gives children the opportunity to deepen and develop their responses, while making preparation more manageable for leaders.

> **Tip: Free response area**
>
> In addition to any other resources you provide, keeping a free response area available every week will give the children the opportunity to create anything they wish in response to the story they've told, building their sense of confidence and personal responsibility. In this area you could simply provide blank paper and crayons, pencils, paints or pastels. If you have them, other interesting media (see p. 256) will provide even more scope for the children to nurture and strengthen their imaginative skills.

Weekly Starter Ideas

Week 1: We're All Saints!

✿ Invite the children to draw a 'saint': this could be themselves, someone they know or a favourite saint. *Provide paper and pencils/crayons. If you like, you could provide a face template or a picture frame template (pp. 267, 275 or website). You could also provide tinfoil, scissors and glue, in case the children would like to use it to make a halo or to create a background that will make their picture look like an icon.*

✿ Give the children the opportunity to make their own halo. *Provide a circle template (p. 266 or website) printed onto card or a paper plate, plus crayons/pencils/paints and scissors. You could also provide glue and gold/silver/yellow collage materials, plus glitter or tinfoil.*

✿ Saints shine like lights in the world. Invite the children to explore showing light shining in the dark by drawing with their choice of media on dark paper. *Provide black or dark blue paper, plus oil pastels, paint, chalk or glitter and glue. Provide a choice if possible.*

✿ Invite the children to make penne pasta haloes. *Provide penne pasta, string/wool/pipe cleaners. You could even dye the pasta yellow beforehand (see p. 257).*

✿ The greatest gift is love. Invite the children to add collage materials of different colours and textures to a heart. For more love-based suggestions, see the Sharing Jesus' Love starter ideas in the Jesus' Wonderful Love unit on p. 80 above. *Provide heart template (p. 270 or website), glue, collage materials (p. 255) and scissors.*

Week 2: We Remember: Remembrance Sunday

✿ Give the children the opportunity to create their own poppy wreath or other poppy-related response by providing simple poppy templates, plus circles for those who would like to make wreaths. *Provide poppy templates, circle templates (pp. 278, 266 or website) or paper plates, plus scissors, glue and pencils/crayons/ paints/pastels. Either print the templates onto green and red card, or onto white card for the children to decorate. If you have red and black tissue paper, you could also provide this for children who would like to create their own poppy shapes or poppy-coloured collages.*

✿ Invite the children to make a bunch of poppies, either freestyle with red paper or using poppy templates. You could invite the children to tape these to a 'stick' or glue them onto a background. *Provide red tissue/ crepe paper or poppy templates (p. 278 or website), straws/lollipop sticks/pipe cleaners, plus masking tape, glue and coloured paper. You could also provide string/wool and/or paper cups for the children to gather their poppies.*

✿ Invite younger children to collage a paper plate poppy with red and black collage. Remember to give them space to explore freely their own idea of a poppy: don't expect every offering to have black (only) in the centre! *Provide pre-prepared paper plates (with a curvy triangle cut from each side to create a large poppy shape), glue, red and black collage materials (p. 255) or tissue paper.*

✿ Invite the children to hand- or finger-paint red poppies onto (pre-drawn) green stalks, or as they wish. *Provide: paper with pre-drawn green lines and red paint. You may even like to use edible cornflour finger paints (p. 258).*

✿ Give the children the opportunity to make salt dough poppies or other red and black poppy-themed creations using red salt dough and black raisins. *Provide: red salt dough (recipe on p. 257), raisins. You may like to provide paper plates to hold the children's creations.*

Week 3: We Remember: All Who've Died

✤ Invite the children to create their own flower picture. They may like to cut out flower templates and use them for collage, or they may like to add green lines to the flower template sheets for stalks. They may like to arrange their flowers in a bunch (2D), or to add a vase to their picture. They may prefer to leave the flowers dotted around as if they're in a garden, or to draw their own flowers freestyle. Encourage the children to explore their own ideas. *Provide flower templates (p. 273 or website) printed onto different-coloured paper or white paper to be decorated, crayons/pencils/pens (especially green), glue, other coloured paper to create vases, more flowers or anything they wish.*

✤ Invite the children to decorate a candle template to remember someone who's died. *Provide: candle templates (p. 269 or website) and crayons/pencils/paints/pastels. For more candle-based ideas, see the Jesus, the Light of the World starter ideas on p. 211 below.*

✤ Give the children an opportunity to make a picture of someone they know or have heard of who's died. It's important to handle this opportunity sensitively, including any drawings of animals or pets that are precious to the child. *Provide picture frame templates (p. 275 or website), plus crayons/pencils. If you have pastels/paints or other interesting media available (p. 256), this would be a lovely opportunity to offer them.*

✤ Invite the children to make their own tealight or candle holder from salt dough to take home and remember someone who's died. *Provide different colours of salt dough for the children to mix and create with as they choose (recipe on p. 257). You may also like to provide tealights or candles and glitter to decorate the salt dough.*

✤ Give the children an opportunity to imagine heaven. Leave this as much to their imagination as possible, providing a range of materials. *Provide interesting media (p. 256), or construction toys such as wooden blocks, Lego, Duplo, Mega blocks, Stickle Bricks, Kapla, K'Nex, Polydron.*

✤ We can feel lots of different things when we remember someone who's died, and that's all right. Give the children the opportunity to explore their feelings with one of the Exploring Our Feelings starter ideas from the Jesus' Wonderful Love unit on p. 80.

✤ Give the children the opportunity to discover that beautiful things can be fleeting and last only a moment through 'ephemeral' or 'transient' art. We don't need to be afraid of the idea that things may not last: we can still celebrate their beauty. *Provide media for creating ephemeral art such as dyed salt, rice or pasta (see p. 256), or objects from the natural world, depending on the season: pressed flowers, leaves, grasses, blossom, twigs, sand, stones, shells. Check that nothing presents a safety hazard. See p. 256 for more ideas of media for ephemeral art.*

✤ Some cultures use stones to remember people who have died. You could invite the children to build little cairns from stones, to decorate a stone with beautiful patterns, or discover their own way to respond with stones. At the end of the session, encourage the children to take a stone home and ask their parents or carers to tell them about someone who's died that they enjoy remembering. *Provide stones. Optional: felt tip pens or paints.*

Week 4: We Remember Christ the King

✤ Invite the children to design a crown fit for King Jesus. *Provide crown templates (p. 279 or website) and pencils/crayons. If you have glue, scissors and a range of collage materials (p. 255), you could also provide these.*

✤ For option 1 of the storytelling: invite the children to design a chalice fit for a king. *Provide chalice templates (p. 280 or website) plus pencils/crayons. Optional: scissors, glue and collage materials (p. 255), including gold, silver (e.g. tinfoil), coloured foil, foil or cellophane sweet wrappers, glitter.*

✤ For option 2 of the storytelling: invite the children to develop the pictures you've used for the storytelling or to create their own. *Provide 'Christ the King' pictures (website only), plus crayons/pencils.*

✤ Invite the children to make a cross beautiful and fit for a king. *Provide cross template, pencils/crayons/ pens. Optional: scissors, glue and collage materials (p. 255) including gold, silver (e.g. tinfoil), coloured foil, foil or cellophane sweet wrappers, glitter.*

✤ Jesus was given a crown of thorns by the Romans. Invite the children to transform a crown of thorns into a crown of victory like the laurel crowns of winners in the Olympic games by adding green leaves to a crown. *Provide crown templates (p. 279 or website), glue, green leaves (either real or cut from green paper by the children).*

Sensory Starter Ideas

These ideas are particularly suitable for babies and toddlers. You could provide:

- battery tealights for the children to explore, plus a piece of fabric that they can be placed on. At St Peter's, Walworth, we have a wooden tealight holder that has holes for six tealights, which the children can explore and use to arrange their candles;

- a range of autumn leaves that have died (you may like to laminate some);

- dry autumn leaves and a large piece of fabric. The children can explore the leaves, or wave the fabric with an adult and send the leaves up into the air. Collect and repeat;

- card leaf shapes or laminated real leaves with holes punched into them and shoelaces for threading;

- pictures of fireworks to explore;

- child-friendly poppies (we laminate pictures of poppies);

- dressing up materials: crowns, robes, and haloes;

- Jesus said heaven is like a palace with many rooms. Provide construction toys (e.g. Mega blocks, Duplo, Stickle Bricks, Kapla, K'Nex, Polydron) and invite the children to build a Palace or 'Heaven' from them;

- pictures of saints, especially the saints you sang about together in week 1;

- 'small world' people (small plastic figures such as those from Happyland or Fisher Price, or wooden/knitted figures). You could even provide a 'small world' church (e.g. Happyland);

- All the saints shine like lights in the world. You might like to take a look at the light-themed Sensory Explorer starter ideas in the Getting Ready for Baby Jesus (Advent) unit (p. 211).

Unit Starter Ideas

- Give the children the opportunity to discover that beautiful things can be fleeting and last only a moment by creating 'ephemeral' or 'transient' art. We don't need to be afraid of the idea that things may not last: we can still celebrate their beauty. *Provide media for making ephemeral art such as dyed salt, rice or pasta (see p. 257), or objects from the natural world, depending on the season: for example, pressed flowers, leaves, grasses, blossom, twigs, sand, stones, shells. Check that nothing presents a safety hazard.*

- Invite the children to create their own firework pictures to remember in November. *Provide dark paper or card plus paint, glitter, chalk or pastels.*

UNIT 4
GETTING READY FOR BABY JESUS (ADVENT AND CHRISTMAS)

This unit gives your group the opportunity to prepare for the arrival of Baby Jesus, the Light of the World, who will shine in the darkness, like the Christmas lights that shine around us at this time of year.

The four stories from this unit all come from Luke's Gospel. We made a conscious decision to keep them together (including the less familiar story of Zechariah) to respect Luke's careful choice of birth narratives, which show God coming to – and working through – all kinds of different people in all kinds of different places:

> Week 1: an old respected man in the Temple
>
> Week 2: a young, disgraced woman at home
>
> Week 3: two unborn babies on a journey
>
> Week 4: the despised 'outsider' shepherds in the fields

Through the stories and supporting material of this unit, the children are encouraged to make sense of and take part in the celebratory mood of this time of year, but also to find space in the busyness to remember and spend time with the tiny baby, the Light of the World, at the centre of it all.

Note: The story of the Magi (or three kings/Wise Men) from Matthew's Gospel features in the Jesus, Light of the World! (Epiphany) unit, which continues immediately after this 'Getting Ready for Baby Jesus' unit in *Diddy Disciples: January to August*. Some groups may prefer to use stories from this unit during the Advent/Christmas season.

Section 1

The Building Blocks, Getting Ready for Baby Jesus unit

Pick and choose from these Building Blocks and their various options to build sessions for your group. Whatever choices you make, we suggest you keep to that pattern for the whole of the unit as this will open up opportunities for the children to participate fully and confidently during your time together.

> **Build your own Diddy Disciples session** (p. 6) provides an overview of the Building Blocks and a short introduction to fitting them together, along with examples.
>
> **A Guide to the Building Blocks** (p. 215) provides a step-by-step guide to each Building Block.

Tip

If your church sings 'O come, O come Emmanuel' (trans. John Mason Neale, 1818–66) during Advent, you may like to sing this Diddy Disciples verse along with the traditional refrain at some point during your session, for instance immediately after the Peace. At St Peter's, Walworth, we include the verse in our singing of 'O come, O come Emmanuel' in our main Sunday service. Having sung it in our session, the children are confident not only in singing the verse itself, but in joining in with the 'Rejoice!' refrain all the way through the hymn.

→ **Song: The Diddy Disciples 'O Come' Antiphon. Words © Sharon Moughtin-Mumby**
→ **Tune:** *Veni Emmanuel* (unknown)

O Come, O little baby, come!
Rock Baby Jesus gently in your arms.
Come play with us
Hold hands out and move up and down as if dancing with the toddler Jesus.
and make our home your home.
Point to yourself, then to the toddler Jesus.
This world can feel as dark as night.
Hands over eyes.
Light of the world, come shine on us your light!
Sun rising action.

Rejoice! Rejoice!
Hands up in 'Alleluia' sign or waving.
Emmanuel shall come to thee, O Israel!
Rock Baby Jesus in your arms.

Welcome

→ **Guide: p. 218**

Welcome your group.

Let's start by going round the circle
and saying our name out loud.
My name's _____.

Go round the circle so that every adult and child has the chance to say his or her name (and introduce any dolls, teddies, or toys). If any of the children don't want to say their name or aren't able to, you (or a parent or carer) could say it for them and wave.

It's time to sing our Welcome Song!

Welcome Song: Option 1

→ **Song: 'The Diddy Disciples welcome song'. Words © Sharon Moughtin-Mumby**
→ **Tune: 'Glory, glory, alleluia!' (traditional). For the music see p. 259, or for a taster see the Diddy Disciples website. For tips on teaching songs for the first time, see p. 215.**

Go around the circle the same way as above. See if you can remember each other's names and insert them into the song.

Welcome *Name 1* **to** *St Peter's**
Welcome *Name 2* **to** *St Peter's**

Welcome *Name 3* **to** *St Peter's**
you are welcome in the name of the Lord!

* Insert the name of your church or children's group, or sing 'our worship'.

Welcome Song: Option 2

→ **Song: 'You are welcome in the name of the Lord' (traditional)**
→ **Tune: Traditional. For the music see p. 262, or for a taster see the Diddy Disciples website. For tips on teaching songs for the first time, see p. 215.**

Let's wave with one hand. *Lead waving*

Then with our other hand. *Lead waving*

Then let's choose someone and show them God's 'glory'!

Move arms up and down in front of you with fingers wiggling, palms facing out, towards one person.

And someone else! *Repeat*

Then let's wave with both hands all around the circle.

Lead waving.

We're ready to sing!

You are welcome in the name of the Lord!
Wave with right hand to one person.
You are welcome in the name of the Lord!
Wave with left hand to another person.
I can see all over you the glory of the Lord,
Move arms up and down in front of you with fingers wiggling, palms facing out, towards one person and then another.
you are welcome in the name of the Lord!
Wave with both hands all around the circle.

Getting Ready to Worship

→ **Guide: p. 218**

Choose one of the following greetings according to which is familiar in your church. (If your church uses a different greeting, you could use that here instead.)

Getting Ready to Worship: Option 1

→ **Action: The sign of the cross. Words © Sharon Moughtin-Mumby**

Invite the children to make the sign of the cross slowly with you. As the children become more confident, invite a child to lead the action as the whole group says the words and makes the sign of the cross.

In my head,	*Touch head*
in my heart,	*touch chest*
and all around me,	*Touch shoulders one by one*
Jesus is here.	*Open hands in front facing upwards*

Getting Ready to Worship: Option 2

→ **Action: 'The Lord be with you' (open hands)**

Let's start by clenching our hands together tightly.

Lead children in clenching fists against your body to show a defensive posture.

When we close ourselves up like this,
it's hard to let anyone into our heart.
It's hard even to let God into our heart!

When we get ready to worship,
we show that we're open to God and to each other.

Open your hands out, facing up.

Can you show me your open hands?
We're ready to let God and each other in!

The Lord be with you.
Hold hands open to the children.

And also with you.
Invite the children to open their hands towards you.

Introducing the Unit

→ **Guide: p. 218**

Introducing the Unit: Option 1

It's time to get ready for Christmas!
Baby Jesus is coming!

Introducing the Unit: Option 2

→ **Focus: the liturgical colour, purple**

Who can tell us what colour season we're in now?
>   *If appropriate:* You may have seen it in church.

The colour purple
reminds us it's time to 'get ready'!
Baby Jesus is coming at Christmas!

>   *If appropriate:* Let's all look out for purple when we go back into church.
>   *Or:* Let's remember to look and see what colour we're in next time we go into church.

Introducing the Unit: Option 3

For Christmas Day or the week after Christmas

It's Christmas!
Baby Jesus is here!

>   *If appropriate:*
>   We have our Baby Jesus doll here to remind us.

>   *If your church uses visible liturgical colours:*
>   Who can tell us what colour Christmas is?
>   *If appropriate:* You may have seen it in church . . .

>   *Invite a child to respond and accept his or her response.*

>   Gold and white are the colours of joy!
>   Baby Jesus is here!

Gathering Song

→ **Guide: p. 219**

In week 1, skip the Gathering Song, including the introduction, and move straight into the storytelling, which will introduce the Gathering Song for the rest of Advent.

Gathering Song: Option 1

→ 'Busy, busy, busy, getting ready for Christmas!' Words © Sharon Moughtin-Mumby
→ Tune: 'What shall we do with the drunken sailor?' (traditional). For a taster see the Diddy Disciples website.

Baby Jesus is the Light of the World!
Let's close our eyes and feel the dark . . .

We're waiting for Baby Jesus, the Light of the World,
to shine in the darkness!
Let's open our eyes again.

You might like to show the children a picture of the sun rising, if you used one in the storytelling for week 1.

Like we wait for the sun to 'dawn',
to come up, in the morning.

If you're using imaginative aids, ask two or three children to give them out.

Let's show the sun 'dawning' with our bodies.
Let's crouch down low . . .
Let's close our eyes . . . it's dark!
Let's show the sun coming up and up and out . . .
in the morning.
Lead the children in showing the sun rising with your hands as you stand up.

The sun is 'dawning'!
Now let's do that as we sing our song,
'Jesus, Light of the World'.

> *If you're singing this song for the first time with your group, you may find the following introduction helpful.*
>
> We have a new song about 'Jesus, Light of the World'.
> Let's learn it 'my turn' *both hands to self*, 'your turn' *hands out to group*
>
> *Sing the words with the tune to the group.*
> Je-sus, Light of the World, *Both hands to self to show your turn*
> Je-sus, Light of the World
> **Je-sus, Light of the World,** *Both hands to group to show their turn*

Je-sus, Light of the World,
Je-sus, Light of the World is *Both hands to self to show your turn*
dawning in the darkness!
Je-sus, Light of the World, is *Both hands to group to show their turn*
dawning in the darkness!

Let's sing that all together and add our actions.
Je-sus, Light of the World, *Sun dawning action*
Je-sus, Light of the World, *Sun dawning action*
Je-sus, Light of the World, is *Sun dawning action*
dawning in the darkness! *Sun dawning action*

Don't worry about teaching the 'Busy, busy, busy' words. These are very repetitive, so that the children will pick them up as they go, and the tune is the same as the 'Jesus, Light of the World' refrain.

Je-sus, Light of the World, *Sun dawning action*
Je-sus, Light of the World, *Sun dawning action*
Je-sus, Light of the World, is *Sun dawning action*
dawning in the darkness! *Sun dawning action*

Getting ready for Christmas can be very busy!
What have we been doing to get ready for Christmas?

Either invite the children to make suggestions, or choose from the suggestions below. For each activity sing the 'Busy, busy, busy, getting ready for Christmas!' verse with an appropriate action designed by the children, followed by the 'Jesus, Light of the World' refrain:

• *hanging lights on the Christmas tree . . . (we use lights at Christmas to remember that Jesus is the Light of the World!)*
• *opening our Advent calendars*
• *writing Christmas cards*
• *cleaning our home*
• *baking and cooking*
• *wrapping presents*
• *dancing at parties.*

Busy, busy, busy, getting ready for Christmas!
Busy, busy, busy, getting ready for Christmas!
Busy, busy, busy, getting ready for Christmas!
The Light of the World is dawning! *Sun dawning action*

Je-sus, Light of the World, *Sun dawning action*
Je-sus, Light of the World, *Sun dawning action*
Je-sus, Light of the World, is *Sun dawning action*
dawning in the darkness! *Sun dawning action*

Getting ready for Christmas can be very busy!
You might see your parents or carers at home running around
and getting very busy!

> *If appropriate:* Or your teachers at school getting stressed
> about the Christmas/Nativity play!

Let's all look busy and stressed like the adults!
Lead children in waving imaginative aids or arms around madly and running on the spot.

Let's sing 'Busy, busy, busy, getting ready for Christmas' again.

Busy, busy, busy, getting ready for Christmas!
Busy, busy, busy, getting ready for Christmas!
Busy, busy, busy, getting ready for Christmas!
The Light of the World is dawning!

Je-sus, Light of the World, *Sun dawning action*
Je-sus, Light of the World, *Sun dawning action*
Je-sus, Light of the World, is *Sun dawning action*
dawning in the darkness! *Sun dawning action*

My goodness, that was busy!
Who's feeling tired?
When we're getting ready for Christmas
it can get really busy and really exciting!
Who's excited about Christmas?
In all the busyness,
let's remember to also have time for some quiet.
Let's remember to get ready for the very special baby
that's coming: Baby Jesus.

Let's sit quietly now and close our eyes . . .
Let's imagine holding Baby Jesus in our arms
and singing to him quietly and gently.
Baby Jesus will be born at Christmas!

Lead the children rocking a baby and singing quietly.
Je-sus, Light of the World,
Je-sus, Light of the World,
Je-sus, Light of the World, is
dawning in the darkness!

One of the ways we get ready inside *Trace a circle on your heart*
is to tell stories about Baby Jesus.
We're going to tell one of those stories today.

Gathering Song: Option 2

For Christmas Day or the week after Christmas

→ **Song: 'Joy! Joy! Joy! It's Christmas! Christmas!' is the alternative refrain for 'Busy, busy, busy, getting ready for Christmas!'**
  Words © Sharon Moughtin-Mumby
→ **Tune: 'What shall we do with the drunken sailor?' (traditional). See Option 1 above for music**

Baby Jesus is the Light of the World!
Let's close our eyes and feel the dark.

Lead the children in closing eyes.

Let's imagine Jesus shining like a tiny star in the sky.
Now let's imagine that light growing brighter and brighter and brighter –
until its light fills the whole world!
So bright we can't even look at it!
Let's open our eyes again.

Baby Jesus, the Light of the World, is
shining. *Jazz hands*
Let's show jazz hands for Jesus' light. *Jazz hands*

Before Christmas, we were 'busy, busy, busy'
Move arms as if running
getting ready for Jesus, Light of the World,
to DAWN in the darkness.
Show the sun rising up and out with your arms

Jesus' light was just beginning to show, like the sun in the morning.
Now Jesus' light is SHINING, bright!
Lead the children in jazz hands

Let's sing our Jesus, Light of the World, song again.
This time, at the end let's sing 'SHINING in the darkness'
Lead the children in jazz hands
And show our jazz hands.

Lead the children in singing:

Je-sus, Light of the World, *Sun dawning action*
Je-sus, Light of the World, *Sun dawning action*
Je-sus, Light of the World, is *Sun dawning action*
SHINING in the darkness! *Jazz hands*

Christmas is an amazing time!
Who's having fun at Christmas?

Let's sing our 'Busy, busy, busy' song,
But with new Christmas words!
Can you say after me?
'Joy! Joy! Joy! It's Christmas! Christmas!'
Joy! Joy! Joy! It's Christmas! Christmas!

And don't forget our *jazz hands* for
'The Light of the World is shining!' at the end.

Joy! Joy! Joy! It's Christmas! Christmas!
Joy! Joy! Joy! It's Christmas! Christmas!
Joy! Joy! Joy! It's Christmas! Christmas!
The Light of the World is shining! *Jazz hands*

Je-sus, Light of the World, *Sun dawning action*
Je-sus, Light of the World, *Sun dawning action*
Je-sus, Light of the World, is *Sun dawning action*
shining in the darkness! *Jazz hands*

Let's think of some of the things we've done this Christmas.

Either invite the children to make suggestions, or choose from the suggestions below. For each activity sing 'Joy! Joy! Joy! It's Christmas, Christmas! with an appropriate action designed by the children, followed by the 'Jesus, Light of the World' refrain:

* *opening stockings*
* *dancing at parties*
* *unwrapping presents*
* *eating lots of tasty food*
* *chocolate, chocolate everywhere!*

My goodness! That was exciting!
But in all that excitement,
let's remember to also have time for some quiet.
Let's remember to welcome Baby Jesus inside. *Trace circle on heart*
Let's sit quietly now and close our eyes . . .
Let's imagine holding Baby Jesus in our arms
Model rocking Baby Jesus.
and singing to him quietly and gently.
Sssssssssh!

Joy! Joy! Joy! It's Christmas! Christmas! *Rock Baby Jesus*
Joy! Joy! Joy! It's Christmas! Christmas! *Rock Baby Jesus*
Joy! Joy! Joy! It's Christmas! Christmas! *Rock Baby Jesus*
The Light of the World is shining! *Jazz hands*

Je-sus, Light of the World, *Sun dawning action*
174 **Je-sus, Light of the World,** *Sun dawning action*

Je-sus, Light of the World, is *Sun dawning action*
shining in the darkness! *Jazz hands*

Getting Ready for Bible Storytelling

→ **Guide: p. 221**

Getting Ready for Bible Storytelling: Option 1

→ **Action: opening your group's box and naming this week's object**

See the beginning of the weekly storytelling material for ideas of items to place in your box. Invite one of the children to open the box.

What's in the box? *Ask the child to respond*

Getting Ready for Bible Storytelling: Option 2

→ **Song: 'Jesus, open up my eyes'. Words © Sharon Moughtin-Mumby**
→ **Tune: 'Michael, row the boat ashore' (traditional). For the music, see p. 262, or for a taster see the Diddy Disciples website. For tips on teaching songs for the first time, see p. 215.**

It's time to tell our Bible story.
Let's get ready!
Let's take our thumb *Lead children in showing thumb*
and draw our cross on our eyes, *Draw cross*
and our lips, *Draw cross*
and our heart. *Draw cross*
Let's ask Jesus to help us get ready to listen out for God!

Jesus, open up my eyes. Alleluia!
Trace a cross between your eyes.
Jesus, open up my lips. Alleluia!
Trace a cross on your lips.
Jesus, open up my heart. Alleluia!
Trace a cross on your heart.
Jesus, help me hear your voice. Alleluia!
Cup your hands behind your ears.

Interactive Bible Storytelling

→ **Guide: p. 221**

See the Bible Storytelling material in Section 2 of this unit.

Saying Sorry to God

→ **Guide: p. 222**

Invite the children to sit in a circle for a moment of quiet.

In Advent we get ready to welcome Baby Jesus into the world.
One way we do this is by tidying up our home.
We can also get ready by asking God to help us tidy up our hearts.
It's time to sing our Sorry Song.

Option 1

→ Song: 'The Diddy Disciples sorry song'. Words © Sharon Moughtin-Mumby
→ Tune: © Sharon Moughtin-Mumby. For the music see p. 259, or for a taster see the Diddy Disciples website. For tips on teaching songs for the first time, see p. 215. For a description of the 'I'm Sorry' and 'New Start' signs, see p. 225 or the website.

Let's put our hands on our head.
I wonder if there's anything we've thought this week
that we wish we hadn't thought?

Lead the children in placing your hands on head, singing.
With my hands on my head,
I remember the things I've thought today,
I remember the things I wish I'd thought a different way.

I'm sorry, I'm sorry, *Diddy Disciples 'I'm Sorry' sign (see p. 225).*
I wish I could start again. *Diddy Disciples 'New Start' sign (see p. 225).*
I'm sorry, I'm sorry, *'I'm Sorry' sign.*
I wish I could start again. *Repeat 'New Start' sign.*

Let's put our hands by our mouths.
I wonder if there's anything we've said this week
that we wish we hadn't said?

With hands by mouth, singing . . .
With my hands on my mouth,
I remember the things I've said today,
I remember the things I wish I'd said a different way.

Repeat 'I'm Sorry' and 'New Start' signs as above.
I'm sorry, I'm sorry,
I wish I could start again.
I'm sorry, I'm sorry,
I wish I could start again.

Let's cross our hands on our chest.
I wonder if there's anything we've done this week
that we wish we hadn't done.

With hands crossed on chest, singing . . .
With my hands on my chest,
I remember the things I've done today,
I remember the things I wish I'd done a different way.

Repeat 'I'm Sorry' and 'New Start' signs as above.
I'm sorry, I'm sorry,
I wish I could start again.
I'm sorry, I'm sorry,
I wish I could start again.

Continue with a Saying Sorry Action or move straight to God Gives Us a New Start below.

Option 2

→ Song: 'We need a new start'. Words © Sharon Moughtin-Mumby
→ Tune: Molly Malone (traditional). For the music see p. 259, or for a taster see the Diddy Disciples website. For tips on teaching songs for the first time, see p. 215. For a description of the 'I'm Sorry' and 'New Start' signs, see p. 225 or the website.

> ### Tip
>
> This song can be sung using 'we're sorry' as indicated, or as 'I'm sorry', adapting the material accordingly.

Let's put our hands on our head.
I wonder if there's anything we've thought this week
that we wish we hadn't thought?

Lead the children in placing your hands on head, singing.
For the things we have thou-ght
that we wish we'd not thou-ght,
we're sor-ry, we're sor-ry, *Diddy Disciples 'I'm Sorry' sign twice (see p. 225).*
we need a new start. *Diddy Disciples 'New Start' sign (see p. 225).*

Let's put our hands by our mouths.
I wonder if there's anything we've said this week
that we wish we hadn't said?

With hands by mouth, singing . . .
For the things we have sa-id
that we wish we'd not sa-id,
we're sor-ry, we're sor-ry, *'I'm Sorry' sign twice.*
we need a new start. *'New Start' sign.*

Let's cross our hands on our chest.
I wonder if there's anything we've done this week
that we wish we hadn't done.

With hands crossed on chest, singing . . .
For the things we have do-ne
that we wish we'd not do-ne,
we're sor-ry, we're sor-ry, *'I'm Sorry' sign twice.*
we need a new start. *'New Start' sign.*

Continue with a Saying Sorry Action or move straight to God Gives Us a New Start below.

Saying Sorry Action

→ **Guide: p. 225**

For alternative actions that can be used during any unit at any time of year, see Saying Sorry Actions: options 2, 3, and 4 on pp. 40–43.

Saying Sorry Action: Option 1

→ **Action: placing a battery tealight or paper star on a piece of dark fabric**

> *If you're using battery tealights:*
> *Show the children one or more baskets/trays containing lit battery tealights.*
>
> Let's turn the lights off
> for a moment and look at these candles.
>
> *Ask an adult or child to turn off the lights.*

When we do things that make God or other people feel sad
everything can feel dark and lonely.
The Good News is that Jesus is the Light of the World.
Jesus can shine in any dark place.

In a moment, *Name* and *Name* are going to bring around these candles/stars.
If you like, you could take one
and hold it gently in your hands like this.

Model to the children holding their tealight/star.

Imagine Jesus' love shining on you.

> *If you've turned the lights off:*
> We're going to sing as we wait
> [*if lights are off:* in the dark] for Jesus,
> Light of the World, to come to us.

While all the children and adults who wish to take a candle/star do so, lead the group in either:

> *Option 1: singing the 'I'm sorry' refrain, or*
> *Option 2: humming the first two lines of the 'We need a new start' song followed by singing the refrain 'We're sorry, we're sorry, we need a new start'*

God gives us a new start!
Let's hold our candle/star high! *Joyfully, hold candle/star high*
But there are other people
feeling like they're in a dark place.
Let's ask God to help us give other people a new start, too.

Lay a dark piece of fabric in the centre of the circle.

If you like, you can put your candle/star in the centre of the circle
and promise to give other people a new start this week, too,
especially when they've made us feel cross or sad.

Lead the group in singing again as the candles/stars are placed. When all the children and adults who wish to place their tealight/star have done so:

After three, let's say 'God gives us a new start!'
1, 2, 3 . . . God gives us a new start!
Let's use our new start to share God's love this week!

Saying Sorry Action: Option 2

→ **Action: scribbling on a whiteboard/chalkboard then wiping it out**

Place a single collective whiteboard/chalkboard in the centre of the circle, or ask one or more children to distribute individual smaller whiteboards/blackboards. Ask two more children to take around chalk/pens and a piece of kitchen roll to give to each child as you sing.

We all make bad choices sometimes.
When we make bad choices,
it can feel like we've made a big mess.
Let's scribble on our board
to show the mess we can make of things.

While the children and adults scribble, lead the group in either:

> *Option 1: singing the 'I'm sorry' refrain, or*
> *Option 2: humming the first two lines of the 'We need a new start' song followed by singing the refrain 'We're sorry, we're sorry, we need a new start'*

Once all the children and adults have had the chance to scribble:

Look at that mess!
Bad choices can make everything feel messy
and all tangled up.
They can make us feel not ready for Baby Jesus!
The Good News is:
God always wants to give us a new start!
Let's be God, and wipe our scribble away!

Lead the children in wiping away their scribble. If you're using a collective board, invite one or more children to wipe out the scribble on behalf of the group; then invite another child to draw a smile.

Now let's draw a big smile . . .
and after three say 'God gives me/us a new start!'
1, 2, 3 . . . God gives me/us a new start!

Let's use our new start to share God's love this week!

Saying Sorry Action: Option 3
→ **Action: sprinkling water or tracing a smile/cross with water**

> ### Tip
>
> This option is particularly appropriate for churches that use the sprinkling of water (asperges) in Advent. When inviting children to lead by taking the water around, you may find it helps to make it clear to them that they can keep both hands on the bowl while the other children dip their finger in. Standing with the children, with your hands placed over theirs on the bowl, as they offer the water to the first participant may help very young children understand the pattern.

When we make bad choices,
it can feel like we've made a big mess of things.
The Good News is:
God always wants to give us a new start!
Sometimes we use water to show
that God's making us clean again:
not just on the OUTside, *Rub arms*
but on the INside too. *Trace a circle on your heart*

> *Either:*
> In a moment, I'm going to sprinkle us with water.
> When the water splashes us
> let's remember God is making us clean inside and out.
>
> *Or: invite two children to take round bowls of water, going opposite ways around the circle.*
> *Name* and *Name* are going to bring round some water.
> If you like, you can dip your finger in the water
> and draw a smile/cross on your forehead
> to show that God gives you a new start!
> *Model to the children drawing a smile/cross on your own forehead. While the water is taken around, lead the group in either:*
> *Option 1: singing the 'I'm sorry' refrain, or*
> *Option 2: humming the first two lines of the 'We need a new start' song followed by singing the refrain 'We're sorry . . .'.*

Once all the children and adults who wish to have taken some water, or everyone who wishes to has been sprinkled with water:

That's better! Our hearts are lovely and clean again!
After three, let's jump up and say 'God gives me a new start!'
1, 2, 3 . . . God gives me a new start!
Let's use our new start to share God's love this week!

God Gives Us a New Start

→ **Guide: p. 225**

Tip

Every time of Saying Sorry should end by assuring the children that God gives them a new start. Most Diddy Disciples Saying Sorry Actions already include this promise of a new start. If they don't – or if you've created your own Saying Sorry Action – you should choose one from the following New Start options, or create your own assurance of forgiveness. You could also choose to move straight from the Sorry Song to God's promise of a new start, without any Saying Sorry Action.

New Start Action: Option 1

→ **Action: tracing a cross or smile on each other's forehead**

The Good News is:
God always wants to give us a new start!
Let's turn to the person next to us
and show that God gives them a new start.
Let's take our thumb/finger *Show thumb/finger*
and draw a cross/smile on their forehead *Draw a cross/smile in the air*

> *If your group is drawing a smile, add:*
> to show that God is very happy with them!

Let's say 'God gives you a new start!'
Then let them give you a new start, too!

When the group has finished drawing a cross/smile to show each other God's new starts:

Let's use our new start to share God's love this week!

New Start Action: Option 2

→ **Action: standing up and hugging each other**

The Good News is:
God always wants to give us a new start!
Let's help someone next to us stand up from the floor.
Then let them help you stand up too!
Lead the children in helping each other stand up.

Then let's give each other a hug and say:
'God gives you a new start!'

When the group has finished helping each other up to show each other God's new starts:

Let's use our new start to share God's love this week!

New Start Action: Option 3

→ **Song: 'God loves to give me a new start!' Words © Sharon Moughtin-Mumby**
→ **Tune: 'Give me oil in my lamp' (traditional). For the music see p. 260, or for a taster see the Diddy Disciples website. For tips on teaching songs for the first time, see p. 215.**

The Good News is:
God always wants to give us a new start!
Let's sing our New Start song together.

[Yes, my] God loves to give me a new start! *Trace a smile/cross on your own forehead*
How amazing God's love for me! *Cross hands on your chest*

180

[Yes, my] God loves to give me a new start! *Trace a smile/cross on your own forehead*
How amazing is God's love for me!

Sing hosanna! Sing hosanna! *Wave hands in the air*
Sing hosanna to the King of kings!
Wave hands in the air followed by placing crown on head.
Sing hosanna! Sing hosanna! *Wave hands in the air*
Sing hosanna to the King!
Wave hands in the air followed by placing crown on head.

Introduction to Prayers

Before Christmas:
It's time to bring our prayers to Jesus, Light of the World.
Christmas Day and Christmas 1:
It's Christmas! All our waiting is over.
It's time to bring our prayers to the tiny Baby Jesus.

Prayers for Other People

→ **Guide: pp. 223, 225**

Invite the children to sit in a circle for a moment of quiet.

Let's imagine holding our prayer gently,
hands together gently in traditional prayer gesture, but cupped so you can imagine a prayer inside
and then let it go up in prayer to God,
hands opened upwards to God

> *If you're using Option 1 below:*
>
> Jesus *Hands together, cupped*
> hear our prayer *Hands opened upwards to God*
> Let's pray . . .

Prayers for Other People: Option 1

→ Song: 'Jesus, hear our prayer!' Words © Sharon Moughtin-Mumby
→ Tune: 'Brown girl in the ring' (traditional). For the music see p. 260, or for a taster see the Diddy Disciples website. For tips on teaching songs for the first time, see p. 215. For similar words designed to fit with the alternative tune 'He's got the whole world in his hands', see p. 260.

For the world: **Jesus, hear our prayer!**
Make a circle shape   *Open hands upwards to God*
For the Church: **Jesus, hear our prayer!**
Praying hands   *Open hands upwards to God*
For our place, *Walworth**:   **Jesus, hear our prayer!**
Hands down, moving out in   *Open hands upwards to God*
a semi-circle to show the area
around us
Lord Jesus, hear our prayer. Amen.
Open hands upwards to God

* *Insert local area/school/church/community/parish.*

For the sick and lonely: **Jesus, hear our prayer!**
Fingers showing tears falling   *Open hands upwards to God*
down cheeks
For our friends and family: **Jesus, hear our prayer!**
Arms around yourself   *Open hands upwards to God*

For ourselves:	Jesus, hear our prayer!
Both hands on heart	*Open hands upwards to God*

Lord Jesus, hear our prayer. Amen.
Open hands upwards to God

Let's close our eyes for a moment.
I wonder if there's someone special
you'd like to pray for?
Let's imagine them now.

Now, let's imagine Jesus coming to them.
Does Jesus say anything?
Does Jesus do anything?

Let's open our eyes.

Continue with one of the Prayer Action options outlined below. Once the Prayer Action has been completed, you may like to use the following verse to close this time of prayer.

Take our prayers:	Jesus, hear our prayer!
Hands together gently	*Open hands upwards to God*
Make them holy:	Jesus, hear our prayer!
Hands together gently	*Open hands upwards to God*
Make them beautiful:	Jesus, hear our prayer!
Hands together gently	*Open hands upwards to God*

Lord Jesus, hear our prayer! Amen.
Hands together gently, then open hands upwards to God

Prayers for Other People: Option 2

→ **Song: 'The Diddy Disciples little prayers song'. Words © Sharon Moughtin-Mumby**
→ **Tune: 'Frère Jacques' (traditional). For the music see p. 258, or for a taster see the Diddy Disciples website. For tips on teaching songs for the first time, see p. 215.**

These prayers are especially suited to churches that prefer less traditional prayer forms.

> *Either: choose what you'd like the group to pray for before the session.*
> *Or: ask the children at this point if there is anything or anyone that they'd like to pray for. Ask them or others to suggest actions for the prayers.*

You will need two different 'thank you' suggestions and two different 'hear our prayer' suggestions. Try to encourage the offering of at least one prayer for people outside the group.

Invite the children to sing after you, repeating your words and their actions. Sometimes it might be almost impossible to fit the child's own words in! But it's really valuable to do so where possible, resisting the urge to try and 'tidy up' their suggestions. For examples, see Unit 1, 'Jesus' wonderful love', p. 47:

At this point, you could insert a Prayer Action, repeat the process, or move straight on to close with the following (or other words that remain the same each week).

For today,	*Point hands down for 'now'*
For today,	*Point hands down for 'now'*
Thank you, God!	*Open hands upwards to God or hands together in prayer*
Thank you, God!	*Open hands upwards to God or hands together in prayer*
Fo-r your love,	*Cross hands on chest*
Fo-r your love,	*Cross hands on chest*
Thank you, God!	*Open hands upwards to God or hands together in prayer*
Thank you, God!	*Open hands upwards to God or hands together in prayer*

Prayer Actions

→ **Guide: p. 225**

Continue with one of the Prayer Action options outlined below, or you can use the Prayer Action options 3 and 4 on p. 48 at any time of year.

Prayer Action: Option 1

→ **Action: placing candles (battery tealights) on a dark piece of fabric**

We ask an adult to light the battery tealights in advance as we've found younger children can be distracted by attempts to light the tealights themselves.

Show the children one or more baskets/trays containing lit battery tealights.
Now as we pray, we're going to turn the lights off
for a moment and look at these candles.
Ask an adult or child to turn off the lights.

Jesus is the Light of the World!
In a moment, *Name* and *Name* are going to bring around these candles.
If you like, you could take one
and hold it gently in your hands like this.

Model to the children holding their tealight.

Imagine Jesus' love shining on you
and on the special person you're praying for.

We're going to sing
as we wait in the dark for Jesus,
Light of the World, to come to us.

Hum the tune together, with the words 'Jesus, hear our prayer!' as a refrain, until all the children and adults who wish to take tealights have done so.

Lay a dark piece of fabric in the centre of the circle.

Let's give our light prayers to God as we sing.
Let's pray that God's light will shine in every dark place.

Hum the tune together, with the words 'Jesus, hear our prayer!' as a refrain, as you lead the children in placing the candles in the centre of the circle on the dark piece of fabric. Some groups may like to invite two children to go around the circle in opposite directions with trays to collect the candles. The trays can then be placed in the centre. End this time of prayer with the final verse of the Prayer Song you've chosen.

Prayer Action: Option 2

→ **Action: placing paper/material/wooden stars on a dark piece of fabric**

Lay a dark piece of fabric in the centre of the circle.
Show the children one or more baskets/trays filled with stars.

Jesus is the Light of the World!
In a moment, *Name* and *Name*
are going to bring around these stars.
If you like, you could take a star
and hold it up high like this.
Model to the children holding their star up.

You can imagine Jesus' love shining on you
And on the special person you're praying for,
like a star shines in the night sky.

We're going to sing
as we wait in the dark for Jesus,
the Light of the World, to come to us.

Hum the tune together, with the words 'Jesus, hear our prayer!' as a refrain, until all the children and adults who wish to take stars have done so.

Let's give our star prayers to God as we sing.
Let's pray that God's light will shine in every dark place.

Hum the tune together, with the words 'Jesus, hear our prayer!' as a refrain, as you lead the children in placing the stars in the centre of the circle on the dark piece of fabric. Some groups may like to invite two children to go around the circle in opposite directions with trays to collect the responses. The stars can then be placed in the centre. End this time of prayer with the final verse of the Prayer Song you've chosen.

Prayer Action: Option 3

→ **Action: placing paper stars, sun shapes or lit candles (battery tealights) on a world map**

> ## Tip
>
> At St Peter's, Walworth, we've used a map jigsaw (the children can also explore it afterwards). At other times, we've used a laminated Peters World Map that shows the world in its proper proportions.
>
> If you're using battery tealights, we ask an adult to light the battery tealights in advance as we've found younger children can be distracted by attempts to light the tealights themselves.

Place your world map in the centre of the circle.

This is a map of the world.
Jesus is the Light of the World!

Show the children one or more baskets/trays with lit battery tealights, stars, or sun shapes.

> *If you're using battery tealights:*
> Now as we pray, we're going to turn the lights off
> for a moment and look at these candles here.

In a moment, *Name* and *Name*
are going to bring round these candles/stars/sun shapes.
If you like, you could take one.
Let's sing as we wait [*if lights are off:* in the dark].
Let's hold our hands out gently like this
Model cupped hands
as we wait for Jesus to shine in our world.

Hum the tune together, with the words 'Jesus, hear our prayer!' as a refrain, until all the children and adults who wish to take candles/stars/suns have done so.

> *If appropriate, as leader, you could mention specific places for prayer. You could take these from your church's intercessions or other times of prayer:*
>
> At the moment, there's fighting in the world
> here and here. *As leader, place a candle/star/sun on these places on the map.*
> *Name the countries or areas if appropriate.*
> There's been *an earthquake [or other disaster]*
> here. *As leader, place a candle/star/sun on the map*
> There are people who *have no homes* here. *As leader, place a candle/star/sun on the map*
> There are people who need our prayers all over the world.

As we sing again, let's put our lights on the world.
You can put your little light anywhere you like.
Let's ask God to see our lights as prayers for the world.

Hum the tune together, with the words 'Jesus, hear our prayer!' as a refrain, as you lead the children in placing the candles/stars/ suns on the map. We've found that asking the children to do this in age groups helps, as the older children tend to be more intent on finding a location than the others. We invite babies first, then nursery and reception children, then Year 1 and upwards (including the adults). Some groups may like to invite two children to go around the circle in opposite directions with trays to collect the candles/stars/suns. The trays can then be placed in the centre of the map. End this time of prayer with the final verse of the Prayer Song you've chosen.

Prayer Action: Option 4

→ **Action: placing paper stars or shiny (safe) Christmas decorations on a small Christmas tree or a picture of a Christmas tree**

With young children, it's best to have stars/decorations that can simply be balanced on the branches of the tree rather than decorations that need hanging, unless you have a very small group in which each young child can be helped.

Place your Christmas tree in the centre of the circle.
Show the children a basket of stars or Christmas decorations.

Jesus is the Light of the World!
At Christmas, whenever we see stars/shiny decorations,
we remember Jesus the Light of the World.

In a moment, *Name* and *Name*
are going to bring round these stars/decorations.
If you like, you could take one
and hold it up high like this.
Model to the children holding their star/decoration up.

You can imagine Jesus' love shining on you
and on the special person you're praying for

> *If using stars:*
> like a star shines in the night sky.

Let's sing as we wait for Jesus,
the Light of the World, to come to us.

Hum the tune together, with the words 'Jesus, hear our prayer!' as a refrain, until all the children and adults who wish to take stars or decorations have done so.

Let's decorate our Christmas tree
with our prayers as we sing.
Let's pray that God's light will shine in every dark place.

Hum the tune together, with the words 'Jesus, hear our prayer!' as a refrain, as you lead the children in placing the stars/decorations on the Christmas tree. End this time of prayer with the final verse of the Prayer Song you've chosen.

Prayer Action: Option for Christmas Day or the week after Christmas

→ **Action: placing paper hearts, stars, or candles (battery tealights) on a world map**

Tip

If you've been using a map for your Prayer Action during Advent, you could use it again today and place Baby Jesus in his manger at the head of the map. If you're using battery tealights, we ask an adult to light the battery tealights in advance as we've found younger children can be distracted by attempts to light the tealights themselves. We tend to place 3–4 lit tealights on Jesus's manger in advance to show that he is the Light of the World.

Show the children one or more baskets/trays filled with paper hearts/stars/candles.

> *If you're using battery tealights:*
> Now as we pray, we're going to turn the lights off
> for a moment.

> *Ask an adult or child to turn off the lights.*

Jesus, the Light of the World, is here!
In a moment, *Name* and *Name*
are going to bring round these candles/stars/hearts.
If you like, you could take a candle/star/heart
and place it gently on Baby Jesus' manger

> *If appropriate:*
> or on our map
> anywhere you like.

Let's give our prayers to the tiny Baby Jesus as we sing.

Hum the tune together, with the words 'Jesus, hear our prayer!' as a refrain, until all the children and adults who wish to have taken a light and placed it. End this time of prayer with the final verse of the Prayer Song you've chosen.

Thank You, God

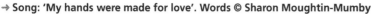

→ **Guide: p. 227**

Thank You, God: Option 1

→ **Song: 'My hands were made for love'. Words © Sharon Moughtin-Mumby**
→ **Tune: 'Hickory, dickory, dock' (traditional). For the music, see p. 262, or for a taster see the Diddy Disciples website. For tips on teaching songs for the first time, see p. 215.**

Invite the children to sit in a circle for a moment of quiet.

It's time to remember all the things we've done this week.
It's time to say 'thank you' to God
for when we've been part of showing God's love.

Let's wiggle our fingers!
I wonder when you've shown love
with your hands this week?

Wiggle fingers as you sing.
My hands were made for love!
My hands were made for love!
Thank you for the love they've shown.
My hands were made for love!

Let's wiggle our feet!
I wonder when you've shown love
with your feet this week?

Wiggle feet as you sing.
My feet were made for love!
My feet were made for love!
Thank you for the love they've shown.
My feet were made for love!

Let's put our hands gently on our neck.
Let's sing 'Ahhh!'
Ahhhhh!
Can you feel your throat vibrating and dancing?

I wonder when you've shown love
with your voice this week?

Hold neck and feel your voice 'dancing' as you sing.
My voice was made for love!
My voice was made for love!
Thank you for the love it's shown.
My voice was made for love!

Thank You, God: Option 2

→ **Song: 'For the love we've shown'. Words © Sharon Moughtin-Mumby**
→ **Tune: 'All through the night' (traditional). For the music see p. 259, or for a taster see the Diddy Disciples website.**

Most suitable for use with children over the age of four.

Invite the children to sit in a circle for a moment of quiet.

It's time to remember all the things we've done this week.
It's time to say 'thank you' to God
for when we've been part of showing God's love.

> *Either:* Let's wiggle our fingers.
> *Or:* Let's hold up our hands.

I wonder when you've shown love
with your hands this week?

> *Either:* Let's wiggle our feet.
> *Or:* Let's show our feet.

I wonder when you've shown love
with your feet this week?

Let's put our hands gently on our neck.
Let's sing 'Ahhh!'

Ahhhhh!
Can you feel your neck vibrating and dancing with your voice?
I wonder when you've shown love
with your voice this week?

Let's sing our 'thank you' song to God
For the times we've been part of sharing God's love.

For the love we've shown with our hands, *Hold hands up or wiggle fingers*
thank you, God!
For the love we've shown with our feet, *Point to feet or wiggle feet*
thank you, God!
When we love all those around us, *Cross hands on chest*
it's the same as loving Jesus!
For the love we've shown with our voice, *Hands on neck or point to singing mouth*
thank you, God!

Creative Response

→ **Guide: p. 228**

See the Creative Responses in Section 3 of this chapter.

Sharing God's Peace

→ **Guide: p. 231**

This Building Block is particularly designed for children's groups that join the adult congregation to share communion, but it can also be used to end any session or Service of the Word. During Advent and Christmas, you might like to keep to your normal option for Sharing God's Peace. Alternatively, if you have a peace cloth of blue sparkly fabric, you could use the special Peace for Advent and Christmas that uses the carol 'Silent night' (Option 4).

Introduction to the Peace in Advent

We're getting ready for Baby Jesus,
the Prince of Peace, to be born.
Let's sing our Peace Song and imagine
Baby Jesus' peace spreading through the whole world.

Introduction to the Peace on Christmas Day or the week after Christmas

Baby Jesus, the Prince of Peace, is here!
Let's sing our Peace Song and imagine
Baby Jesus' peace spreading through the whole world.

For a special Advent and Christmas option for the Peace, see Option 4 below.

Sharing God's Peace: Option 1

→ **Song: 'I've got peace like a river' (traditional). Isaiah 66.12,** NIV
→ **Tune: Traditional. For a taster, see the Diddy Disciples website. For tips on teaching songs for the first time, see p. 215.**

> *Either: Hold one end of the peace cloth (see Guide, p. 231) and ask one of the older children or an adult to hold the other end. Start singing the Peace Song. As the children begin to gather, invite them to join in holding a small section of the cloth, raising and lowering it so it 'flows' like a river as you sing together.*

> *Or: Invite the children to sit in a circle in the worship space. Start singing the Peace Song. As the children begin to gather, invite them to join in raising and lowering their hands like the waters of a flowing river.*

I've got peace like a river,
I've got peace like a river,
I've got peace like a river in my soul.
I've got peace like a river,
I've got peace like a river,
I've got peace like a river in my soul.

If your group is about to rejoin the adults for communion, when all the children are gathered, continue with the words of the Peace following Option 4 below.

Sharing God's Peace: Option 2

→ **Song: 'Peace is flowing like a river' (traditional). Isaiah 66.12,** NIV
→ **Tune: Traditional. For a taster, see the Diddy Disciples website. For tips on teaching songs for the first time, see p. 215.**

> *Either: Hold one end of the peace cloth (see Guide, p. 231) and ask one of the older children or an adult to hold the other end. Start singing the Peace Song. As the children begin to gather, invite them to join in holding a small section of the cloth, raising and lowering it so it 'flows' like a river as you sing together.*

> *Or: Invite the children to sit in a circle in the worship space. Start singing the Peace Song. As the children begin to gather, invite them to join in raising and lowering their hands like the waters of a flowing river.*

Peace is flowing like a river,
flowing out through you and me.

Spreading out into the desert,
setting all the captives free.

If your group is about to rejoin the adults for communion, when all the children are gathered, continue with the words of the Peace following Option 4 below.

Sharing God's Peace: Option 3

→ **Song: 'I've got peace in my fingers' © 1995 Susan Salidor ASCAP**
→ **Tune: © 1995 Susan Salidor ASCAP**
→ **The words and music can be found on the album *Little Voices in My Head* by Susan Salidor © 2003 Peach Head. They can also be found on iTunes, YouTube, or at www.susansalidor.com**

Invite the children to sit in a circle in the worship space. Start singing the Peace Song. As the children begin to gather, invite them to join in with the song and actions. If your group is about to rejoin the adults for communion, when all the children are gathered, continue with the words of the Peace below (following Option 4).

Peace Song: Option 4

Either: lay the peace cloth (see p. 231) on the floor and invite the children to come and sit around it, and find a sparkle and look at it.

Or: invite the children to lie on the floor and ask two adults to hold either end of the peace cloth at waist height over the children.

Invite the children to imagine the peacefulness of the night sky on the night that Jesus was born. I wonder what it was like to be there? Sing or play a CD of 'Silent Night' (by Joseph Mohr, translated by John Freeman Young) as the children look at their star.

Silent night, holy night,
all is calm, all is bright
round yon virgin mother and child.
Holy infant, so tender and mild,
sleep in heavenly peace,
sleep in heavenly peace.

If your group is about to rejoin the adults for communion, when all the children are gathered, continue with the words of the Peace below.

The Peace

→ **2 Thessalonians 3.16; 1 Peter 5.14**

Once you've finished singing . . .

The peace of the Lord be always with you.
Hold hands open to the children.

And also with you.
Invite the children to open their hands towards you.

Let's shake hands or hug each other
and say 'Peace be with you' as a sign of God's peace.
or whatever is said on sharing the Peace in your church.

Lead the children in giving and receiving the Peace. Immediately following this, at St Peter's, Walworth, we lead the children back to join the rest of the congregation to continue our worship with the Eucharistic Prayer.

Taking God's Love into the World

→ **Song: 'This little light of mine' (traditional)**
→ **Tune: Traditional. For a taster, see the Diddy Disciples website. For tips on teaching songs for the first time, see p. 215.**
→ **Guide: p. 232**

This Building Block is particularly designed for standalone groups or groups that are held during a Service of the Word. Alternatively, you could use one of the Peace Songs above to end your worship.

Our time together is coming to an end.
God has lit a little light of love inside all of us.
Trace a circle on your heart.

Let's make our finger into a candle.
Bring your finger from your heart and hold it out.

Let's be God and light our little light of love together, after three.
Lead the children in lighting their finger candle by striking an imaginary match in the air on a count of three and pretending to light your finger.
1, 2, 3 . . . Tssss!

Let's imagine God's love shining and dancing like light in us.

Wave your finger in front of you as you sing.
This little light of mine, I'm gonna let it shine!
This little light of mine, I'm gonna let it shine!
This little light of mine, I'm gonna let it shine!
Let it shine, let it shine, let it shine!

Blow on your finger as if blowing out a candle on 'puff'. Then hold it up high.
Won't let no one *puff* it out! I'm gonna let it shine!
Won't let no one *puff* it out! I'm gonna let it shine!
Won't let no one *puff* it out! I'm gonna let it shine!
Let it shine, let it shine, let it shine!

Hold your finger behind a cupped hand, then take your cupped hand away to reveal the 'candle' and hold it high!
Hide it under a bushel? No! I'm gonna let it shine!
Hide it under a bushel? No! I'm gonna let it shine!
Hide it under a bushel? No! I'm gonna let it shine!
Let it shine, let it shine, let it shine!

Lead the children in placing your finger back on your heart.

Now let's put our little light of love
back in our hearts, where it belongs.
Let's remember to let our little light shine
in all our playing and working today . . .

If you're building a Service of the Word and this is your final Building Block, you may like to close with a familiar blessing, the Peace, and/or one of the following. If you're introducing one of these call-and-responses to your group for the first time, see p. 53 for an introduction.

Either:	Praise the Lord!	Both hands to self
	Alleluia!	Both arms upwards in 'V' shape
Or:	Let us bless the Lord.	Both hands to self
	Thanks be to God.	Both arms upwards in 'V' shape
Or:	And all the people said . . .	Both hands to self
	Amen!	Both arms upwards in 'V' shape

Section 2

The Bible Storytelling material, Getting Ready for Baby Jesus unit

Week 1: Get Ready! (Baby John's story)

→ Luke 1.5–25, 57–79
→ Song: 'Jesus, Light of the World'. Words © Sharon Moughtin-Mumby
→ Tune: 'What shall we do with the drunken sailor?' (traditional). For a taster, see the Diddy Disciples website.

This week's storytelling involves learning the song that will become the basis of the Gathering Song in the weeks to come. There is therefore no Gathering Song this week and the storytelling is a little longer than usual.

Ask the children to sit for a moment of quiet.

To tell our story today, first we need to learn a song.
It's called 'Jesus, Light of the World!'
Let's close our eyes and feel the dark . . .
Now let's imagine a bright light shining in the darkness!
Wow!
Let's open our eyes again.

In our story, Zechariah sings that Baby Jesus
is like a bright light in the dark,
like the sun rising in the morning.
You might like to show the children a picture of the sun rising at this point.

Let's show the sun 'dawning' with our bodies.
Let's crouch down low . . .
Let's close our eyes . . . it's dark!
Let's show the sun coming up and up and up and out . . .
The sun is 'dawning' in the morning.
Lead the children in showing the sun rising with your hands as you stand up.

Now let's do that as we sing our song,
'Jesus, Light of the World'.

Lead the children in singing quietly.
Je-sus, Light of the World, *Sun dawning action*
Je-sus, Light of the World, *Sun dawning action*
Je-sus, Light of the World, is *Sun dawning action*
dawning in the darkness! *Sun dawning action*

We're ready!

> *If you're using the What's in the Box? option (p. 221), invite one of the children to open the box. Inside will be an angel or a picture of an angel. You might even like to show your group a photograph of an angel depicted somewhere in your church building.*

> What's in the box? *Ask the child to respond.*

> This is the angel Gabriel.
> He's a very special angel.
> Gabriel takes messages from God to people:
> he's like a post-angel.
> Today Gabriel's going to take his first message
> to a man called Zechariah!

Let's tell Zechariah's story together.
Zechariah was a very good man!
Let's be Zechariah. Let's sit up straight!
Show me how you look when you're being good.
Zechariah really, really wanted something.
Can you show me how you feel when you really want something?
Zechariah really, really wanted a baby!
Invite the children to rock their arms like rocking a baby.

But everyone said he was too old.
Can you show me how you feel
when you don't get something
you really, really want?
Lead the children in looking sad, cross, fed up.

Let's sing together in a very quiet, sad voice.
Zechariah wants a baby. *Rock arms looking sad, fed up*
Zechariah wants a baby.
Zechariah wants a baby.
[The] Light of the World is dawning!
Hands up and stretching outwards like the rising sun.

Lead the children in singing a little more excitedly but still quietly.
Je-sus, Light of the World, *Sun dawning action*
Je-sus, Light of the World, *Sun dawning action*
Je-sus, Light of the World, is *Sun dawning action*
dawning in the darkness! *Sun dawning action*

Now Zechariah had a very special job.
He led the prayers at the 'Temple'.

The Temple was God's house, where people went to pray,
a bit like our church.
Zechariah lit some special candles.
The smoke went up to God.
Let's sway our bodies like smoke going up, up, up!
Crouch down low, then reach up tall as you sway.

The prayers went up with the smoke!
Zechariah didn't say anything
but his secret prayer for a baby went up to God, too.
Let's sing quietly again . . .

The prayers are going up to God.
The prayers are going up to God.
The prayers are going up to God.
[The] Light of the World is dawning!
Hands up and stretching outwards like the rising sun.

Lead the children in singing even more excitedly and a little louder:
Je-sus, Light of the World, *Sun dawning action*
Je-sus, Light of the World, *Sun dawning action*
Je-sus, Light of the World, is *Sun dawning action*
dawning in the darkness! *Sun dawning action*

Suddenly, the Holy Place was filled with light!
Shield eyes with your hand.

The brightest light Zechariah had ever seen!
Zechariah saw an angel standing there!
He fell to the floor!
Invite the children to fall to the floor.

We're going to be the angel Gabriel together.
Let's stand up tall and strong and sing nice and loud . . .
'Zechariah! *Point strongly* You will have a baby!'

Lead the children in pointing strongly at someone else each time as you sing:
Zechariah, *point* **you will have a baby!** *Rock arms*
Zechariah, *point* **you will have a baby!** *Rock arms*
Zechariah, *point* **you will have a baby!** *Rock arms*
[The] Light of the World is dawning!
Hands up and stretching outwards like the rising sun.

Go straight into the following without the refrain.
This baby isn't Jesus. *Shake head*
We're not ready for Baby Jesus yet!
This baby will help us get ready for Jesus.
This is Baby John!
The angel says to Zechariah,
'Baby John will get the world ready!'
Diddy Disciples 'New Start' sign (see p. 225) for 'getting ready'.

Let's sing together!

Baby John will get the world ready. *'New Start' sign*
Baby John will get the world ready. *'New Start' sign*
Baby John will get the world ready. *'New Start' sign*
[The] Light of the World is dawning!
Hands up and stretching outwards like the rising sun.

Je-sus, Light of the World, *Sun dawning action*
Je-sus, Light of the World, *Sun dawning action*
Je-sus, Light of the World, is *Sun dawning action*
dawning in the darkness! *Sun dawning action*

But Zechariah shook his head!
Let's shake our heads and look sad.
'I can't have a baby!' said Zechariah.
'I'm too old!'
Zechariah didn't believe the angel!
Look shocked.

The angel said, 'Because you didn't say yes,
you won't be able to open your mouth!'
Let's zip our mouths shut after three:
1, 2, 3 . . . Zip!
Then the angel leaves. Gone!

Zechariah tries to tell everyone about the angel,
Pretend to speak with your mouth closed,
'Mmmmmm', but he can't speak!
Let's be Zechariah trying to tell people about the angel!
Mmmmmmm! Mmmmm! *With frenetic pointing*
Then do you know what happened?
Nine months later, a baby was born!
Lead the children in holding a baby gently.

Let's be Zechariah holding our baby.
Let's sing together really happily and joyfully.

Zechariah has a baby. *Rock arms gently*
Zechariah has a baby. *Rock arms gently*
Zechariah has a baby. *Rock arms gently*
[The] Light of the World is dawning!
Hands up and stretching outwards like the rising sun.

Je-sus, Light of the World, *Sun dawning action*
Je-sus, Light of the World, *Sun dawning action*
Je-sus, Light of the World, is *Sun dawning action*
dawning in the darkness! *Sun dawning action*

Zechariah's friends ask 'What's his name?'
What do you think Zechariah says?

If appropriate, invite the children to guess.

Trick question!
Zechariah can't say anything!
He still can't open his mouth! Mmmmmm!
But his friends give him something to write on
and Zechariah writes 'John' on it!
Let's write John together . . .

Lead the children in writing letters or squiggling in the air. The children may join in with you in spelling the name out. If you know the phonic sounds, it's best to use those. You could always ask a Year 1 or Reception child to help you out.

j . . . o . . . h . . . n

That moment, Zechariah's mouth was opened up!
Let's unzip our mouth . . .
1, 2, 3, zip!

Zechariah sang a beautiful song:
the song we've been singing
about the Light of the World
getting ready to shine in the darkness.

Put your hand up if you've seen Christmas lights being put up!
At Christmas, we have Christmas lights to remind us
that Jesus is the 'Light of the World'.

When we see Christmas lights,
let's remember we're getting ready for Baby Jesus.
Let's sing Zechariah's song together,
this time as loud and joyfully as we can!

Je-sus, Light of the World, *Sun dawning action*
Je-sus, Light of the World, *Sun dawning action*
Je-sus, Light of the World, is *Sun dawning action*
dawning in the darkness! *Sun dawning action*

Je-sus, Light of the World, *Sun dawning action*
Je-sus, Light of the World, *Sun dawning action*
Je-sus, Light of the World, is *Sun dawning action*
dawning in the darkness! *Sun dawning action*

Week 2: 'Yes!' Said Mary

→ **Luke 1.26–38**
→ '"Yes!" said Mary'. Words © Sharon Moughtin-Mumby
→ Tune: '"Pop!" goes the weasel' (traditional). For a taster, see the Diddy Disciples website.

An an-gel came to Ma-ry. 'You will have a ba-by!
He will be the Son of God!' 'Yes!' said Ma-ry.

If you're using the What's in the Box? option (p. 221), invite one of the children to open the box. Inside will be an angel or a picture of an angel. Like last week, you might even like to show your group a photograph of an angel depicted somewhere in your church building.

What's in the box? *Ask the child to respond.*

This is the angel Gabriel.
He's a very special angel.
Gabriel takes messages from God to people:
he's like a post-angel.
Today Gabriel's going to take a message
to a girl called Mary.

To tell our story today, we need to learn a song.

The actions of this song are designed to mirror a jack-in-the-box, with its lid closing and the puppet bursting out at the 'pop' moment. To teach this song, sing it alone the first time, with the children copying your actions. See if they can join in on the second time around.

Start standing on tiptoes with your hands stretched high. You could make angel wings (like butterfly wings) with your hands.
An angel came to Ma-a-a-ry.
Bring hands down from on high and come down from tiptoes.

'You will have a baby!
Rock baby, standing at normal height.
He will be the Son of God!'
Crouch down on the ground like tiny child.
'Yes!' sa-id Mary.
Jump up and shout 'Yes!'
Repeat.

We're going to tell the story of our song together now.
First we need to practise showing
how we feel with just our faces.
Not opening our mouths at all.
Who can show me . . .
As you list the following emotions one by one, give the children time to show each emotion with their face. You might like to point out some good examples given by the children:
sad . . .
happy . . .
confused (when you don't understand) . . .
amazed! . . .
scared.

We're ready to tell our story.

Mary was at home, sweeping the house.
Let's be Mary and sweep together.

Hum the tune of 'Pop goes the weasel' quietly as you sweep.

Suddenly, the room was filled with light!
Shield eyes with hand.

The brightest light Mary had ever seen!
Mary saw an angel standing there!
She fell to the floor!

Lead the children in kneeling.

We're going to be the angel Gabriel together.
These words are very important.
Let's kneel up high on our knees for a moment
to say the angel's words together.
It's 'my turn *point to self* your turn' *leader's hands out to group*

Lead the children in saying the following words.
Hello Mary. *Wave*
Hello Mary. *Wave*
Don't be frightened. *Hands out*
Don't be frightened. *Hands out*
God is very happy with you! *Draw smile on face*
God is very happy with you! *Draw smile on face*
You're going to have a baby: *Rock arms*
You're going to have a baby: *Rock arms*
a little boy called Jesus. *Rock arms*
a little boy called Jesus. *Rock arms*
He's going to be King! *Place imaginary crown on head*
He's going to be King! *Place imaginary crown on head*

Wow!
These words are very special words.
Shall we say them again together?

Hello Mary. *Wave*

Hello Mary. *Wave*

Don't be frightened. *Hands out*

Don't be frightened. *Hands out*

God is very happy with you! *Draw smile on face*

God is very happy with you! *Draw smile on face*

You're going to have a baby: *Rock arms*

You're going to have a baby: *Rock arms*

a little boy called Jesus. *Rock arms*

a little boy called Jesus. *Rock arms*

He's going to be King! *Place crown on head*

He's going to be King! *Place crown on head*

I wonder how Mary's feeling now?

> *Invite the children to explore their feelings or use the following. As you list these emotions one by one, give the children time to show each emotion with their face. You might like to pick out some examples given by the children.*

> Can you show me amazed?
> Show me scared!
> Show me happy!
> Show me excited!

Mary is feeling lots of things!
Mary's also feeling confused.
Show me confused! Mary doesn't understand.
Can you show me how you look
when you don't understand – when you're confused?
Lead the children in looking confused.

Mary says, 'How? I'm not meant to have a baby yet!
I'm just a girl.'
Let's put our hands out like a question and say 'How?'

The angel says, 'The Holy Spirit will come on you . . .'
Let's all raise our hands in the air
and bring them down in front of us
to show the Holy Spirit coming down.
The angel says,
'The Holy Spirit will come down.
Your baby will be very special,
he will be the Son of God!'
Mary's baby isn't going to just be a king,
He's going to be God!
I wonder how Mary is feeling now?
Can you show me?

One last special action! . . .
And then, do you know what Mary says?
She says, 'Yes!' Can you nod your head in a big 'Yes'?
Lead the children in nodding: **'Yes!'**

Mary says, 'I am God's servant.
YES. I will do this!'
Then the angel leaves.
I wonder how Mary is feeling now?
How would you feel,
if an angel came to your home?!
Can you show me?
Accept any responses.

Let's sing our song about Mary's story.

Start standing on tiptoes with your hands stretched high. You could make angel wings (like butterfly wings) with your hands.
An angel came to Ma-a-a-ry.
Bring hands down from on high and come down from tiptoes.
'You will have a baby!
Rock baby, standing at normal height.
He will be the Son of God!'
Crouch down on the ground like a tiny child.
'Yes!' sa-id Mary.
Jump up and shout 'Yes!'

Mary said 'yes' to God!
I wonder how easy you find it to say 'yes'?
I wonder what would have happened if Mary had said 'no!'?
Accept any responses.

Thankfully, Mary said 'yes!'
After three, let's all nod and say 'yes!' together like Mary.
1, 2, 3 . . . Yes!
Let's sing our song one last time to finish
and sing our 'yes' especially loud and clear.
Let's imagine saying 'yes' to God like Mary.

Start by standing on tiptoes with your hands stretched high.
An angel came to Ma-a-a-ry.
Bring hands down from on high and come down from tiptoes.
'You will have a baby!
Rock baby, standing at normal height.
He will be the Son of God!'
Crouch down on the ground like a tiny child.
'Yes!' sa-id Mary.
Jump up and shout 'Yes!'

Week 3: My God is a Topsy Turvy God!

→ Luke 1.39–55
→ Song: 'My God is a topsy turvy God!' Words © Sharon Moughtin-Mumby
→ Tune: 'O the grand old Duke of York' (traditional). For a taster, see the Diddy Disciples website.
→ Poem: 'What can Jesus hear?' © Sharon Moughtin-Mumby

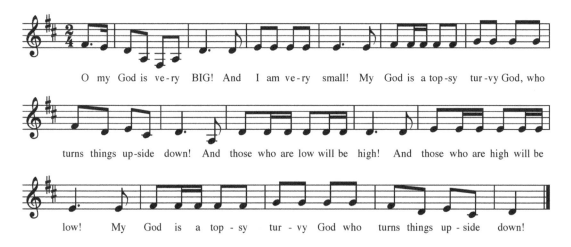

O my God is ve-ry BIG! And I am ve-ry small! My God is a top-sy tur-vy God, who turns things up-side down! And those who are low will be high! And those who are high will be low! My God is a top-sy tur-vy God who turns things up-side down!

To tell our story today,
we need to practise making shapes with our body.
Can you show me the biggest shape
you can make with your body?

Now show me the smallest, tiniest shape
you can make with your body.
Now show me the highest you can reach!
And the lowest you can be!

We need to learn a song.
This is Mary's song.

Talk the children through the song ('my turn, your turn') then add the tune.

[O] My God is very BIG!
Make the biggest shape you can with your whole body.
And I am very small!
Make the smallest shape you can.
My God is a topsy turvy God,
Diddy Disciples 'New Start' sign (see p. 225)
who turns things upside down!
And those who are low will be high!
Start low and end up high.
And those who are high will be low!
Start high and end up low.
My God is a topsy turvy God,
'New Start' sign
who turns things upside down.

We're ready to tell our story.

> *If you're using the What's in the Box? option (p. 221), invite one of the children to open the box. Inside will be two baby dolls or pictures of babies.*

> What's in the box? *Ask the child to respond.*

Our story today is about two babies.
Baby Jesus and Baby John.
But Baby Jesus and Baby John aren't born yet.
They're still inside their mummies' tummies.

> *If appropriate, if there is an expectant mum present:*
> Like *Name* has a baby inside her tummy.

Let's put our hands on our tummy.
Baby Jesus is inside Mary.
And Baby John is inside Elizabeth.

Recap the story from last week by saying these words alone. If the children join in that's great.

An angel came to Mary.
Hands high in the sky and bring them down like angel wings.
[And said,] 'You will have a baby!'
Rock arms as if holding a baby.
'He will be the Son of God!'
'Yes!' said Mary!
After three, let's all shout 'yes!' together.
1, 2, 3 . . . Yes!

Now Mary has Baby Jesus, God, growing inside her! *Hands on tummy*
Mary wants to tell someone!
Her cousin Elizabeth has a baby inside her, too.
Her baby is called Baby John.
So Mary goes on a journey to see Elizabeth.

We're going to imagine Mary's journey together now.
Someone is travelling with Mary, inside her.
Who's inside Mary? *Hands on tummy*
Baby Jesus is inside Mary!

Baby Jesus can't see anything, but he can hear. *Hands behind ears*
Let's imagine together what Baby Jesus hears
on Mary's special journey.

Let's stand up together.
Let's walk on the spot. Ssssh! Be gentle!

We're going to say this 'my turn' *point to self,* 'your turn' *leader's hands out to group.*

Start with a whisper.
We're on the way to Elizabeth's house. *Walk gently on spot*
We're on the way to Elizabeth's house. *Walk gently on spot*
What can Jesus hear? *Hands behind ears*
What can Jesus hear? *Hands behind ears*
Sssh! Sssh! Sssh! Sssh! *Finger on lips*
Sssh! Sssh! Sssh! Sssh! *Finger on lips*
What can Jesus hear? *Walk gently on spot*
What can Jesus hear? *Walk gently on spot*

Lead the children in swaying like trees.
Trees are swaying in the breeze:
Trees are swaying in the breeze:
Wishy, washy, wishy, washy . . .
Wishy, washy, wishy, washy . . .

We're on the way to Elizabeth's house. *Walk gently on spot*
We're on the way to Elizabeth's house. *Walk gently on spot*
What can Jesus hear? *Hands behind ears*
What can Jesus hear? *Hands behind ears*
Sssh! Sssh! Sssh! Sssh! *Finger on lips*
Sssh! Sssh! Sssh! Sssh! *Finger on lips*
What can Jesus hear? *Walk gently on spot*
What can Jesus hear? *Walk gently on spot*

Ask the children for a sign for sheep.

Lead the children in the sheep action.
Sheep are baaing in the fields:
Sheep are baaing in the fields:
Baa! Baa! Baa! Baa!
Baa! Baa! Baa! Baa!

Lead the children in swaying like trees.
Trees are swaying in the breeze:
Trees are swaying in the breeze:
Wishy, washy, wishy, washy.

We're on the way to Elizabeth's house. *Walk gently on spot*
We're on the way to Elizabeth's house. *Walk gently on spot*
What can Jesus hear? *Hands behind ears*
What can Jesus hear? *Hands behind ears*
Sssh! Sssh! Sssh! Sssh! *Finger on lips*
Sssh! Sssh! Sssh! Sssh! *Finger on lips*
What can Jesus hear? *Walk gently on spot*
What can Jesus hear? *Walk gently on spot*

Lead the children in showing birds tweeting with their hands.
Birds are singing in the trees:
Birds are singing in the trees:
Twitter, tweet, twitter, tweet.
Twitter, tweet, twitter, tweet.

Lead the children in the sheep action.
Sheep are baaing in the fields:
Sheep are baaing in the fields:
Baa! Baa! Baa! Baa!

Lead the children in swaying like trees.
Trees are swaying in the breeze:
Trees are swaying in the breeze:
Wishy, washy, wishy, washy.

We're on the way to Elizabeth's . . .
Interrupt yourself!
Look! We're HERE!

Mary calls Elizabeth.
After three, let's call Elizabeth. 1, 2, 3 . . .
Elizabeth! Elizabeth!
Elizabeth hears Mary.
Someone else can hear Mary, too! *Hands on tummy*
Baby John inside Elizabeth!
After three, let's call Elizabeth again with our hands over our mouth.
A bit quieter, like Baby John can hear Mary
inside his Mummy's tummy. 1, 2, 3 . . .
Elizabeth! Elizabeth!'

Baby John hears Mary calling.
Baby John knows that Baby Jesus is here!
And Baby John jumps head over heels for joy
inside his mummy.
'New Start' sign

Let's show baby John with our arms, jumping head over heels,
topsy turvy with joy! *'New Start' sign*

> *If some of your group are familiar with the Sorry Song:*
> Look, it's our 'new start' sign from our Sorry Song!
> Baby John knows that Baby Jesus
> is going to bring a new start when he's born!
> So he's jumping head over heels! *'New Start' sign*
> Amazing!
> Let's show the new start that Baby Jesus will bring
> like Baby John.
> *Lead the children in the 'New Start' sign.*

Elizabeth feels Baby John jumping inside her. *'New Start' sign*

Hold hands on tummy.

She says, 'My baby is jumping for joy!'
And Mary bursts with joy! *Fling arms outwards*
And she sings an amazing song
about God who turns the world upside down. *'New Start' sign*
Like John turning upside down,
head over heels, in his Mummy's tummy! *'New Start' sign*

Let's sing Mary's song
about our topsy turvy God together.

My God is very BIG!
Make the biggest shape you can with your body.
And I am very small!
Make the smallest shape you can.
My God is a topsy turvy God,
'New Start' sign
who turns things upside down!

And those who are low will be high!
Start low and end up high.
And those who are high will be low!
Start high and end up low.
My God is a topsy turvy God,
'New Start' sign
who turns things upside down!

Repeat.

Ask the children to sit down for a moment of quiet.

Let's close our eyes.
I wonder if there are times when you feel small?
So small you don't matter?
To God the smallest people
are the most important people of all!

Let's open our eyes.
God came to us as a tiny baby.
Let's put our hands on our tummies to remember Baby Jesus.

And the first person to recognize Jesus
was another tiny baby, not born yet –
not even able to see yet!
Baby John, inside his mummy's tummy!
Baby Jesus came to Baby John first!
Small people are very, very important to Jesus.
Next time you feel small remember that!

Let's sing our song one last time.
Let's sing 'My God is very big and I am very small'.
This time, let's not sing as Mary,
Let's sing as ourselves:
Mary's song is going to become our song!

My God is very BIG!
Make the biggest shape you can.
And I am very small!
Make the smallest shape you can.
My God is a topsy turvy God,
'New Start' sign.
who turns things upside down!

And those who are low will be high!
Start low and end up high.
And those who are high will be low!
Start high and end up low.
My God is a topsy turvy God,

'New Start' sign
who turns things upside down!

If you like, you could repeat the song, changing the words 'high/low' to 'rich/poor', 'strong/weak', etc. Invite the children to make up their own actions for the new words.

Week 4: Gloria! Gloria!

→ **The shepherds' story, Luke 2.8–16a**
→ **Song: a 'Gloria'**
→ **Tune: At St Peter's, Walworth, we use the tune from 'The clapping Gloria' by Mike Anderson © 1999 Kevin Mayhew Ltd (964 in *Complete Anglican: Hymns Old and New*)**

Tip

One of the reasons we use Mike Anderson's 'Clapping Gloria' at St Peter's is because it's often sung in our Sunday morning main service. We've also found this version works well with young children who are unfamiliar with the Gloria, for instance those in our nursery and reception classes at school. If you prefer, you could use another straightforward Gloria that you're familiar with. Or you could use the words 'Gloria! Gloria! In excelsis Deo!' without a tune. Your group may prefer to use the English ('Glory to God in the highest'), but we like to use this opportunity to familiarize the children with words that they will hear repeatedly in Christmas carols as well as in church services throughout the year.

If appropriate, before the story begins, ask an adult to stand by the light switch and be ready to turn the light off, then later turn it on again (or even flash the light on and off a few times).

> *If you're using the What's in the Box? option (p. 221), invite one of the children to open the box. Inside will be the angel Gabriel (or a picture of the angel Gabriel) and lots of other angels. As in previous weeks, you might like to show your group a photograph of angels depicted somewhere in your church building. Or, if you are providing paper angels that fold out like paper dolls for one of your Creative Response starter ideas, you could use these.*

What's in the box? *Ask the child to respond.*

It's the angel Gabriel.
He's a very special angel who takes messages
from God to people, like a post-angel.
But look! Today's Gabriel's not the only angel!
There are lots and lots and lots of angels!
A whole sky full of angels!
Shall we tell the story of the night when the whole sky was full of angels?

If appropriate:
It's nearly Christmas!
Baby Jesus, the Light of the World, is about to come.
And our story today is all about light:
darkness and light!
Has anyone noticed how dark
it's getting at the moment?
Before we go to bed, it's already dark!
When people decided what day Christmas should be on,
they chose it because it was the darkest time of the year.
Jesus, the Light of the World, is born
in the deep, deepest dark.
Our story today is all about darkness and light.

All groups:

For our story today, we need to practise two things.
First, we need to learn a song:
the song of the angels!

At this point, teach the children the Gloria words:
So let's do 'my turn' *point to self*, 'your turn' *leader's hands out to group*
Gloria! *Clap, clap* Gloria! *Clap, clap*
Gloria! *Clap, clap* **Gloria!** *Clap, clap*
In excelsis Deo! *Palms up, raise arms heavenwards*
In excelsis Deo! *Palms up, raise arms heavenwards*
That means Glory to God!
Glory in the highest! *Show the raising arms action*
The Gloria is really important.
It's the song of the angels.

If you're using a tune, teach it to the children at this point.
Let's sing it (*or* chant it) together:

Quietly . . .
Gloria! *Clap, clap* **Gloria!** *Clap, clap*
In excelsis Deo! *Palms up, raise arms heavenwards*

Loudly . . .
Gloria! *Clap, clap* **Gloria!** *Clap, clap*
In excelsis Deo! *Palms up, raise arms heavenwards*

Really loudly! . . .
Gloria! *Clap, clap* **Gloria!** *Clap, clap*
In excelsis Deo! *Palms up, raise arms heavenwards*

Second, we need to practise 'freeze frames'.
Freeze frames are when you show an action . . . *demonstrate*
then freeze! *demonstrate* Keeping absolutely still!

Let's have a go at freeze-framing. Can you show me . . .
Scared . . .
Ready to run . . .
Amazed . . .
Happy! Full of joy and excited . . .
Asleep . . .

We're ready to tell our story.

Ask helper to turn the light off.

Our story begins in the dark.
We're shepherds, looking after our sheep.
That's our job. It's not a job anyone else wants.
Let's shake our heads to show it's a job no one wants. *Lead the children in shaking heads*
It's dangerous and cold! Can you show me cold?
But we're poor and it's the only job we can get.

So we're shepherds and we're looking for wolves and bears.
Can you show me a 'looking out for wolves' freeze-frame?
And another one, looking that way?
Suddenly, the skies are filled with light!
The brightest light the shepherds have ever seen!
Shield eyes with hand.

Then the light of God's glory began to flash all around.
Ask the adult to turn the light on, or even flash it on and off.

The shepherds were terrified. Very, very scared!
Can you show me terrified and scared?
They looked into the light.
Let's hold our hand over our eyes to see.
An angel was standing there!

Let's stand up tall and strong and be the angel Gabriel.
Can you say after me?
'My turn' *point to self*, 'your turn' *leader's hands out to group*
Don't be frightened! *Hold hands out and smile*
Don't be frightened! *Hold hands out and smile*
I have Good News. *Thumbs up*
I have Good News. *Thumbs up*
There's a new baby king! *Place imaginary crown on head*
There's a new baby king! *Place imaginary crown on head*
Go! *Point*
Go! *Point*
Find him!
Find him!

Suddenly the skies were filled with noise.
It was all God's armies of angels singing!
We're going to be the angels.
Not pretty, baby angels, but soldiers of light,
warriors in an army! Super-powerful!
Can you show me a super-powerful pose and freeze!
We're super-powerful angels.
We're far away at the moment, so let's sing really quietly.

Gloria! *Clap, clap* **Gloria!** *Clap, clap*
In excelsis Deo! *Palms up, raise arms heavenwards*

We're getting a bit closer so let's sing a little louder . . .
Gloria! *Clap, clap* **Gloria!** *Clap, clap*
In excelsis Deo! *Palms up, raise arms heavenwards*

If your group includes children who are unsettled by loud noises, you could keep to clapping at this point.

And even louder. This time let's stamp our feet!
Gloria! *Stamp, stamp* **Gloria!** *Stamp, stamp*
In excelsis Deo! *Palms up, raise arms heavenwards*

Then the angels came right up to the shepherds!
It was the loudest noise of praise and joy
the shepherds had ever heard!

> *If appropriate:*
> Let's sing as loud as we have ever sung.
> Let's use our whole bodies to sing!

Gloria! *Stamp, stamp.* **Gloria!** *Stamp, stamp*
In excelsis Deo! *Palms up, raise arms heavenwards*
And again! Louder!
Gloria! *Stamp, stamp.* **Gloria!** *Stamp, stamp*
In excelsis Deo! *Palms up, raise arms heavenwards*

Then all of a sudden . . . the angels had gone.
Silence!
The shepherds were amazed!
Let's crouch down and be the shepherds, amazed!

The shepherds looked at each other.

Let's look right, then left. *Lead the children in looking side to side*

What shall we do?

What did the angel say to do?

Can anyone remember?

Accept the children's responses.

Go! *Point away.* Find him!

So what are we waiting for?

After three, let's get up and run like the shepherds

And find the baby King!

Let's run as fast as we can on the spot.

1, 2, 3 . . . Run!

Faster! Faster!

Freeze!

We'll find out what the shepherds

found in Bethlehem on Christmas Day!

Week 5: Meet Baby Jesus!

→ **Christmas, Luke 2.16–20**

> ## Tip
>
> During the Christmas period, we keep a Baby Jesus doll in a manger in the centre of our circle from the beginning of the session. We're very happy for the toddlers to take him out every now and then for a cuddle at any point of our session. We place lit battery tealights in the manger throughout to remind us that Jesus is the Light of the World.

This session's storytelling is much shorter than other weeks to open up the opportunity for a longer Creative Response time. You may wish to use this time for the children to make their own presents for Baby Jesus.

The shepherds are running!

After three, let's jump up and run on the spot

as fast as we can.

1, 2, 3 . . . Run! Faster! Faster!

Freeze!

Let's sit down for a minute.

The shepherds are running to find a very special baby!

Which baby has been born at Christmas?

Give the children the chance to answer.

Baby Jesus!

The shepherds want to see Baby Jesus.

They want to see Jesus with their own eyes.

After three, let's jump up again and run on the spot.

As fast as we can to find Baby Jesus.

1, 2, 3 . . . Run! Faster! Faster!

Freeze!

Look! It's a stable!

Who do you think is inside?

Give the children the chance to say who they think is inside.

Look! It's a little baby! Baby Jesus!

Shall we tiptoe on the spot

like we're going into the stable.
Ssssh! Let's be quiet. As quiet as we can.
Tiptoe, tiptoe, tiptoe . . . Ssssh!

Look! It's Baby Jesus! *Point to Baby Jesus*
The shepherds see Baby Jesus.
And they kneel down and they worship him.
Let's kneel down. Let's worship Baby Jesus.
Let's sing Baby Jesus a song,
Like a lullaby, ever so gently.

Lead the children in singing 'Away in a manger' or another appropriate song that they can sing together or listen to.

Section 3

Creative Response starter ideas, Getting Ready for Baby Jesus unit

→ **Guide: p 228**

These starter ideas are designed to spark imaginations and open up opportunities for the children to respond creatively in their different ways to the worship and storytelling you've taken part in together.

Tip

As outlined in the Guide (from p. 228), we've found the following rules of thumb helpful for fostering an environment where children are encouraged to engage personally and openly:

1 Encourage the children to make their own choices.
2 Give the children space to develop their response as they wish.
3 Create space for 'bridge building'.
4 It's the act of responding that matters, not the final result.
5 These responses are 'holy ground'.

Weekly Starter Ideas relate directly to the Bible storytelling of each session, and include a print-and-go option (indicated by the printer icon).

Sensory Starter Ideas are designed for sensory explorers, including babies and toddlers. These can remain the same through the whole unit.

Unit Starter Ideas are designed to remain relevant throughout the whole unit. Keeping these resources available each week gives children the opportunity to deepen and develop their responses, while making preparation more manageable for leaders.

Tip: Free response area

In addition to any other resources you provide, keeping a free response area available every week will give the children the opportunity to create anything they wish in response to the story they've told, building their sense of confidence and personal responsibility. In this area you could simply provide blank paper and crayons, pencils, paints, or pastels. If you have them, other interesting media (see p. 256) will provide even more scope for the children to nurture and strengthen their imaginative skills.

Weekly Starter Ideas

The four nativity stories told in this unit share a number of strong themes and memorable characters. For this reason, there are more unit starter ideas than weekly starter ideas for this unit, so do take look at pp. 211–12 as well.

Week 1: Zechariah's Story

➤ Invite the children to make a representation of the angel Gabriel, providing angel templates for those who'd like a starting point but also encouraging free exploration of what an angel might look like. *Provide paper, pencils/crayons, scissors, glue, angel templates (p. 283 or website). Optional: collage materials (p. 255), ribbon/string/wool, in case the children would like to convert the angel into a Christmas tree decoration.*

➤ If your church uses an Advent wreath, give the children an opportunity to design their own wreath or wreath hat. Traditionally, four purple candles (or three purple and one pink: check your church's wreath) are placed around the wreath, standing for the four weeks of Advent, with one white central candle. However, the children might like to explore their own symbolism. *Provide candle templates (p. 269 or website) and glue, paints/pens/crayons/pencils. You could also provide green paper strips to make hatbands, circle templates (p. 266 or website), and/or paper plates.*

➤ Invite the children to make little bags that smell like incense from squares of fabric, filled with pleasant-smelling spices that you have in the cupboard (e.g. cinnamon, allspice) and tied together with a pipe cleaner. Encourage the children to imagine the smell of the Temple as the prayers go up to God with the incense. *Provide fabric squares, pipe cleaners, cupboard spices. Little socks can also make great incense bags when tied with a pipe cleaner. If you prefer, you could add popcorn and a few drops of essential oil to the bags.*

Week 2: Mary's Story

➤ Invite the children to make a puppet of Mary. 'I wonder what Mary looked like?' For other print-and-go options, see week 1. *Provide body template (p. 264 or website), crayons/pencils/pastels, masking tape, lollipop sticks/straws/twigs.*

➤ Invite the children to paint Mary's face with pastels or paints. 'I wonder what Mary looked like?' Encourage the children to think of a 'strong woman' they know who would be brave enough to say 'yes' to God like Mary (their mum, teacher, aunt, head teacher, granny, a friend) to use as a model. Or the children might like to let their imagination go wild. *Provide paper, crayons/pencils or paints/pastels, or other interesting media (p. 256). Optional: you may like to provide face templates (p. 267 or website) as a guide.*

Week 3: Baby Jesus Meets Baby John

➤ Give the children the opportunity to make Christmas cards, or to send a Christmas postcard to someone to share the Good News that Baby Jesus is coming! *Provide card-making materials. You might also provide scissors, glue, and last year's Christmas cards with characters from the Nativity story in case the children would like to cut them up to use on their own cards. Optional: you may like to provide postcard templates (p. 271 or website).*

Week 4: The Shepherds' Story

≋ Give the children the opportunity to make paper angels that multiply before their eyes. *Provide fold-out paper angel templates (p. 284 or website, instructions on p. 263), scissors, and pencils/crayons/pastels.*

≋ Invite the children to make their own sheep to retell the story at home. *Provide sheep template (p. 265 or website), pencils/crayons. Optional: glue and collage materials (p. 255), including cotton wool and black/ brown crepe or tissue paper.*

≋ Give the children the opportunity to explore van Gogh's picture *The Starry Night* and then to paint or draw their own night sky filled with the light from stars and angels. *Provide copies of van Gogh's* The Starry Night *(available online).*

≋ Invite the children to turn pre-made (or bought) gingerbread people into shepherds or angels with icing and sprinkles. Try to leave as much space as possible for their own imagination and interpretation. If you have the facilities, you could even make the gingerbread shapes together using Nativity dough cutters. *Provide: pre-made (or bought) gingerbread people (or dough and cutters), bowls of different coloured icing with teaspoons, sprinkles.*

Sensory Starter Ideas (including for babies and toddlers)

Note: Some of these Creative Responses can remain the same for the Jesus, the Light of the World (Epiphany) unit in the weeks immediately after Christmas.

You could provide:

≋ a Baby Jesus doll along with a Moses basket, manger, or cardboard box. You could even provide real hay for the children to explore;

≋ Christmas cards of famous Nativity paintings or major characters from the stories. You could also provide a box with a slot cut into it for the children to post the cards, or make them into sewing cards by punching holes and providing shoelaces for threading;

≋ a durable Nativity set (we use PlayMobil 123's Christmas manger);

≋ a range of animals (either plastic or soft) from the Nativity stories: sheep, a donkey, cows, hens;

≋ Nativity figures in a cloth bag, box or socks for the children to discover and explore;

≋ torches, battery tealights, or sensory light toys like flashing stars or light sticks;

≋ board books with Nativity stories, or *That's Not My Angel* by Fiona Watt and Rachel Wells (London: Usborne, 2009; 2012).

≋ dressing up materials: tea towels, nativity outfits, angel outfits (white fairy costumes with a halo), sheep or donkey masks;

≋ a light box. Put battery fairy lights (or similar) into a transparent plastic box and tape the lid firmly shut. Provide different coloured cellophane paper, tissue paper, or other child-safe items that light can shine through. Include some items that no light shines through to create a contrast;

≋ a small durable Christmas tree to decorate with Nativity characters cut from old Christmas cards and attached to curling ribbon;

≋ building bricks (or other construction toys, e.g. Mega blocks, Duplo, Stickle Bricks, Kapla, Polydron) and 'small world' figures. Invite the children to build the Temple, Mary's house, a shepherd's hut, the stable – anything they like;

≋ wooden, plastic, or jigsaw numbers. You could even use these to count down the weeks (or days, if from ten) to Christmas together;

≋ a range of different Christmas smells for the children to explore. Add drops of essential oils to scraps of material and place in little pots for the children to investigate. Or make baby-safe versions of the bags from week 1 above, using small socks and tightly tied string.

Unit Starter Ideas

Jesus, the Light of the World

✎ Invite the children to make a darkness/light collage by decorating one half of a piece of paper with dark colours and the other half with light colours. *Provide white/dark paper folded in half, glue, dark collage materials and gold, white, yellow, orange and silver collage materials (p. 255; e.g. tinfoil).*

✎ Invite the children to explore light shining in the darkness by creating their own 'light' patterns with oil pastels, paint, chalk or glitter on dark paper. *Provide dark paper plus oil pastels/paint/chalk/glitter.*

✎ Invite the children to create a collage of the sun rising behind a silhouetted building. *Provide: white card, glue, orange/pink/yellow/red tissue or crepe paper squares to create a sunrise collage, the shape of a silhouetted building on black paper, as well as blank sheets of black paper for children who prefer to create their own silhouette. For the silhouetted building, you may like to use the church template (see website), or you may prefer to ask an artistic adult or child to make a simple outline of your own church or a local building. Note: the silhouette only needs to be drawn once (on black or white paper) and placed on the top of a pile of black paper: the sheets of paper can then all be cut at the same time.*

✎ You may like to put a candle out of reach in a safe place and invite the children to make an observational drawing of it. Talk with them about what colours they can see in the light. *Provide pastels/chalks/glitter on dark paper, or crayons/felt tips/pencils on white paper.*

Christmas tree and other decorations

✎ Invite the children to make foil decorations by cutting different shapes from metal pie plates and asking an adult to add a hole before threading a pipe cleaner through. *Provide metal pie plates, pipe cleaners (or curling ribbon/ wool/string), hole punch. Optional extras: glitter and glue.*

✎ Invite the children to make pasta decorations by threading a pipe cleaner through penne pasta then shaping it. *Provide dried penne pasta, pipe cleaners. Optional extras: glitter and a curling ribbon/string/wool to hang. You could dye the pasta beforehand if you like (see p. 257).*

✎ Give the children the opportunity to make tree decorations from last year's Christmas cards. Encourage them to explore the cards and cut out different shapes. Once an adult has made a hole, they could then thread a pipe cleaner through to hang the decorations. *Provide Christmas cards, scissors, hole punch, pipe cleaners (or wool/ string/curling ribbon). Optional extras: glue and glitter.*

God's messenger angels

✎ Invite the children to make their own angel mobile from simple angel templates hung with curling ribbon. *Provide wire coat hangers (or two sticks covered in tinfoil and fastened in a cross with a pipe cleaner), angel templates (p. 283 or website), pencils/paints/crayons, glue, collage materials and glitter, hole punch, pipe cleaners/curling ribbon/string.*

✎ Give the children the opportunity to explore an angel detail from a famous painting (or a photograph), or an angel in your church building, then invite them to create their own painting. Encourage them to use their imaginations freely. *Provide an angel detail from a painting, interesting media (p. 256).*

✎ Invite the children to collage their own angel: 'I wonder what angels might look like?' *Provide: angel templates (p. 283 or website), glue, scissors, collage materials (p. 255).*

✎ Give the children the opportunity to make gingerbread people into angels. Encourage them to use their imaginations freely. *Provide pre-made (or bought) gingerbread people, bowls with different coloured icing, a range of sprinkles.*

✎ See also the Weekly starter ideas for week 1.

Nativity characters

✎ Invite the children to make their own Nativity puppet sets so they can tell the story themselves at home. Remember to encourage the children to develop the resources in their own ways and to make their own connections. *Provide finger puppet templates (p. 268 or website), scissors, crayons/pencils.*

✎ Give the children the opportunity to experiment and create with Nativity stencils. *Provide nativity stencils, paper paint or pencils.*

✎ Invite the children to create their own Nativity scene using Nativity paint stamps. *Provide paper, paint, Nativity paint stamps (e.g. those from Baker Ross).*

✎ Invite the children to create their own nativity scene. *Provide modelling clay or playdough (which is softer for little fingers). Optional extras: rolling pins, playdough tools, or even Nativity-themed animal and people dough cutters.*

Part 3
Additional information and resources

TEACHING YOUR GROUP NEW SONGS

Many of the songs from the Diddy Disciples Building Blocks remain the same every week even when the units change. Still, there will always be a first time these songs need to be learned. Here are some tips for learning new songs that we've found helpful at St Peter's, Walworth.

Use a call-and-response formula: 'my turn' *both hands to yourself*, followed by 'your turn' *both hands out to the group*. This helps the children understand when your line has stopped and theirs is starting.

Example: The Welcome Song (Option 2)

We've got a new song to learn!

Let's say/sing the words
'my turn' *both hands to yourself,* 'your turn' *hands out to the group*
You are welcome in the name of the Lord! *both hands to yourself*
You are welcome in the name of the Lord! *both hands out to the group*

You are welcome in the name of the Lord! *both hands to yourself*
You are welcome in the name of the Lord! *both hands out to the group*

I can see all over you the glory of the Lord. *both hands to yourself*
I can see all over you the glory of the Lord. *both hands out to the group*

You are welcome in the name of the Lord! *both hands to yourself*
You are welcome in the name of the Lord! *both hands out to the group*

If you think your group will find either the words or the tune challenging, introduce them separately: first the words, then the tune second time around.

Example: The Welcome Song (Option 2)
Use the 'say' version above. At the end:
Now let's add the tune.
Repeat as above, this time singing. At the end:
Now let's try that altogether and add the actions.

Lead the group in singing:
You are welcome in the name of the Lord! *Wave with right hand*
You are welcome in the name of the Lord! *Wave with left hand*
I can see all over you the glory of the Lord. *Move arms up and down*
You are welcome in the name of the Lord! *Wave with both hands*

If you think the tune will be extremely familiar to the group and the words are very repetitive, you might find that you can simply begin singing and the children will instinctively join in once they're told the words.

Example: 'If you're rich and you know it', which is sung to the tune of 'If you're happy and you know it'.
Who likes going on holiday?
Ask for an action for going on holiday.
Can you sing with me and use our action?

Simply start singing and the children will gradually join in.
If you're rich and you know it, go on holiday!
If you're rich and you know it, go on holiday!
If you're rich and you know it,
and you really want to show it . . .
If you're rich and you know it, go on holiday!

With longer songs, at first the children may only join in with the parts of the song that are repeated: for instance the 'Jesus, hear my prayer' refrain in the Prayers for Other People song or the 'I'm sorry' refrain in the Sorry Song. Over time, you'll probably find that they begin to join in with more and more of the song. When you're teaching the song for the first time, you might find it helpful to introduce those sections first to give the children confidence.

Example: 'Jesus, open up my eyes' from the Getting Ready for Bible Storytelling Building Block (Option 2)

We're going to learn a new song.
There's one word in it that's very important: Alleluia!
After 3, can you say 'Alleluia!'
1, 2, 3 . . . Alleluia!
Let's try that again.
1, 2, 3 . . . Alleluia!

'Alleluia' is a very important word in our song.
Let's say the words 'my turn' *both hands to yourself,* 'your turn' *both hands out to the group*

Jesus, open up my eyes. Alleluia! *both hands to yourself*
Jesus, open up my eyes. Alleluia! *both hands out to the group*
Jesus, open up my lips. Alleluia! *both hands to yourself*
Jesus, open up my lips. Alleluia! *both hands out to the group*
Jesus, open up my heart. Alleluia! *both hands to yourself*
Jesus, open up my heart. Alleluia! *both hands out to the group*
Jesus, help me hear your voice. Alleluia! *both hands to yourself*
Jesus, help me hear your voice. Alleluia! *both hands out to the group*

Now let's add the tune.

Repeat as above, this time singing.
At the end:
Now let's try that altogether and add the actions!

For the first few sessions that you sing the song, you may find your group singing it as follows, with only a few singing the words in normal type, and others joining in with the words in bold. At St Peter's Walworth, we've found that over time the children join in with more and more of the song until we are all singing the whole song together.

Jesus, open up my eyes. **Alleluia!** *Trace a cross between your eyes*
Jesus, open up my lips. **Alleluia!** *Trace a cross on your lips.*
Jesus, open up my heart**. Alleluia!** *Trace a cross on your heart.*
Jesus, help me hear your voice. **Alleluia!** *Cup your hands behind your ears*

The first few times, some children may only join in with the actions rather than singing. If you find yourself singing with only a couple of others to begin with, don't worry. This is why the actions are included: so everyone can join in at their own level. Gradually over the weeks encourage the children to join in: 'Thank you for helping with the actions. Now who can help me with the singing, too?'

To learn longer songs like the Sorry Song, your group might like to put aside a whole session. You could keep your usual pattern for the session but introduce the new song at the point at which you would normally hold the Bible Storytelling.

A GUIDE TO THE BUILDING BLOCKS

There's no single way of holding a Diddy Disciples session. At St Peter's, Walworth, we're continually faced both with developing and adapting our pattern of worship as our group grows in number, experience and age range, and with adapting to new waves of children who have different gifts and ways of being. Every group really is unique, and it will be for your own group to work out over time what Diddy Disciples will look like. Below is a description of the way we've tended to do things at St Peter's, Walworth. This is intended as a guide and reference point, not as an instruction manual as to how Diddy Disciples must be done. We ourselves do things differently in nursery and reception at St Peter's Primary School, as will become clear.

If your group is held during a church service

At St Peter's, Walworth, we begin our worship with the rest of the congregation in the main church building, emphasizing that we're all one Church. All the children's groups go out for their sessions after the first hymn and welcome, during a prayer for the children's worship that's said by the whole congregation.

We carry with us a symbol that helps us remember we're part of this whole gathering. For you it could be a Bible, a cross, a banner, candles, or another symbol your group might find helpful. At St Peter's, we use two battery candles. We're a church that uses candles and servers, and the candles help the children understand that our time together is in step with the service taking place upstairs. These little candles have already been carried by two younger children (or by babies held by parents or carers) during the procession into the church, accompanied by an older Diddy Disciple carrying a colourful wooden cross. The cross and candles will also be used in the procession at the end of the service, when they are carried by three different children. We always invite newcomers, visitors, or people we haven't seen for a while to carry the candles and crosses, to emphasize that these people are not just onlookers but a welcome and active part of the group. Using battery candles instead of real candles means that babies, more adventurous toddlers, and newcomers can take this leading role in the same way as everyone else.

Tip

We started with a smallish wooden cross, but found it was still too cumbersome for the smallest children, who tended to drop it. Having two smaller symbols (our candles or tealights) has meant that children who are able to walk can hold hands in the procession, holding the symbols in their other hands, and so gain confidence (and direction!) from each other.

Entering the worship space

As the children (some with parents or carers) enter the room, we encourage everyone to sit in a circle with all the children seated on the floor. We use chairs as little as possible, both to make setting up easier and to make it easier to move around the room, but some of the parents or carers with babies use a chair. Our meeting space is relatively small, which means it's obvious where the children should sit – against the walls – and I would recommend that the group sit near at least one wall to help the children find their place. If you're using a large room, try sectioning part of it off with chairs to create a clear boundary within which the children are free to move around. We try to leave some spaces by the door as our group inevitably tends to grow during the session. We encourage all children to come and join us, no matter what time their families arrive. The set rhythm of the service means the children can usually slip in and take part without any explanation, as they can see where we're up to. In the school hall, where the space is less clear, and there are no extra adults to help gather the children, we tend to mark out a square (easier than a circle) in masking tape.

 With children, what is heard spiritually is usually less influential than what is seen or touched. It makes sense therefore to consider the focal point of the room – what you see when you enter. REBECCA NYE[1] "

At St Peter's we find liturgical colours helpful, and so we place a cloth matching the colour of the liturgical season on a small focal table. We add our two tealights to the focal table as we enter the room, though some very young children prefer to keep hold of theirs or take them from the table during the session.

Welcome

> " Jesus said, 'Whoever welcomes a little child, welcomes me.' MATTHEW 18.5 "

We begin with the same welcome every week as we've found this is important for helping the children to feel at home. We first go round the circle, inviting each child to say his or her own name. This isn't just an opportunity to learn each other's name. It's shaped by our belief that God knows our name, and calls each of us by name (Isaiah 43.1). We've also found this is a good opportunity for children to hear their own voices within the group and to experience being heard by everyone.

To begin with, some children may be shy, but it's wonderful to see them grow in confidence as they realize that it's all right for their voice to be heard. Even the smallest babies can be seen to respond to a group that's looking at them, and we encourage parents and carers to help them join in actively with a wave. We ask any helpers and parents or carers present to take part in the naming to underline that they're full members of the group and that this is their worship too: there are no observers in Diddy Disciples, only participants. If children have brought along a doll or figure, we also ask the child to give the toy's name: this can be a helpful signal to children that the things that are important to them are accepted and welcome in the group. Some weeks nowadays, when there's a longer story for us to tell, or a more involved Creative Response, we skip the naming around the circle – having grown from 5 children to 30 to 40 weekly has changed the dynamic of our group! – but it's still good to do it when possible.

After the naming, we sing a Welcome Song together. We find that the smallest children particularly enjoy this part of our session, as it remains exactly the same each week. We used to sing Option 1, in which all the children and adults in the group are named in turn and welcomed. Sadly, it now takes far too long to go around both naming and singing in our group. For this reason, we have included Option 2 for bigger groups.

In Option 2, we encourage the children to wave at different individual people within the circle. We also encourage them to choose a particular person across the circle to 'show the glory' to (by waving their arms up and down while wiggling their fingers). Through this we try to encourage the sense that we're all individuals before God, even when there are many of us present. It can be really meaningful for the leader to choose someone 'to show the glory' to: it opens up the possibility of choosing a child who is new, sad, or feeling unsettled. As the children have become more familiar with the introduction to the song, we often ask toddlers to help us remember the waving actions and lead the group.

Getting Ready to Worship

> " When two or three are gathered in my name, I am there with them . . . MATTHEW 18.20 "

Immediately after welcoming each other in God's name, we remind ourselves that we're not the only ones here: Jesus is also here with us. At St Peter's, in both church and school, we use the sign of the cross (Option 1) because this is how our main acts of worship begin. We would encourage your group to begin with whatever greeting is used in your church, whether it's one of those indicated in the material, or a more informal 'good morning'.

> " Christian work with children faces the temptation of putting children in the centre in such a way that Jesus himself is marginalised. The child placed by Jesus among the disciples does not displace Jesus, but stands beside him, to point to truths about God's unexpected way of reigning in the now-and-not-yet world. BILL PREVETTE[2] "

> " *For Option 2:*
>
> Dear God,
> I am so afraid to open my clenched fists!
> Who will I be when I have nothing left to hold on to?
> Who will I be when I stand before you with empty hands?
> Please help me to gradually open my hands
> and to discover that I am not what I own,
> but what you want to give me.
> HENRI NOUWEN[3] "

Introducing the Unit

'Introducing the Unit' and the Gathering Song are designed to be used together (though they can stand alone). In some units the introduction is longer; in others, the Gathering Song takes more time. Both of these Building Blocks set out the main theme of the unit in simple, accessible, repetitive words and body language. By returning to the same pattern each week, this material presents the children with the opportunity to strengthen and deepen their understanding of the theme and – in time – to begin to anticipate the pattern and words, possibly even beginning to lead the group by preparing everyone for the next words or action.

Tip: Presentation folders

Presentation folders can really help with the leading of Diddy Disciples. They allow leaders to have the Building Blocks and options they've chosen to hand in a way that's easy to hold while performing actions. They're much easier to manage than loose sheets, and they look neater. They can also remain the same for the whole six weeks, making weekly preparation more manageable. At St Peter's, Walworth, we use two presentation folders: one that contains the Building Blocks we've chosen for our session; the other for the Bible storytelling material.

Option 1 of the introduction is short and designed for groups with time limitations, or those belonging to churches that don't use liturgical colours. Option 2 is designed for groups who wish to follow the seasons and/or colours of the Church year. The children are invited to tell us what colour we're in at the moment (this is clearly apparent on our focal table, in the church, and in the clergy vestments). Colours are something that many young children are encouraged to notice and name, so being asked to notice colours in a church environment seems to be a very natural activity for many children. We've found that this too can be a great opportunity to give the younger children a chance to lead the group confidently.

Gathering Song

Diddy Disciples encourages the use of imaginative aids during the Gathering Song to send a strong signal that this is an environment where imagination is celebrated. Imaginative aids can be anything that the children can use to make shapes and show feelings. At St Peter's Church, we tend to use streamers, ribbons and dance scarves, but the aids you choose will depend on your space, numbers, imagination and budget. In St Peter's nursery class, we've used fallen autumn leaves to wave during our God the Maker unit.

> "At first I didn't like the bit that they [the children] do different things with the streamers. It didn't have any relevance to the subject and just seemed a bit irrelevant. I was completely wrong. After a few sessions I realized that that was the point. It encourages confidence, and helps everyone move away from having to always have a well thought out religious answer to be accepted.
> DIDDY DISCIPLES LEADER FOR THE PARISH OF BUNBURY, CHESTER"

Imaginative aids can help children fire up their imaginations, get used to participating actively, and worship God in ways that aren't wholly dependent on words. We've found that they open up a space where children and babies can find the confidence to use their whole bodies, to move freely, and – in time – to become lost in the moment. They also cut down on preparation time for adults, as the imaginative aids can become anything that you want them to be.

> "Children need every encouragement to get into the habit of using their imaginative faculties in the service of spiritual life. It is this that will help them both now, and in later years, to engage with the elements of religious practice. Encouraging real imagination will develop the spiritual skills they need as they sift through layers of meaning and make new discoveries.
> REBECCA NYE[4]"

If your church uses liturgical colours, you may wish to use imaginative aids that correspond to the season's colour. Since children are so aware of and responsive to colour, changing colours with each season can help them to make connections between their children's session and what is happening in church. If your church doesn't use liturgical colours, it may still be worth using only one colour at a time, to prevent upset about which colour each child is given. This will help to keep the emphasis on the children's imagination and how they use the aid rather than on the choice set before them. Alternatively, your group may choose to use hand actions instead of imaginative aids for some or all of the seasons; or may choose to stay with one set of aids for the whole year.

> ### Tip
>
> The imaginative aids that we've found to work at St Peter's are:
>
> - purple hand scarves: Advent and Lent (10 weeks in total);
> - yellow ribbons threaded onto rings: Easter, Christmas, Epiphany (around 12–17 weeks in total);
> - green streamers on sticks: Green Time/Ordinary Time (around 30 weeks in total).
>
> The Diddy Disciples website contains up-to-date suggestions of where to purchase imaginative aids and options for making your own.

To prepare for the use of imaginative aids, we've found ourselves naturally introducing an 'imagination warm-up' immediately before the Gathering Song. During this time, we encourage the children to explore the imaginative aids freely and see what their bodies can do. We've found that this warm-up also sends a useful and important signal to children, parents, carers and leaders alike that our session is a space where there are no 'right' answers, all contributions are welcome, and our imagination can be freed up.[5]

This warm-up will almost certainly take longer for groups who are new to Diddy Disciples. At St Peter's, we've found that our warm-up has become shorter; children begin warming up themselves naturally as the streamers are given out and no longer need to be led. Every so often, however, if we have more than three or four new children at any one time, we spend a little longer on warming up.

> ### Tip
>
> Ideas for using the scarves or ribbons in the warm-up include:
>
> - single swishes: swish one scarf/the ribbon up/down or left/right;
> - rainbow: swish a rainbow shape over your head;
> - fireworks: wave the scarf/ribbon fast high above the head;
> - circle/square/triangle: draw the shape in the air;
> - thunder: move the scarves/ribbon quickly to make a cracking sound.
>
> With scarves you can also make:
>
> - pompoms: Shake the scarves like pompoms with arms outstretched;
> - double swishes: as above, but with both scarves;
> - a roly-poly action, hand rotating over hand, while holding the scarves.

The use of imaginative aids during the Gathering Song provides a wonderful opportunity to include any babies who are present and encourage them to take a leading role. Many babies when handed a streamer or dance scarf will instinctively shake it, hide behind it, or make some really interesting shapes. We've found that the older children really enjoy copying a baby in her or his innovative action. They seem to love to discover that babies are individuals, and it's always wonderful to see the reaction of small babies as they realize that everyone is looking to them and following their lead. This is always a 'topsy-turvy' moment for us at St Peter's, Walworth. It can also be a great time to encourage a newcomer or child who may be feeling a little shy to take a lead, where appropriate.

> " To participate in the Eucharist is to live inside God's imagination. It is to be caught up into what is really real, the body of Christ. WALTER BRUEGGEMANN[6] "

> ### Tip
>
> For groups that are building a children's service to reflect *Common Worship* or BCP 2004, the Gathering Song can act a little bit like the Collect: gathering up both the theme of the day and ourselves before God as we prepare to open the Bible together. It also provides the children with the chance to release some energy in preparation for the Bible storytelling!

If your group wishes to use an alternative Gathering Song, make sure that the words are repetitive and easy for even the youngest children (and the most forgetful adults!) to pick up quickly and join in with fully. Even if all your group are familiar with a particular song that you've learned together, make sure it's accessible to those beyond the group, and always be ready for visitors and newcomers to join you. We've experimented with using other songs (for instance, songs that the nursery and reception children were learning in school). However, we found that the amount of new words involved – or the unfamiliar tune – became a stumbling block for the youngest children and discouraged newcomers and visitors (both children and adults) from fully participating.

Getting Ready for Bible Storytelling

Following the Gathering Song, the 'Getting Ready for Bible storytelling' Building Block provides a short moment for the children to refocus and prepare to take part in the Bible storytelling. This isn't a Building Block to linger on and is very easy to incorporate into a session.

Option 1: What's in the Box is particularly helpful for younger children, children with special needs, and those for whom English is not a first language. It provides the children with a visual stimulus and opens up an opportunity to introduce some vocabulary, for instance 'poppy' or 'shepherd'. We use a box that looks special and place inside it items relevant to the theme of the Bible storytelling (suggestions are given at the beginning of each story in the Interactive Bible Storytelling material). Before the storytelling itself begins a child is invited to open the box – as indicated in the material – and describe what he or she sees. If a baby opens the box, you could invite another child to describe what he or she sees. The storytelling continues from there.

The items taken from the box can be placed on the focal table during the storytelling, or given to any babies or children with special needs who are present (depending on numbers). If your group includes children who attend frequently, you could even let these items accumulate week by week through each unit to give the children a visual reminder or hint of what the previous weeks have been about. Another alternative is to use a children's picture Bible with strong, colourful pictures to identify characters (like Gabriel the angel) or objects (like a crown) before beginning your storytelling.

Option 2: 'Jesus, open up my eyes' is a calming and focusing song that's particularly appropriate for groups held during Sunday morning worship where 'Alleluias' are sung before the reading of the Gospel. If you keep your Bible storytelling in a separate book, you could ask a child to bring out the book as you sing to show that this is a special part of the session when the Bible is read.

> " Then he opened their minds to
> understand the scriptures. LUKE 24.45 "

In churches where the congregation or leaders trace crosses on their forehead, lips and chest at the words 'Hear the Gospel of our Lord Jesus Christ', the song helps to introduce this symbolic action in a meaningful way. If your church stops singing 'Alleluia' during Lent, you could join them by changing to Option 1 at this time.

Bible Storytelling

Central to any Diddy Disciples session is the Bible Storytelling (see Section 2 of each unit). At St Peter's, Walworth, we keep this material in a separate book

decorated by the children and bring it out as we get ready to tell the Bible story. For us it's important that the children see with their own eyes that the stories we're telling together come from the Bible. These aren't stories we're making up! They're not even stories we need to know by heart in order to have access to them. They're stories that the children can find for themselves in their picture Bibles at home, or can have read to them by their parents or carers. They're stories that have been passed down for hundreds of years in a book.

It can also be valuable for the children to see adults moving from reading to action, then back to reading again. These movements from book to real life can begin to model to them what reading the Bible is actually about: something that begins on the page, but through our participation, imagination and the breath of the Spirit ends up being embodied in us, in our actions. We don't need to hide the fact that our faith has been passed down and shared and grown through writing and reading in all sorts of ways before it has been brought to life in us. For these reasons – and many others – we encourage our leaders not to feel self-conscious about reading from the material during the session, although it's natural to ad lib at times.

Diddy Disciples storytelling is closely modelled on biblical storytelling in all sorts of ways. Perhaps most importantly, it is:

- our shared story
- rooted in and connected to our everyday lives.

Our shared story

Diddy Disciples storytelling is always interactive. We never begin with 'let me tell you a story', but always 'let's tell the story together'. Storytelling in this way isn't a passive experience, where children are asked to sit and listen or observe. Nor is it a drama or performance where some of us act and the rest of us watch. In Diddy Disciples *all* children and adults present are invited to take an active part in the storytelling, using their bodies, facial expressions and voices to participate in their own way. This is about 'embodied reading', where the biblical stories become our stories, where the expectation that these stories will begin to shape our actions and lives is made clear, and where that process is begun.

In this way, Diddy Disciples storytelling has strong echoes with biblical models of storytelling. When Moses talks about God's covenant in Deuteronomy 5.3, he speaks to the people gathered before him: 'The LORD didn't make this covenant with our parents, but with *us*, those *here*, all of *us* alive *today*. The Lord spoke to *you*, *face to face*, at the mountain from out of the fire . . .' The

Hebrew couldn't be more emphatic: *you* were actually there at the mountain when God made the covenant. The irony is that a closer look at the story reveals that most of the people present were *not* actually there at the mountain. This is, in fact, the next generation; it was their *parents* who were at the mountain. Moses hasn't made a mistake: he's making a vital point to God's gathered people about storytelling in God's family. These stories are not just their parents' stories, which happened long ago to be passed on and remembered: these stories are to become *their* story, and – as children adopted into God's family – *our* story. When we tell these stories together, it's because we too were there at that mountain when God spoke to us, face to face, out of the fire.

This understanding of what it means to tell stories as the people of God is fundamental to our storytelling in Diddy Disciples and can be seen coursing through the material. In telling those stories, we're not simply remembering something that happened to someone else. We ourselves are becoming part of that story, finding ourselves in it in all sorts of different places. And as we tell the story together, it is to us that God is speaking.

> "People have an idea that the preacher is an actor on a stage and they are the critics, blaming or praising him. What they don't know is that they are the actors on the stage; he (the preacher) is merely the prompter standing in the wings, reminding them of their lost lines. SØREN KIERKEGAARD[7]"

Diddy Disciples storytelling repeatedly invites the children to enter into the story and explore its feelings and emotions for themselves by asking questions such as 'How do you think the little Lost Sheep feels?' or 'I wonder how Mary's feeling now?' Most young children will naturally prefer to use their bodies and facial expressions to respond, which is wonderful. Sometimes children may offer a single word, or more – and these should be accepted with joy – but on the whole, Diddy Disciples expects and encourages babies and young children to use their most fluent language (their bodies, see p. 23) to respond to any questions. This is often indicated in the script with the question 'Can you show me . . . ?' The added advantage of encouraging 'body responses' is that this can enable lots of children to respond at the same time, at an age when many children are still learning to take turns. Sitting and listening to another young child as he or she formulates a sentence can be challenging for young children. Taking turns plays an important role in other parts of Diddy Disciples sessions, but, on the whole, we've found it helpful

during the storytelling to let the children all respond at the same time in their different ways, with their bodies.

For this reason, we don't tend to use props in our storytelling at St Peter's. Our group has grown to be fairly large and includes many babies and toddlers, as well as a number of children with special needs. We've found that taking turns and sharing is still a learning process that can distract from the storytelling itself. We also prefer not to encourage some children to 'watch', while just one or two of them use the props and become the storytellers. Instead, we like to encourage everyone to take part the whole time, often changing from all being one character to all being another. Diddy Disciples does encourage the use of objects to introduce the stories, however (see What's in the Box, see p. 221), and the use of more props is suggested for storytelling when only babies and toddlers (see p. 232) are involved, where the dynamics are different.

Tip

At St Peter's, Walworth, we've found that questions like 'Who can tell me what story we told last week?' can lead some children who weren't present for that story to disengage, as if 'this has nothing to do with me'. For this reason, the storytelling material avoids these kinds of questions (although in a school situation where the children are the same every week we sometimes use them). Units that involve an ongoing story that unfolds over a few weeks tell the whole story from the beginning each week in abbreviated form, as if it hasn't been told before (a little like a recap sequence at the beginning of some TV series). This allows those who weren't present at previous sessions to take full part in the storytelling, while giving those who were there the opportunity to recall, strengthen, and deepen their knowledge of the story.

Rooted in and connected to our everyday lives

Another way in which Diddy Disciples storytelling echoes biblical storytelling is in its use of tunes from traditional songs and nursery rhymes. Of course, these tunes are catchy, and singing is an effective way of storytelling with young children (see 'Diddy Disciples celebrates our voices', p. 24). More importantly, however, these traditional songs make vital connections with the children's everyday lives, helping to build confidence and a sense of belonging among the children and parents who recognize them: these stories are connected with songs we know and tunes we sing ourselves.

Using the everyday to make connections between our daily lives and the life of God echoes Jesus' insistent use of what was the 'everyday' for those he met (bread, water, wine, wineskins, sheep, goats, vineyards) and Paul's use of the everyday for people living in a Roman world (architecture, war, Greek games, agriculture, trading, and the distinctive Roman practice of adoption). Similarly, one of the ways in which the Diddy Disciples storytelling material repeatedly aims to help young children connect their everyday life to the stories of God and the stories of God to their everyday life is via the use of familiar tunes that they hear around them. For more on the ways in which Diddy Disciples storytelling is modelled on biblical storytelling, see 'More than storytelling' in *Diddy Disciples: January to August*.

> Community is first of all a quality of the heart. It grows from the spiritual knowledge that we are alive not for ourselves but for one another. Community is the fruit of our capacity to make the interests of others more important than our own. The question, therefore, is not 'How can we make community?' but, 'How can we develop and nurture giving hearts?'
> HENRI NOUWEN[8]

Tip

The interactive Bible Storytelling sometimes ends with a quieter, more reflective moment. At times, we've found it helpful to lead into this moment with a basic breathing exercise to help the children to calm and refocus themselves. For instance:

> *Speaking quietly and slowly.*
> Let's close our eyes . . .
> Let's breathe in through our nose . . .
> and out . . .
> and in . . .
> and out . . .
> *Continue with the reflective material from the Bible storytelling.*

The Prayer Building Blocks: Saying Sorry to God, God Gives Us a New Start, Prayers for Other People, Thank You, God

Prayer is a vital part of Christian life. The Prayer Building Blocks each open up space for a time of prayer, enabling children to experience what are commonly viewed as the three most important aspects of Christian prayer: (1) saying sorry to God, (2) asking God for help, and (3) saying 'thank you' to God. They're also designed to help children reflect on their relationships with other people and the world before God: another vital part of Christian discipleship.

As the Prayer Building Blocks are more substantial, we recommend that you use only one of them in any session and that you wait until the children are familiar with the basic pattern of your session before introducing them. You could even teach the songs for these Building Blocks in the place of the Bible storytelling in the week

that you first introduce them, so that the children (and leaders!) are not overwhelmed by new material. Using the Prayer Blocks may feel challenging for the first two to three weeks, while the songs and actions are new. Once the children are used to the material, however, this can become a time for the whole group – including parents, carers and leaders – to relax into the familiar pattern and spend time with God. At St Peter's, Walworth, we've found that these more reflective resources can provide a little oasis of quiet singing and reflection (where everyone knows what they're doing) after the newness of the storytelling, opening up space to reflect on what the storytelling might mean for us.

Saying Sorry to God

> If we confess our sins, God who is faithful and just will forgive us our sins and cleanse us from all unrighteousness. 1 JOHN 1.9
>
> Let us therefore approach the throne of grace with boldness, so that we may receive mercy and find grace to help in time of need. HEBREWS 4.16
>
> My grace is sufficient for you, for power is made perfect in weakness. 2 CORINTHIANS 12.9

The 'Saying Sorry to God' Building Block is an important part of Diddy Disciples. It provides children with the opportunity to experience the joy of saying sorry and being given a new start, and to reflect on the transformative power of God's forgiveness in the world. Reflecting on our own lives in the light of Bible stories and being given a new start to change the way we live is an integral part of being a Christian disciple. We believe it's important to discover meaningful ways of saying sorry together – for the smallest things as well as for the big things – on a regular basis from the very earliest age.

The 'Saying Sorry to God' Building Block is also designed to open up opportunities for children to explore and begin to name negative feelings, to understand that these emotions are part of being human, and to become familiar with bringing them before God, confident of God's power to transform every part of us into something beautiful and life-giving.

> " Grace means there is nothing I can do to make God love me more, and nothing I can do to make God love me less. PHILIP YANCEY[9] "

Early childhood is a time when we explore the range of human emotions with which we've been created. This can be unsettling, even overwhelming, for some children as they seek to navigate the breadth and strength of human emotions (and disconcerting for many first-time parents, as these emotions can seem much bigger than the children themselves!). Earlier, we touched on the importance of following the Bible's lead in bringing all our emotions – both positive and negative – before God to be transformed (see p. 25). There are times when all of us feel guilty or 'wrong' in ourselves, when we want to hide, when we feel as if everything is dark, when we feel that we've made a mess or 'ruined' everything, when we're feeling angry or destructive. These negative feelings are echoed throughout the stories and songs of the Bible. Having named these emotions in its Bible storytelling, Diddy Disciples gently recalls them within the 'Saying Sorry to God' Building Block, opening up opportunities for young children to begin to recognize their negative feelings and bring them before God in hope and trust.

> " No part of a life cannot be transformed by God's love. Even the aspects of ourselves that we consider worthless, or sinful, can be made worthwhile and holy. As the proverb has it, God writes straight with crooked lines. JAMES MARTIN[10]
>
> God is the perfect Recycler, and in the economy of grace, nothing is wasted, not even our worst sins nor our most stupid mistakes. RICHARD ROHR[11] "

At St Peter's, Walworth, we've found that the most effective way to cultivate quietness for this part of the session is for all the adults – including the leaders – to close their eyes and focus on their own prayers. It was only when we did this for the first time (instead of worrying about engaging children who were finding it difficult to focus) that all the children fell silent and began to join in. The sight of us all saying sorry to God in a quiet way was far more effective than our attempts to tell the children how to take part. Our leaders and adults now really appreciate this moment within the session where the atmosphere changes. Even the youngest children seem to sense this and respond with hushed quiet. At times, there may be a visitor or newcomer who is restless for a little while, being unfamiliar with this part of the session. It's amazing how soon they also join in, however, when they see all the adults and other children singing with their eyes closed.

The 'Saying Sorry to God' Building Block is made up of two parts:

1 The Diddy Disciples Sorry Songs in both options invite children and adults to reflect on what they've 'thought and said and done' in the past week, with accompanying signs. These songs remain the same for every unit, giving even the youngest children the opportunity to become familiar with the words and their pattern. When first teaching the song for Option 1, you may prefer to omit the verses ('With my hands on my head . . .'), simply using the spoken words (Let's put our hands on our head . . .') followed by the 'I'm sorry' refrain the first couple of times to build confidence in the pattern.

2 The Saying Sorry Action enables the children to participate in this time of prayer actively in ways beyond words. The themes and symbols lying behind these actions are drawn from a wide range of places:

- the biblical storytelling (wanting to run away or hide, being in a dark cave);
- looking at God's world around us (blossom, rubbish, weeding, mess);
- wider biblical imagery as indicated throughout the material (God taking our burdens, sprinkling us with water, blotting out sins, casting them into the ocean, shining like light upon us);
- moments of Christian life (like baptism).

All the actions, however, share an emphasis on God's power to transform our lives, the world and broken situations into places of hope and promise.

> If forgiveness is liberation, it is also the recovery of the past in hope, a return of memory, in which what was potentially threatening, destructive, despair-inducing, in the past is transfigured into the ground of hope. ROWAN WILLIAMS[12]

Depending on which options you choose, the Saying Sorry Action can involve distributing symbols or objects. We encourage the children, especially newcomers and those who find it hard to sit still, to do the distributing whenever possible: this is a good moment for newcomers to feel they belong and for the particularly active to celebrate their love of being 'on the go' by taking a lead. When a child hasn't experienced leading in this way before, we've found it's helpful to be very clear who does what, not only with our words but by walking alongside the child and showing him or her in practice until he or she seems confident to continue independently.

Signs for the Sorry Song

The 'I'm Sorry' and 'New Start' signs from the Sorry Song are among the very few Diddy Disciples signs and actions that are fixed. It's worth learning these well from the first time you use the Sorry Song, as they become important in a number of units. Videos of both signs can be found on the website next to the Sorry Song Building Block in any of the units.

The Diddy Disciples 'I'm Sorry' sign

Start with your hands lightly crossed in front of your forehead, then move them in opposing arcs downwards towards your chest and round in opposing circles, and back just in front of your forehead.
This opposing circular motion is the 'I'm Sorry' sign. It's designed to convey sadness as well as calling to mind splashing our face with water. There are also echoes of an 'X' shape in the sign to show that we know we've got something 'wrong'.

> **Tip**
>
> This description is not designed to be used within the group – we would simply make the sign in front of the children and encourage them to imitate it. If at all possible, go to the website to see this sign in practice – it's far easier to do than to describe!

The Diddy Disciples 'New Start' sign

The 'New Start' sign can best be described as the 'winding' action from the nursery rhyme 'Wind the Bobbin Up'. Repeatedly rotate your arms around each other in front of your body.

> **Tip**
>
> Groups with large numbers of children may find it helpful to choose options or actions where all the children can respond at the same time (such as growing like a seed together), rather than actions where turn-taking is required (such as pulling a 'weed' from a 'garden'). Where actions suggest that the children place a symbol (for instance, crumpled paper) in the centre of the circle, larger groups may find it easier to ask a child or adult to carry a tray or bowl around the circle so the children can place their paper without leaving the circle. You may even like to use two trays going opposite ways. At St Peter's, Walworth, we have found that we have had to continually adapt as our group has grown in number, working out new ways of actively involving all those present in this time of prayer.

God Gives Us a New Start

It's vital to end this time of Saying Sorry with the reminder that God loves to give us a new start. Many of the Saying Sorry Actions suggested within the material come with this hope of a new start already included. Where they don't, one should be added. This hope of a new start – won by Jesus when he rose from the dead – is central to our Christian life and is the Good News we're sent to share with everyone.

> However we put it – and there are countless ways – God's loving kindness is there ahead of us. Forgiveness is never a matter of persuading God of something but of discovering for myself that there is no distance to be crossed, except that long journey to that which gives trust and reality to my very self. ROWAN WILLIAMS[13]

Prayers for Other People

Diddy Disciples aims to encourage a multifaceted experience of prayer from the very earliest age. The material opens up opportunities for us to pray in all sorts of different ways: using our bodies, minds, imagination, senses, and silence as well as a wide range of symbols, objects and words. Option 1 moves through five short steps which take the children on a journey through different ways and experiences of praying. Option 2 is provided for groups who prefer a more word-based option.

In Option 1 the children are invited to imagine they're holding their prayers gently in their cupped hands. They're then invited to open their hands to let their prayers go up to God, giving meaning to the actions that will be used in the song.

We next sing 'Jesus, hear our prayer!', which introduces the children to praying in a familiar pattern: for the world, the Church, their community, the sick and lonely (including those who mourn), their friends and family, themselves. Similar patterns lie behind many intercessions in *Common Worship*, BCP 2004, and other Christian prayer traditions. The 'Jesus, hear our prayer!' refrain also echoes the 'Lord, hear our prayer!' and 'Lord, graciously hear us' responses from *Common Worship* and BCP 2004.

Our aim was to create a prayer time that the children could grow into, not out of. We were looking for a time of prayer that would make connections with the intercessions that the children might take part in on an average Sunday morning at our church – and, indeed, in other churches throughout the world. Over time, we've appreciated the way in which this familiar prayer pattern reminds us first to look outwards to the world around us, before looking inwards and bringing to God the things and people that immediately matter to us. Using this familiar pattern of prayer has also meant that our children have felt confident in leading the Prayers for Other People for the whole church during all-age services. If your church follows a different pattern, you may wish to adapt the song accordingly.

At the centre of the Prayers for Other People is a second invitation for the children to imagine. The children are invited to imagine a person they'd like to pray for. They're then invited to see Jesus with that person: 'Does Jesus say anything? Does Jesus do anything?' In this short moment children are encouraged to see Jesus' presence in the world, particularly alongside those who need our prayers: a habit that might nourish them throughout life. Influenced by Ignatian forms of prayer, this moment also encourages children to understand prayer not simply as giving God a 'wish list' of things that need 'fixing', but about beginning to see Jesus' transforming presence in the situation. There is no invitation to share out loud with the group this moment of imagining: this is special time with God.

> " Praying . . . is equally a learning to look at the world as if with God's eyes. ROWAN WILLIAMS[14]
>
> When I pray for another person, I am praying for God to open my eyes so that I can see that person as God does, and then enter into the stream of love that God already directs toward that person. PHILIP YANCEY[13] "

Following this brief moment of imagining comes an invitation to use an object or body movement as a prayer. This Prayer Action gives children the opportunity to pray in ways completely beyond words. It underlines that our prayers don't need to be spoken out loud to be heard or seen by God: they don't even need to be thought in words.

> One of the most significant 'prayers' in the Bible – sparking off the great story of the exodus – is not spoken in words but is still heard by God. In Exodus 2.23–25, the Israelite slaves 'groan' in pain and suffering. There is no reference to this groan being addressed to God: indeed, the Israelites have not met God yet. Nevertheless, 'Out of their slavery their cry of help rose up to God. God heard their groaning, and God remembered his covenant with Abraham, Isaac, and Jacob. God looked upon the Israelites, and God took notice of them.'

One way we can move beyond the limitations of words in our prayers is through using actions or objects. Diddy Disciples offers groups a wide range of Prayer Actions to choose from. Alongside opportunities which can help make traditional symbols (such as candles or water) meaningful to young children, there are opportunities for children to use everyday objects (poppies, blossom, Christmas lights) to enrich their prayer life. The Bible also provides a rich source of imagery for the Prayer Actions, as is indicated throughout the material. For example, the imagery of the blossoming crocus in Isaiah 35.1–2 and of our lives as a 'watered garden' in Jeremiah 31.12 has inspired our action of placing flowers in a garden and offering them to God as prayers for other people.

The Prayer Action is the longest part of Prayers for Other People, and large groups, or groups limited by time, will need to take this into account when choosing from the various Prayer Actions: some take more time than others.

> Their life shall become like a watered garden . . . JEREMIAH 31.12
>
> The wilderness and the dry land shall be glad,
> the desert shall rejoice and blossom;
> like the crocus it shall blossom abundantly,
> and rejoice with joy and singing. ISAIAH 35.1–2

> It is obvious that spirituality at any age, but most of all in childhood, exists on both verbal and non-verbal planes. It can be so tempting to value verbal over non-verbal, or non-verbal only to the extent that we hear it put into words. One consequence of this temptation is that the spiritual life of less verbal (often younger) children is overlooked and that their journey begins with the negative lesson that a central core of their spiritual engagement is both invisible to others and presumably of lesser value. REBECCA NYE[16]

We end our Prayers for Other People with a final verse of the 'Jesus, hear our prayer!' song, which gathers up the group's prayers before God. This final step can also provide an opportunity for us to focus on what has been created during the Prayer Action, to appreciate its beauty, and to see it offered up to God as a shared prayer. In this moment, we can see 'my' prayer become 'our' prayer.

Tip

At St Peter's, Walworth, we treasure these Prayer Actions as a time when all those of whatever age in our varied group – parents and carers as well as babies and school-age children – are equal before God, expressing themselves in the same way. We've found the Prayer Actions to be as meaningful to the adults as to the children and would encourage your group to give everyone who is present, not just the children, the opportunity to pray with whatever object or action you choose.

Option 2 is designed for groups from churches which don't use a formal prayer pattern and tend to pray using words. While the children can pray for anything they wish, we would still encourage the leaders to gently draw the children beyond prayers only for themselves and those close to them, to pray for other people and all creation also.

> Mission then is less about the transportation of God from one place to another and more about the identification of a God who is already there . . . You see God where others don't. And then you point him out. So the issue isn't so much taking Jesus to people who don't have him, but going to a place and pointing out to the people the creative, life-giving God who is already present in their midst. ROB BELL[17]

Thank You, God!

> Giving thanks to God the Father at all times and for everything in the name of our Lord Jesus Christ. EPHESIANS 5.20

Thank You, God encourages the children to focus on those times when they've been part of sharing God's love. Love comes from God and without God we cannot love (1 John 4.7–12). This Building Block gives children the opportunity to say 'thank you' to God for the times they've been part of sharing that love. Although thanking God in this way doesn't specifically reflect any part of a usual *Common Worship* or BCP 2004 service, we believe that forming the habit of looking back on our week in God's presence and learning to see ourselves and our actions through God's eyes is an important part of Christian discipleship, one that should be encouraged from the very earliest age.

We believe it's just as important to say 'thank you' for when we have been part of sharing God's love as it is to say 'sorry' when we have not lived God's way of love. This time of review – leading to showing thanks or sorrow to God – is by no means an innovation and has been particularly important within Ignatian approaches to prayer for centuries.

Option 1 is designed for groups that include younger children. Option 2 is designed for older children and also introduces the important concept that 'when we love all those around us, it's the same as loving Jesus'.

> Truly I tell you, whatever you did for one of the least of these brothers and sisters of mine, you did for me. MATTHEW 25.40

"
Did I offer peace today? Did I bring a smile to someone's face? Did I say words of healing? Did I let go of my anger and resentment? Did I forgive? Did I love? These are the real questions! I must trust that the little bit of love that I sow now will bear many fruits, here in this world and in the life to come. HENRI NOUWEN[18]
"

Creative Response

Diddy Disciples aims to encourage personal engagement and a personal response from the very earliest age. Opening up space and time to give young children the opportunity to reflect on the storytelling for themselves can be an important part of doing this. Alongside the Prayer Building Blocks (see above), one way in which Diddy Disciples seeks to create this kind of space for children is through the time set aside for Creative Responses.

Tip

Imagination and creativity can be vital to our relationship with God. After all, we're made in the image of God the Maker.

Section 3 of each unit provides a wide range of starter ideas that aim to spark the children's imaginations as well as one or more 'print-and-go' options for each week. Drawing on these ideas and beyond, there are a myriad of ways in which young children might respond creatively and imaginatively to the biblical storytelling. Ensuring that this time of Creative Response is set aside for the children to respond for themselves, however, can be more of a challenge. Over time, we've found the following rules of thumb helpful.

1 Encourage the children to make their own choices

Inviting children to make a choice encourages them to begin to take responsibility for their own responses and their own relationship with God. Learning to make choices is an important part of learning who 'I' am: what my interests and gifts are, as well as my questions, joys, hopes and fears.

You may find if your group contains mainly older children that you can simply provide a range of creative materials, encouraging the children to choose freely for themselves how to respond creatively. This may not be appropriate for all groups, however. Some young

children can be overwhelmed by too much choice, or may spend just a few seconds with a blank sheet of paper and pencils before disregarding it for the next thing that attracts their attention.

At St Peter's, Walworth, we've found that even some older pre-school children aren't used to holding a crayon or a pair of scissors, and haven't yet experienced using their own initiative to create something. We've found that beginning by offering the children two or three starting points to choose from helps to build their confidence in making choices and taking responsibility, as well as experience in exercising their imagination. Over time, we've found that the children become less and less reliant on our starting points and become wonderfully creative with the range of materials we provide, often mixing and matching resources from different tables and creating things we would never have dreamt of. These children then become wonderful role models of open creativity to any visitors or new children joining the group. We're often amazed at the range of different responses that are created during a session from the same choice of materials.

Tip

Offering choice doesn't have to mean lots more preparation for leaders: in fact, it can mean the opposite. At St Peter's, Walworth, we always leave at least one table which gives the children opportunity to respond creatively in whatever way they'd like. On this table, we tend to provide play dough (which always seems popular), plus different-coloured paper and drawing or painting media (see interesting media on p. 256). We actively encourage the children to respond however they wish.

Tip

As your group develops and the children grow in confidence, try providing only open-ended resources (paints, clay, play dough, collage materials (p. 255) and glue, recycling materials, Lego, Kapla blocks, etc.) for at least one week per unit. Some groups may find this works for them and gradually increase this approach to more weeks per unit. Every group is different, and it will be for you to find the right balance for your group. It helps to remember that the overall aim is for children to feel confident – indeed energized – when invited to respond however they'd like: the starter ideas are about building that confidence and sense of choice and personal responsibility.

2 Give the children space to develop their response as they wish

This is their response; not our response as leaders, nor their parents' or carers' response. This means it will almost certainly not look as we imagined it. Diddy Disciples deliberately offers very simple templates or other open-ended activities as starting points or ideas for the children to explore for themselves. Our hope is that in their hands these resources and initial ideas will be transformed into wholly unique and individual responses, according to the children's gifts, interests and abilities. For this reason, we never show the children an example of what a response 'should' look like, as this is likely to limit their creativity, but rather leave how they will develop the resources to their own imagination.

> Keep a space where God can let something totally new take place.
> HENRI NOUWEN[19]

3 Create space for 'bridge building'

If our aim is to build a people of God who naturally make connections between their relationship with God and their learning and home life, then we need to encourage children to do this from the earliest age. Throughout the Bible Storytelling and other Building Blocks we aim to model all sorts of ways of going about 'building bridges' between our life with God and our everyday lives (see p. 25). It's in this Creative Response time, however, that children can be really set free to embark on exploring bridge building independently and for themselves.

Some of the ideas suggested for each unit are specifically designed to encourage this kind of bridge building. For instance, puppet making will mean that the children can retell the stories for themselves at home. Exploring the weather or colours might resonate with the kinds of things the children talk about in nursery or school, and encourage them to make connections between that time and their time with God. In providing these ideas, however, it remains important to remember that this is about providing opportunities for the children to build their own bridges and make their own connections: this is their response and we should give them the space and time to develop it as they wish.

4 It's the act of responding that matters, not the final result

If a child finds herself caught up 'in the moment' watching glue drip off a glue stick or discovering that he can change the shape of paper with scissors, or learning that she has the power to create lots of things from one by knocking blocks over, we need to respect this as a time of wonder. If the child wishes to repeat this moment, then it's for us to encourage that (even if it means slipping extra paper under the child's picture to contain the glue, or making sure the child has a safe space to use the scissors, or an appropriate space to build up the bricks and then knock them down again). Whether the children 'complete' the activity that we'd imagined for them is not the point: the moment of wonder that they've found for themselves is priceless in itself. This can be a moment when the children find time to glory in the gifts God has given them, as well as an opportunity to process the story you've told together at a deeper level, making it their own. As so many others have said: it's the process, not the product that matters.

5 These responses are 'holy ground'

The Creative Response time is about giving the children space to open up their own conversations with God. As they explore expressing their feelings, emotions, ideas and reflections in ways beyond words, the responses they create can act as a bridge between their inner and outer worlds, making glimpses of their inner life visible. For this reason, we believe it's essential that every response is treated with respect and wonder, as 'holy ground' where the child has met with God.

We need to tread carefully here. On the one hand, these responses are intensely personal and private: they're conversations with God and not with us. On the other hand, some young children can be very keen to show an adult what they've created. To avoid sharing this moment of intimacy may send the wrong message. In these situations, we've found it helpful to treat any child's response as we would want a personal contribution of our own to be treated in a church setting, preparing ourselves to learn from this opportunity to see God's world from another perspective. Instead of responding with a 'Well done!' or 'Very good!', we respond with a 'Thank you for letting me see this' or another response we might offer adults who have opened themselves up to us and shared something about their journey with God.

Section 3 of each unit lays out options for:

A **Weekly starter ideas**, which relate directly to the Bible storytelling for that session and include a print-and-go option.
B **Sensory starter ideas** designed for sensory explorers, including babies, and which remain the same through the whole unit.
C **Unit starter ideas**, also designed to remain relevant throughout the whole unit. Keeping the same options available each week gives children the opportunity to deepen and develop their responses, while making preparation more manageable for leaders.

Tip for sensory explorers

At St Peter's, Walworth, we prepare the activities we've chosen for sensory explorers on a builder's mixing tray, then place the tray on the floor during the Creative Response time. These responses stay the same for every week of the unit. During the unit, we keep the responses in a designated drawer of our filing cabinet so they can be easily put on the builder's tray at the beginning of each session.

Background music

Over the years that we've held Diddy Disciples at St Peter's, Walworth, we've experimented with the use of background music during our time of Creative Response. At times we've found the presence of quiet music helpful; at other times we've preferred to remain without. The decision is largely informed by the particular dynamics of the group at the time. When we first began to include babies and toddlers along with their parents and carers, for instance, we found that background music helped to send a clear signal that the time for Creative Response was still very much part of our worship. Now that our group has grown (in both maturity and numbers), we find that we prefer to have no music playing in what feels like quite a small space.

Tip

It will be for your group to work out whether the presence of background music adds to or detracts from your worship. Whatever your decision, we suggest that the music is set to a background level and chosen to encourage a meditative, reflective atmosphere. At St Peter's, Walworth, we've found that worship songs, Taizé chants and classical music have all, at different times, enriched our worship together.

Sharing God's Peace

 Peace is a full-time vocation that includes each member of God's people.
HENRI NOUWEN[21]

For many churches, sharing God's Peace with each other in a 'sign of peace' (such as shaking hands) is an important part of the service. This Building Block gives young children the opportunity to experience the Peace in a smaller, more familiar group, where taking part by

" Now may the Lord of peace himself give you peace at all times in all ways. The Lord be with all of you. 2 THESSALONIANS 3.16

Greet one another with a kiss of love. Peace to all of you who are in Christ. 1 PETER 5.14 "

shaking hands or hugging each other (or whatever the custom of your church is) might feel less daunting.

Options 1 and 2 are designed for groups where a wide range of age groups, including babies and toddlers, are represented. At St Peter's, we let the children (who are engaged in their Creative Response) know when there's around two minutes to go before Sharing God's Peace will begin.

Two adults then stand one at either end of the peace cloth and begin singing and waving the cloth. This is a familiar signal to children of any age to finish what they're doing. We repeat the song as the children begin to gather around the cloth to join in with the gentle waving and singing. We've found that this is a calm but clear way to let the children know that our session is about to end. Once all the children are gathered, we ask them to let go of the cloth and one of the adults gathers it in. The leader then says the simple words, 'The peace of the Lord be always with you,' and a growing number of children and adults respond 'And also with you'. We then invite the children and adults to 'show each other a sign of peace' and lead them in shaking hands with each other, saying 'Peace be with you'. We like to use the same words and handshake that we use in our main communion service, so that the children are familiar with them when we worship together as a whole congregation and can join in actively.

Option 3 is designed for groups with children mostly over the age of three. This song gives children the opportunity to explore how peace starts with us as individuals: with our own hands, mouths and hearts.

Tip: Peace cloth

Groups that choose to use a peace cloth for the 'Sharing God's Peace' Building Block will need a long piece of blue fabric. The fabric needs to be long enough for all the adults and children to stand around it, and to allow each child to hold a section of the fabric with both hands. It helps to have an adult or older and experienced Diddy Disciple standing at each end. At St Peter's, Walworth, we found some sheer blue fabric at the local market. As it also looks like the night sky, we've used our peace cloth in the Advent and Christmas seasons. Bear in mind that your children's group might grow in numbers!

> " For this is what the LORD says: 'I will extend peace to her like a river, and the wealth of nations like a flooding stream . . .' ISAIAH 66.12, NIV "

Timing a Diddy Disciples session to coincide with a main Sunday service

At St Peter's, Walworth, it's important to us that all our groups – of all ages – are gathered and present ready to pray the Eucharistic Prayer and share communion together. To help us time our session to coincide with the adult worship upstairs, we ask an adult to tell us (1) when the sermon is starting and (2) when the sermon has ended. Over time, this has helped us to gauge how long we have left for the session. When the second signal comes, we let the children know that they have around two minutes more with their Creative Response. After those two minutes, we begin singing our Peace Song. Having shared the Peace, we join the adults, who are either in the process of sharing the Peace or singing the offertory hymn. We are then all present as a gathered church for the Eucharistic Prayer.

Taking God's Love into the World

This is designed as the final Building Block for groups that are not held during a communion service. We've found ending the session with the same song each week very helpful for our youngest children. Over time, they begin to recognize the signal that the session's coming to an end, while their familiarity with the song means they can participate fully and confidently in this time of 'sending out'. In nursery and reception at school, our sending out song has come to be 'This little light of mine'. Its promise to 'let it shine' reminds us that we don't just tell Bible stories to learn about God, but to let those stories shape the way we live. In this way, the song echoes the closing words of many church services where God sends us out 'to live and work to your praise and glory'. At various times we've experimented with other closing songs, but the children have always insisted on singing 'This little light' after any replacement. In the end, we've followed the children's lead, and it means that our sessions always finish with a sense of joy and celebration.

Including babies in mixed groups

Some suggestions from St Peter's, Walworth:

- We've found it helpful to clarify both to the parents or carers of babies, and to the older children, the different expectations we have for the various ages in the group. For instance, those who are crawling are free to wander within the circle until they're able to understand how to keep a circle. This includes taking objects from the focal table: we understand this as an attempt to join in. As we have a lot of children at the crawling and toddling stage during our Sunday morning worship, we've sectioned off the part of the room that our circle is in with chairs to help keep the idea of a circle as much as possible.

- We let those under two hold on to the imaginative aids for the whole session instead of collecting them in at the end of the Gathering Song.

- We keep simple sensory objects relevant to the story or unit ready to pass to particularly restless babies and for the handful of times when it might not be appropriate for roaming toddlers to take a focal object (e.g. during the storytelling on Remembrance Sunday). For example, we have available:

  - baby-safe mirrors for exploring facial expressions for the Jesus' Wonderful Love unit;

  - soft butterflies, caterpillars, and other soft animal toys for the God the Maker unit;

  - plastic bottles filled with water and glitter for stories from the Getting Ready for Baby Jesus (Advent) unit and Jesus, the Light of the World (Epiphany) unit;

  - a variety of board books that resonate with the content of the various units.

- When we're using streamers, or singing a particularly active song, we ask our school-age children to gather together on one side of the room, creating space for the babies to join in safely on the other side. We then reform our usual circle at the end of the song.

- We've found it helpful to recognize that it's completely natural for babies and toddlers to dip in and out of the session, as they would in any other group. Many of our parents and carers have expressed surprise that their two-year-old will talk about a story or sing a song from the session that they seemed to show no interest in at all at the time. It can be helpful to remember that just because babies and toddlers are not sitting still or 'paying attention' in the way an older child might, this does not mean that they're not engaging or feeling part of the experience.

DIDDY DISCIPLES STORYTELLING WITH BABIES AND TODDLERS

At St Peter's, Walworth, we've tended to hold mixed groups for babies, toddlers and young school-age children because we've found that both the babies and the older children gain so much from the experience (see pp. 3–4). If your group is made up only of babies and toddlers under two and a half, however, you may wish to adapt the sessions accordingly. For a group like this, I would build a simple baby singing session as follows. However, feel free to use any of the material to complement your session as it stands.

Welcome

→ **See Guide, p. 218.**

Welcome your group.

Let's start by going round the circle
and saying our name out loud.
My name's _____.

Go round the circle so that every adult and child has the chance to say his or her name (and introduce any dolls, teddies or toys). If any of the children don't want to say their name or aren't able to, you (or a parent or carer) could say it for them and wave.

Welcome Song: Option 1

→ **Song: 'The Diddy Disciples welcome song'. Words © Sharon Moughtin-Mumby**
→ **Tune: 'Glory, glory, alleluia!' (traditional). For the music see p. 259, or for a taster see the Diddy Disciples website**

Go around the circle the same way as above. See if each of you can remember the others' names and insert them into the song.

Welcome *Name 1* to *St Peter's**
Welcome *Name 2* to *St Peter's**
Welcome *Name 3* to *St Peter's**
You are welcome in the name of the Lord!

* Insert the name of your church or children's group, or sing 'our worship'.

Bible Storytelling

> ### Tip
>
> Choose a suitable number of songs from the material for the unit you've chosen. Aim to move through these songs in the same order each week. Punctuate the singing with getting ready for the next song by using the visual aids or imaginative aids suggested. Keeping the songs the same each week will give the children (and adults) plenty of time to familiarize themselves with the songs and begin to join in actively. You may like to make simple song sheets for parents for each unit, but most of the songs provided here simply repeat the first line, making it easy to join in.

Thank You, God

→ Song: 'My hands were made for love'. Words © Sharon Moughtin-Mumby
→ Tune: 'Hickory, dickory, dock' (traditional). For the music, see p. 262, or for a taster see the Diddy Disciples website.

If you'd like to include a time of prayer to follow the Bible Storytelling, you may find the following material from the 'Thank You, God' Building Block helpful. Having said this, we've found that the 'Sorry song' (p. 37) and the 'Jesus, hear our prayer!' song (p. 44) are the parts of Diddy Disciples that our youngest babies engage with most.

Invite the children to sit in a circle for a moment of quiet.

It's time to remember all the things we've done this week.
It's time to say 'thank you' to God
for when we've been part of showing God's love.

Let's wiggle our fingers!
I wonder when you've shown love
with your hands this week?

Wiggle fingers as you sing.
My hands were made for love!
My hands were made for love!
Thank you for the love they've shown.
My hands were made for love!

Let's wiggle our feet!
I wonder when you've shown love
with your feet this week?

Wiggle feet as you sing.
My feet were made for love!
My feet were made for love!
Thank you for the love they've shown.
My feet were made for love!

Let's put our hands gently on our neck.
Let's sing 'Ahhh!'
Ahhhhh!
Can you feel your throat vibrating and dancing?
I wonder when you've shown love
with your voice this week?

Hold neck and feel your voice 'dancing' as you sing.
My voice was made for love!
My voice was made for love!
Thank you for the love it's shown.
My voice was made for love!

Feast

Eat, drink and sit together as a sign of what God's kingdom looks like (Luke 14.15–24). This may be a simple snack (for instance, a drink and pieces of fruit or a biscuit). Aim to provide for everyone, including adults. You may instead prefer to hold your feast after your closing song.

Closing song

→ Song: 'I've got peace like a river' (traditional)
→ Tune: Traditional. For a taster, see the Diddy Disciples website.
→ See Guide, p. 231.

Either: invite the children each to hold a small section of the peace cloth (p. 231), helped by adults, and to raise and lower it so it 'flows' like a river as you sing.

Or: Invite the children to lie beneath the peace cloth (p. 231) as two adults wave it over their heads.

Or: If you don't have a peace cloth, invite the group to join in raising and lowering their hands like the waters of a flowing river as you sing.

I've got peace like a river,
I've got peace like a river,
I've got peace like a river in my soul.
I've got peace like a river,
I've got peace like a river,
I've got peace like a river in my soul.

Jesus' Wonderful Love: storytelling with babies and toddlers

Introducing the Unit

Jesus loved to tell stories!
Lots of Jesus' stories are about how much God loves us.
Let's tell some of Jesus' stories together.

Choose however many songs you like from the following material.

Song 1: 'The Good Shepherd song'

→ John 10.11–15
→ Tune: 'Mary had a little lamb' (traditional). Words © Sharon Moughtin-Mumby. For the music see p. 65, or for a taster, see the Diddy Disciples website. Alternatively, use the tune for 'Have you seen the muffin man?'

Give out sheep (either toy sheep, or laminated/card sheep) to the children. Encourage them to move the sheep around on the floor.

Jesus told a story about some sheep!

We are a-ll little sheep, *Move sheep around*
little sheep, little sheep!
We are a-ll little sheep!
Baa, baa! Bleat! Baa, baa!

Hold your hands out like claws, ready to pounce on the word 'wolf'.
Look! Here comes a big, bad wolf, *Pounce*
a big, bad wolf, *Pounce* **a big, bad wolf!** *Pounce*
Look! Here comes a big, bad wolf! *Pounce*
Baa, baa! Bleat! Baa, baa! *Sounding scared*

Move the sheep around the floor, or run your fingers around to show the sheep running away as you sing.
[The] sheep, they ran and ran and ran,
ran and ran, ran and ran!
[The] sheep, they ran and ran and ran!
Baa, baa! Bleat! Baa, baa!

Oh dear! Poor sheep!
Jesus said, 'Then there were some different sheep.'
These sheep had a GOOD shepherd! *Thumbs up*
Shall we see what happens to these sheep?

We are a-ll little sheep, *Move sheep around*
little sheep, little sheep!
We are a-ll little sheep!
Baa, baa! Bleat! Baa, baa!

Hold your hands out like claws, ready to pounce on the word 'wolf'.
Look! Here comes a big, bad wolf, *Pounce*
a big, bad wolf, *Pounce* **a big, bad wolf!** *Pounce*
Look! Here comes a big, bad wolf! *Pounce*
Baa, baa! Bleat! Baa, baa! *Sounding scared.*

Make the Good Shepherd from two fingers standing on the floor like a person. Show the shepherd standing firm by lifting your fingers slightly and putting them down again as you sing.
The Good Shepherd, he did not run!
did not run, did not run!
The Good Shepherd, he did not run!
Baa, baa! Bleat! Baa, baa!

Show the wolf with your downturned hand running all over you (a bit like a spider) as you sing.
The wo-lf ran and ran and ran,
ran and ran, ran and ran!
The wo-lf ran and ran and ran!
Baa, baa! Bleat! Baa, baa!

You may like to end with the following:
Jesus says, 'I am the Good Shepherd.'
We're Jesus' little sheep.
Jesus loves us and will never leave us.
Let's be Jesus.
Let's sing to each other, 'I will never, never leave'.
Instead of singing our 'baas' at the end,
Let's sing 'thank you, thank you, Jesus'.

I will never, never leave! *Shake head gently*
Never leave! Never leave!
I will never, never leave! *Shake head gently*
Thank you, thank you, Jesus!

Song 2: 'The lost sheep song'

→ Luke 15.3–7
→ **Tune: 'Little Bo Peep' (traditional). Words © Sharon Moughtin-Mumby. See the music on p. 54, or for a taster, see the Diddy Disciples website.**

In our song, some of the first sheep ran off!
Jesus told a story about a little Lost Sheep!
Shall we be the Good Shepherd
and go on a sheep hunt for the Lost Sheep?
Let's pick up our crook. *Mime picking up an imaginary crook*
A crook is like a stick to hook the sheep and bring them back.
Demonstrate hooking a sheep with your crook.

You may like to use toy animals or pictures as props to help you tell the story as suggested below. If your group doesn't have the animals used in the story, you could adapt the material with your own ideas.

Searching and searching everywhere, *Hand sheltering eyes, looking*
ready with my shepherd's crook. *Get ready to hook a sheep*
What is that moving over there? *Point in surprise to a place in the circle*
Let's tiptoe and take a look!
Tiptoe on the spot, or make two fingers into a 'shepherd' and tiptoe with them on the floor.
Spoken in rhythm: **tiptoe, tiptoe, tiptoe . . .** *Tiptoe on the spot*

I can see . . . *Hand sheltering eyes*
A snake! *Pull a toy snake, or a picture of a snake, out of your bag*
Tssss!

That's not my sheep! *Shake head and look surprised*
We need to keep on looking . . .

Searching and searching everywhere, *Hand sheltering eyes, looking*
ready with my shepherd's crook. *Get ready to hook a sheep*
What is that moving over there? *Point in surprise to a place in the circle*
Let's tiptoe and take a look!
Tiptoe on the spot or make two fingers into a 'shepherd' and tiptoe with them on the floor.
Spoken in rhythm: **tiptoe, tiptoe, tiptoe . . .** *Tiptoe on the spot*

I can see . . . *Hand sheltering eyes*
A _____!

Repeat with different animals that a shepherd might encounter when searching for a sheep: a bear, a lion, an owl, a crocodile, etc.
Make the animal's sound.

That's not my sheep! *Shake head and look surprised/scared*
We need to keep on looking . . .

The last time you do this, find the sheep!
I can see . . . *Hand sheltering eyes*
the Lost Sheep!
We've found the Lost Sheep!
Sometimes we feel lost.
When we're lost, God comes looking for us
like we looked for the sheep.
And God is always very excited to find us!

Song 3: 'The lost coin song'

→ Luke 15.8–10
→ Tune: 'Oh dear! What can the matter be?' (traditional). Words © Sharon Moughtin-Mumby. For the music see p. 58, or for a taster, see the Diddy Disciples website.

Jesus told another story about lost things.

Show a doll or teddy and a large coin shape.

Doll's/teddy's name has lots of coins like this.
But she's lost a coin!
Let's help her find her coin!

'Hide' a large card coin under a cushion in the centre of the circle.

Let's sing with *Doll's/teddy's name* and help her look.

Lead the parents, babies and toddlers in an appropriate 'looking around' action as you sing.
Oh dear! Where can my coin be?
Oh dear! Where can my coin be?
Oh dear! Where can my coin be?
I'm turning my house upside down! *Find the coin*

As you sing 'upside down', you could encourage the children to lift up the cushion and find the coin. Don't worry if the toddlers can't wait! Let them find the coin at any point, but pretend yourself not to see it until the end of the verse.

Let's sing 'Hooray! Hooray!' with *Doll's/teddy's name*
and dance and wave our hands in the air.
Hooray! Hooray! I did it! I did it!
Hooray! Hooray! I did it! I did it!
Hooray! Hooray! I did it! I did it!
Hooray! Hooray! Hooray!

Let's tell the story again! *Hide coin under cushion*
Doll's/teddy's name has lost her coin!
Let's sing our song and help her look for it!

Lead the parents, babies and toddlers in an appropriate 'looking around' action as you sing.
Oh dear! Where can my coin be?
Oh dear! Where can my coin be?
Oh dear! Where can my coin be?
I'm turning my house upside down! *Find the coin*

To end:
Hooray! We've found the Lost Coin!

Sometimes we feel lost.
When we're lost, God comes looking for us
like we looked for the coin.
When God finds us, God says 'Hooray!'

Let's stand up tall and be God!
Let's sing 'Hooray! Hooray! I did it! I did it!' and dance and wave our hands.

Hooray! Hooray! I did it! I did it! *Waving hands throughout*
Hooray! Hooray! I did it! I did it!
Hooray! Hooray! I did it! I did it!
Hooray! Hooray! Hooray!

Song 4: 'Look how much Jesus loves me!'

→ **Tune: 'Here we go Looby Loo' (traditional). Words © Sharon Moughtin-Mumby. For the music see p. 33, or for a taster see the Diddy Disciples website.**

> *If appropriate for the age group:*
> Jesus loves us!
> Let's make our body into the biggest shape we can!
> Even bigger!
> 'Look how much Jesus loves me!'

Let's sing our 'Higher than the stars' song.

You may find it helpful to pause or interrupt singing as indicated each time to remind the children 'big shape!' If this action isn't appropriate for your age group, you could stretch your arms out as wide as possible.

Higher than the stars! *Reach up high with 'twinkle' hands*
Deeper than the sea! *Crouch down low showing rippling waters*
Wider than the sky! . . . *Reach out wide and upwards*
Spoken: Big shape!
Look how much Jesus loves me!

If appropriate for your group, you may also wish to explore different feelings with this song, as exemplified here. Alternatively, you may simply wish to simply sing the refrain 'Higher than the stars . . .' as above.

Let's all be cross! Can you show me cross?

Lead the children and parents in singing along, with their chosen facial expression and action.
When I'm feeling cross, *Cross action and face*
When I'm feeling cross, *Cross action and face*
When I'm feeling cross . . . *Cross action and face*
Spoken: Big shape!
look how much Jesus loves me!

Repeat for different feelings. For instance:
When I'm feeling happy . . .
When I'm feeling sad . . .

When I'm feeling surprised . . .
When I'm feeling scared . . .
When I'm feeling excited . . .
When I'm feeling poorly . . .

You may like to repeat the 'Higher than the stars' refrain after each verse or after every couple of verses.

You may like to end with:
So many different feelings!
Yawn I'm feeling tired after all that. Are you?
Can you show me tired?
Let's all go to sleep and sing again.
This time at the end we won't make our 'big shape'.
Let's fall fast asleep instead . . .

When I'm feeling tired,
When I'm feeling tired,
When I'm feeling tired . . .
look how much Jesus loves me! *Yawn*

Sing more reflectively while still miming falling asleep. Slow down towards the end as if going to sleep at night.
Higher than the stars!
Deeper than the sea!
Wider than the sky! . . .
Look how much Jesus loves me!

End with a moment of sleepy silence.

God the Maker: storytelling with babies and toddlers

Introducing the Unit

At the moment, we're telling stories
about God the Maker who made the whole world!

Choose however many songs you like from the following material. You may like to create two units from the material – one of them focusing on Harvest and the other on creation more generally – holding each of them over six weeks.

Song 1: 'And it was good!'

→ Genesis 1.1—2.3
→ Tune: 'Here we go round the mulberry bush' (traditional). Words © Sharon Moughtin-Mumby. For the music see p. 104, or for a taster, see the Diddy Disciples website. For tips on teaching songs for the first time, see p. 215.

The song below is based on the song from week 1 of the God the Maker unit, which tells the Genesis 1 story of God the Maker making the world in seven days. Here it's adapted for very young children, focusing on day six and the creation of animals. Your group may prefer to sing the original version instead (see p. 104).

Let's sing our story
about the day God made the animals.

For each verse, you might like to pull an animal out of a bag, asking the toddlers for an action for each animal. A later song will focus on farm animals, so you might like to keep to wild or zoo animals for this song. However, encourage the children to choose which animals they'd like to sing about.

'Let there be elephants!' And there were elephants!
There were elephants! There were elephants!
'Let there be elephants!' And there were elephants!
[And] it was good! *Thumbs up action*

'**Let there be tigers!' And there were tigers!**
There were tigers! There were tigers!
'**Let there be tigers!' And there were tigers!**
[And] it was good! *Thumbs up action*

'**Let there be crocodiles!' There were crocodiles!**
There were crocodiles! There were crocodiles!
'**Let there be crocodiles!' There were crocodiles!**
[And] it was good! *Thumbs up action*

Continue for as many verses as you like.

To end, sing about the creation of people, who are also part of day six in Genesis 1. If you're pulling animals out of a bag for this song, you could use a child-safe mirror for the children to see themselves in, or 'small world' people (e.g. those from Happyland or Fisher Price, or knitted figures).

'**Let there be people!' And there were people!**
There were people! There were people!
'**Let there be people!' And there were people!**
[And] it was good! *Thumbs up action*

But wait: this time it wasn't good.
God looked at people and saw that it was VERY good.
Let's sing the end again, but this time let's sing
(sing) 'And it was very good!' *Thumbs up even higher*
[And] it was VERY good! *Thumbs up even higher*

You might like to end by resting, inviting the babies and toddlers to go to sleep on the floor.

Time to rest now. Ssssh! Ssssh!
Ssssh! Ssssh! Ssssh! Ssssh!
Time to rest now. Ssssh! Ssssh!
And it was VERY GOOD! *Thumbs up above head action*

Song 2: 'Little hands, little hands'

→ **Genesis 1.27–31**
→ **Tune: 'Peter Pointer'. Words © Sharon Moughtin-Mumby. For a taster, see the Diddy Disciples website. For tips on teaching songs for the first time, see p. 215.**

Lit-tle hands, lit-tle hands, what can you do? I can clap! I can clap! Can you clap too?

God the Maker made people and they were VERY GOOD!
Look at your body!
Look at your own hands, arms and legs.

It's amazing!
Let's sing a song to say 'thank you' to God the Maker
for our amazing body!

Little hands, little hands, *Wave hands*
what can you do?
I can clap! I can clap! *Clap on the word 'clap'*
Can you clap too?

Little eyes, little eyes, *Point to eyes*
what can you do?
I can blink! I can blink! *Blink on the word 'blink'*
Can you blink too?

Little nose, little nose, *Point to nose*
what can you do?
I can *Atchoo!* **I can** *Atchoo!*
Can you *Atchoo!* **too?**

Little mouth, little mouth, *Point to mouth*
what can you do?
I can *blow a raspberry*, **I can** *blow a raspberry*
Can you *blow a raspberry* **too?**

Stand up or wiggle feet in front of you.
If more appropriate, use 'stamp' or 'wiggle'.
Little feet, little feet, *Point to feet*
what can you do?
I can jump! I can jump! *Jump on the word 'jump'*
Can you jump too?

Song 3: 'Everything in all the world sings "Alleluia!"'

→ **Psalm 148**
→ **Tune: 'Old Macdonald had a farm' (traditional). Words © Sharon Moughtin-Mumby. For the music, see p. 112, or for a taster, see the Diddy Disciples website. For tips on teaching songs for the first time, see p. 215.**

God the Maker made us!
And God made all the animals!
Let's sing about how
everything in all the world sings 'thank you' to God,
with a special 'thank you' word:
'Alleluia!', 'Praise God!' *Arms raised in 'V' shape*

Choose animals as you would for 'Old Macdonald had a farm'. For each verse, you might like to pull an animal out of a bag then ask the toddlers for a sound and action for each animal. If you focused on wild or zoo animals in the first song, you may like to focus on farm animals here. However, encourage the children to choose which animals they'd like to sing about. You may like to end with 'Children always love to sing Alleluia!', choosing a noise to show how your babies and toddlers sing 'Alleluia!', e.g. 'Ba! Ba!' or Clap! Clap! Or by blowing a raspberry, etc. You might like to use toy animals for this song, or keep to actions.

Everything in all the world *Circle action* **sings 'Alleluia!'** *Arms raised in 'V' shape*
[The] *horses* **always love to sing 'Alleluia!'** *Arms raised in 'V' shape*
With a ____! ____**! here!** *Add the children's sound and action*
And a ____! ____**! there!**
Here a ____! There a ____!
Everywhere a ____! ____**!**
Everything in all the world *Circle* **sings 'Alleluia!'** *Arms raised in 'V' shape*

Song 4: 'It's raining, it's raining!'

→ **Tune: 'A-tisket, a-tasket' (traditional). Words © Sharon Moughtin-Mumby. For the music see p. 85, or for a taster see the Diddy Disciples website. For tips on teaching songs for the first time, see p. 215.**

God the Maker made the weather!
Let's thank God for every kind of weather.

If you have imaginative aids (see p. 219), give these out and encourage the children to explore movements for the different kinds of weather. You might like to pull different weather symbols out of a bag for each verse. Introduce each verse by inviting the children (or their parents or carers) to show the kind of weather mentioned with their imaginative aids, hands or bodies.

Let's start off by imagining it's raining outside!
Can you show me rain?

Continue with the action as you sing:
It's *raining*, **it's** *raining*.
Outside it is *raining*.

God the Maker made the world.
Thank you, God the Maker!

Now let's imagine it's sunny outside!
Can you show me sunny?

Continue with the action as you sing:
It's *sunny*, it's *sunny*.
Outside it is *sunny*.
God the Maker made the world.
Thank you, God the Maker!

Look! I can see a rainbow!
Can you show me a rainbow!
Let's sing 'a rainbow, a rainbow!
Outside there's a rainbow!'

Continue with the action as you sing:
A rainbow, a rainbow.
Outside there's a rainbow.
God the Maker made the world.
Thank you, God the Maker!

Oh my goodness, now there's thunder!
Can you show me thunder with your feet?
And lightning! Can you show me lightning?
It's stormy!

Continue with the action as you sing:
It's *stormy*, it's *stormy*.
Outside it is *stormy*.
God the Maker made the world.
Thank you, God the Maker!

And now listen. *Hand over your ear*
Lead the children in blowing.
Can you hear that?
It's windy outside! Can you show me wind?

Continue with the action as you sing:
It's *windy*, it's *windy*.
Outside it is *windy*.
God the Maker made the world.
Thank you, God the Maker!

> *If appropriate:*
>
> Last of all, what's the real weather like today?
> Can anyone tell me?
> Today, it's _____.
> Can you show me _____?
> Let's sing one more time.
> Let's thank God the Maker for today's weather.
>
> *Continue with the action as you sing:*
> **It's _____, it's _____.**
> **Outside it is _____.**
> **God the Maker made the world.**
> **Thank you, God the Maker!**

Song 5: 'On the Sea of Galilee'

→ The Calming of the Storm, Luke 8.22–25 (also Matthew 8.23–27 and Mark 4.35–41)
→ Tune: 'The big ship sails on the Ally, Ally-O' (traditional). Words © Sharon Moughtin-Mumby. For the music see p. 115, or for a taster see the Diddy Disciples website. For tips on teaching songs for the first time, see p. 215.

God the Maker
made all the different kinds of weather!
Let's tell the story
of when Jesus stopped the storm!
And Jesus' friends knew that he was God the Maker.

Lead the group in a 'Row, row, row your boat' kind of action as you sing to the tune of 'The big ship sails on the Ally, Ally-O'.
[Let's] row, row, row on the Sea of Galilee,
the Sea of Galilee, the Sea of Galilee!
[Let's] row, row, row on the Sea of Galilee,
on the Sea of Galilee!

But look! *Point in shock*
There's a storm coming!

And the wind goes 'Whoosh!' *Fling arms outwards*
and the waves go 'Crash!', *Waves crashing action*
the waves go 'Crash!', the waves go 'Crash!'
And the wind goes 'Whoosh!' *Fling arms outwards*
And the waves go 'Crash!' *Waves crashing action*
on the Sea of Galilee!

Help! Where's Jesus?
Lead the group in looking around with hand shielding eyes.

Look! *Point* Jesus is sleeping *Sleeping action*
at the bottom of the boat!

Sleeping action throughout.
Jesus is sleeping at the bottom of the boat,
the bottom of the boat, the bottom of the boat!
Jesus is sleeping at the bottom of the boat,
on the Sea of Galilee!

And the wind goes 'Whoosh!' *Fling arms outwards*
and the waves go 'Crash!', *Waves crashing action*
the waves go 'Crash!', the waves go 'Crash!'
And the wind goes 'Whoosh!' *Fling arms outwards*
and the waves go 'Crash!' *Waves crashing action*
on the Sea of Galilee!

Let's wave our hands in the air to show we're scared!
'Come on Jesus! Help! Wake up!
'Help! Wake up! Help! Wake up!
'Come on Jesus! Help! Wake up!'
on the Sea of Galilee!

And the wind goes 'Whoosh!' *Fling arms outwards*
and the waves go 'Crash!', *Waves crashing action*
the waves go 'Crash!', the waves go 'Crash!'
And the wind goes 'Whoosh!' *Fling arms outwards*
and the waves go 'Crash!' *Waves crashing action*
on the Sea of Galilee!

Jesus says, 'Be calm! *Palms outwards* **Be still!'** *Palms downwards*
'Be calm! *Palms outwards* **Be still!'** *Palms downwards*

'**Be calm!** *Palms outwards* **Be still!**' *Palms downwards*

Jesus says, '**Be calm!** *Palms outwards* **Be still!**' *Palms downwards*

on the Sea of Galilee!

And the winds are calm, *Palms outwards*

and the waves are still, *Palms downwards*

the waves are still, the waves are still! *Palms downwards*

And the winds are calm, *Palms outwards*

and the waves are still, *Palms downwards*

on the Sea of Galilee!

That was the day that Jesus' friends

knew that Jesus was God the Maker!

> *This optional ending can be lovely to do even with the smallest babies and their parents or carers.*

Do you ever feel a bit stormy?

Sometimes, it can feel like there's a storm inside us.

Hands on stomach.

It can feel a bit scary.

Next time you feel stormy inside,

maybe you could ask Jesus to say 'Be calm! Be still!'

Let's sing about the storms we can sometimes feel inside ourselves.

Instead of 'on the Sea of Galilee',

let's sing 'inside me'. *Both hands on stomach*

And the wind goes 'Whoosh!' *Fling arms outwards*

and the waves go 'Crash!', *Waves crashing action*

the waves go 'Crash!', the waves go 'Crash!'

And the wind goes 'Whoosh!' *Fling arms outwards*

and the waves go 'Crash!' *Waves crashing action*

inside me. *Both hands on stomach*

Now let's imagine Jesus there,

calming the storm inside us.

Lead the children in singing.

Jesus says, '**Be calm!** *Palms outwards* **Be still!**' *Palms downwards*

'**Be calm!** *Palms outwards* **Be still!**' *Palms downwards*

'**Be calm!** *Palms outwards* **Be still!**' *Palms downwards*

Jesus says, '**Be calm!** *Palms outwards* **Be still!**' *Palms downwards*

inside me. *Both hands on stomach*

And now let's imagine our storm calming inside us. Ssssh!

And the winds are calm, *Palms outwards*

and the waves are still, *Palms downwards*

the waves are still, the waves are still! *Palms downwards*

And the winds are calm, *Palms outwards*

and the waves are still, *Palms downwards*

inside me. *Both hands on stomach*

Song 6: 'This is the way we sow the seed'

→ **Tune: 'Here we go round the mulberry bush' (traditional). Words © Sharon Moughtin-Mumby. For the music, see p. 104, or for a taster see the Diddy Disciples website. For tips on teaching songs for the first time, see p. 215.**

Show some bread.

God the Maker made the world!

God helps everything around us to grow!

Let's sing a song about how we grow

the wheat to make our bread.
Let's remember to say 'thank you' to God the Maker for our bread.

Choose an action for saying 'thank you'. It could be folding your hands as if for prayer, holding them up in an 'Alleluia' sign, or the Makaton 'thank you'.

This is the way we sow the seed, *Sowing action*
sow the seed, sow the seed.
This is the way we sow the seed.
Thank you, God the Maker! *Thank you sign*

Curl up in a ball and grow up like the seed, or make your fist into a seed then open it out and let it grow upwards as you sing.
This is the way the wheat seed grows,
the wheat seed grows, the wheat seed grows.
This is the way the wheat seed grows.
Thank you, God the Maker! *Thank you sign*

It's harvest time! Let's harvest our wheat!
Let's cut it down.

This is the way we cut the wheat, *Slashing action*
cut the wheat, cut the wheat.
This is the way we cut the wheat.
Thank you, God the Maker! *Thank you sign*

Now we need to grind our wheat into flour.

This is the way we grind the flour, *Grinding action*
grind the flour, grind the flour.
This is the way we grind the flour.
Thank you, God the Maker! *Thank you sign*

This is the way we make the bread, *Kneading action*
make the bread, make the bread.
This is the way we make the bread.
Thank you, God the Maker! *Thank you sign*

This is the way we say thank you to God, *Thank you sign*
thank you to God, thank you to God!
This is the way we say thank you to God!
Thank you, God the Maker! *Thank you sign*

If you have a 'feast' at the end of your session, you could share bread in the weeks you're singing this song.

In November, We Remember: storytelling with babies and toddlers

This is an optional unit for groups who wish to mark All Saints, Remembrance Sunday, All Souls and Christ the King. There is no tailored material for babies and toddlers. However, you may like to explore the storytelling for November laid out for mixed groups from p. 143. Alternatively, with this very young age group, you may prefer to continue with the theme of God the Maker (see pp. 239ff.).

Getting Ready for Baby Jesus: storytelling with babies and toddlers

Introducing the Unit

Before Christmas:
Christmas is coming!
Someone very special is coming at Christmas:
Baby Jesus!

On or after Christmas Day:
Baby Jesus is here!

Following Christmas, you may like to place a Baby Jesus doll in a manger/Moses basket/cardboard box in the centre of the circle. If the children like playing with Baby Jesus, you might like to have more than one doll ready!

Choose however many songs you like from the following material.

Song 1: 'Busy, busy, busy, getting ready for Christmas!'

→ Luke 1.78–79
→ Tune: 'What shall we do with the drunken sailor?' (traditional). Words © Sharon Moughtin-Mumby. For the music see p. 171, or for a taster see the Diddy Disciples website.

Before Christmas only:
Everyone's very busy getting ready!
Let's sing our 'Busy, busy, busy' song.
Let's start off by decorating our Christmas tree
while we sing.

Act out decorating a Christmas tree, or provide a little Christmas tree with wooden decorations for the children to hang as you sing.

Busy, busy, busy, getting ready for Christmas!
Busy, busy, busy, getting ready for Christmas!
Busy, busy, busy, getting ready for Christmas!
[The] Light of the World is dawning!
Hands together in front of your chest then reaching up and out, like the sun dawning. Toddlers might want to crouch down with the same action, then stand up as they bring their arms up and out.

Je-sus, Light of the World, *Sun dawning action*
Je-sus, Light of the World, *Sun dawning action*
Je-sus, Light of the World, is *Sun dawning action*
dawning in the darkness! *Sun dawning action*

Either invite the toddlers, parents or carers to make suggestions about what they've been doing that week at home, or choose from some of the following suggestions. For each activity sing 'Busy, busy, busy, getting ready for Christmas' with an appropriate action, followed by the 'Jesus, Light of the World' refrain:

- *opening Advent calendars*
- *making Christmas cards*
- *cleaning*
- *baking and cooking*
- *wrapping up presents*
- *dancing at parties*

To end:
Getting ready for Christmas can be very busy!
You might see your parents or carers at home running around
and getting very busy!
Let's look all busy and stressed like the adults!

Lead children in waving imaginative aids or arms around madly and running on the spot.

Let's sing 'Busy, busy, busy, getting ready for Christmas' again.
Continue 'very busy' action as you sing.
Busy, busy, busy, getting ready for Christmas!
Busy, busy, busy, getting ready for Christmas!
Busy, busy, busy, getting ready for Christmas!
[The] Light of the World is dawning!
Crouch down then arms up and out like sun dawning

Je-sus, Light of the World, *Sun dawning action*
Je-sus, Light of the World, *Sun dawning action*
Je-sus, Light of the World is *Sun dawning action*
dawning in the darkness! *Sun dawning action*

My goodness, that was busy!
In all the busyness,
let's remember to also have time for some quiet.
Let's imagine holding Baby Jesus in our arms
and singing to him quietly and gently.

Lead the children rocking a baby and singing quietly.
Je-sus, Light of the World,
Je-sus, Light of the World,
Je-sus, Light of the World, is
dawning in the darkness!

Let's get ready for Baby Jesus today
by singing our songs about when Baby Jesus was born.

After Christmas:
Let's sing our 'Busy, busy, busy' song,
But with new Christmas words!
We're going to sing:
'Joy! Joy! Joy! It's Christmas! Christmas!'
And instead of 'the Light of the World is dawning',
let's sing 'the Light of the World is shining!' *Twinkle hands*

Joy! Joy! Joy! It's Christmas! Christmas!
Joy! Joy! Joy! It's Christmas! Christmas!
Joy! Joy! Joy! It's Christmas! Christmas!
The Light of the World is shining! *Twinkle hands*

> *Either invite the toddlers, parents or carers to make suggestions about what they've been doing over Christmas, or choose from the following suggestions. For each activity sing 'Joy! Joy! Joy! It's Christmas! Christmas!' with an appropriate action, followed by the 'Jesus, Light of the World' refrain:*
>
> - *opening stockings*
> - *dancing at parties*
> - *unwrapping presents*
> - *eating lots of food*

Je-sus, Light of the World, *Sun dawning action*
Je-sus, Light of the World, *Sun dawning action*
Je-sus, Light of the World, is *Sun dawning action*
shining in the darkness! *Twinkle hands*

My goodness, that was busy!
In all the busyness,
let's remember to also have time for some quiet.

Let's imagine holding Baby Jesus in our arms
and singing to him quietly and gently.

Lead the children rocking a baby and singing quietly:
Je-sus, Light of the World, *Sun dawning action*
Je-sus, Light of the World, *Sun dawning action*
Je-sus, Light of the World, is *Sun dawning action*
shining in the darkness! *Twinkle hands*

Song 2: '"Yes!" said Mary'

→ **Luke 1.26–38**
→ **Tune: '"Pop!" goes the weasel' (traditional). Words © Sharon Moughtin-Mumby. For the music, see p. 196, or for a taster see the Diddy Disciples website.**

Show an angel.
Shall we sing the story together of when an angel went to Mary?

The actions of this song are designed to mirror a jack-in-the-box, with its lid closing and the puppet bursting out at the 'pop' moment. Encourage the children to stand with their hands stretched high, or hold your hands high over the babies. You could make angel wings (like butterfly wings) with your hands if you like.

An angel came to Ma-a-a-ry. *Hands come down from on high*
'You will have a baby! *Rock like a baby standing at normal height*
He will be the Son of God!' *Crouch down on the ground like tiny child*
'Yes!' sa-id Mary! *Jump up and shout 'Yes!'*

You may like to continue with the following, sung to the second verse of 'Pop goes the Weasel': 'Up and down the City Road . . .'

Angels singing in the sky, *Hands come down from on high*
came down to shepherds . . . *Wave arms like wings standing at normal height*
'Come and meet the new-born King!' *Beckoning gesture and point to king*
Up jumped the shepherds! *Jump up*

Song 3: 'My God is a topsy turvy God!'

→ **Luke 1.39–55**
→ **Tune: 'O, the grand old Duke of York' (traditional). Words © Sharon Moughtin-Mumby. For the music see p. 200, or for a taster see the Diddy Disciples website.**

Mary was so excited about her special baby!
She sang a beautiful song to say 'thank you' to God.
Let's sing Mary's song together!

O my God is very BIG! *Make the biggest shape you can*
And I am very small! *Make the smallest shape you can*
My God is a topsy turvy God, *Diddy Disciples 'New Start' sign (see p. 225)*
who turns things upside down!
And those who are low will be high! *Start low and end up high*
And those who are high will be low! *Start high and end up low*
My God is a topsy turvy God, *'New Start' sign*
who turns things upside down!

If you like, you could repeat the song, replacing 'high/low' with 'rich/poor' and 'strong/weak'.

Song 4: 'Little donkey'

→ **Luke 2.1–5**
→ **Tune and words: Eric Boswell © Warner Chappell Music, 1959**

Mary was going to have a baby.
But first she had to go on a journey to Bethlehem
with Joseph. *Show a donkey*

Let's sing our story about Mary and Joseph
travelling with a little donkey!

Sing Eric Boswell's 'Little donkey'. This song is under copyright but can be found in many hymn and carol books. If you have imaginative aids, you might like to distribute them for this song and encourage the children to use them as donkey's tails, long donkey's ears, ringing bells, etc. for different verses through the course of the song.

Song 5: 'The cow in the stable'

→ Luke 2.6–7
→ Tune: 'The wheels on the bus' (traditional). Words © Sharon Moughtin-Mumby. For a taster, see the Diddy Disciples website.

When Mary and Joseph arrived at Bethlehem,
There was nowhere for them to stay. *Shake head*
Just a stable full of animals!
Let's sing our song about the animals in the stable.

For each verse, you might like to pull a toy animal or picture of an animal out of a bag and give it to a child, or place it in or next to a 'stable'. You could use the animals that follow, or go wherever your imagination takes you.

**The cow in the stable goes 'Moo, moo, moo!
Moo, moo, moo! Moo, moo, moo!'
The cow in the stable goes 'Moo, moo, moo!'
all night long!**

**The sheep in the stable goes 'Baa, baa, baa!
Baa, baa, baa! Baa, baa, baa!'
The sheep in the stable goes 'Baa, baa, baa!'
all night long!**

**The fly in the stable goes 'Bzzz! Bzzz! Bzzz!
Bzzz! Bzzz! Bzzz! Bzzz! Bzzz! Bzzz!'
The fly in the stable goes 'Bzzz! Bzzz! Bzzz!'
all night long!**

**The goat in the stable goes 'Bleat! Bleat! Bleat!
Bleat! Bleat! Bleat! Bleat! Bleat! Bleat!'
The goat in the stable goes 'Bleat! Bleat! Bleat!'
all night long!**

**The mouse in the stable goes 'Squeak, squeak, squeak!
Squeak, squeak, squeak! Squeak, squeak, squeak!'
The mouse in the stable goes 'Squeak, squeak, squeak!'
all night long!**

And in that dark, dark stable,
Baby Jesus was born.

Show the children a Baby Jesus doll. Ask one of the children to hold the baby, or place him in something that represents a manger (this could be as simple as a cardboard box).

**The baby in the stable goes 'Waa! Waa! Waa!
Waa! Waa! Waa! Waa! Waa! Waa!'**

The baby in the stable goes 'Waa! Waa! Waa!'
all night long!

Song 6: 'Silent night'

→ Tune: Franz Xaver Gruber. Words: Joseph Mohr, translated by John Freeman Young

For groups that don't choose 'The cow in the stable' (Song 5):

And in a dark, dark stable,
Baby Jesus was born.

Show the children a Baby Jesus doll.
Ask one of the children to hold Baby Jesus, or place him in something that represents a manger (this could be as simple as a cardboard box).

For groups that do choose 'The cow in the stable':

But sssh! Baby Jesus has fallen asleep!
In all of that noise, there was also silence.
Silence and peace! Sssh!
Let's sing 'Silent night' together!

For this song you might like to use the peace cloth (see p. 231). Depending on the age of the children present, you could encourage them to each hold a small section of the cloth and raise and lower it over Baby Jesus (as for the Peace Song), or you might like to encourage the children to lie underneath the peace cloth along with Baby Jesus instead.

Silent night, holy night,
all is calm, all is bright
round yon virgin mother and child.
Holy infant so tender and mild,
sleep in heavenly peace,
sleep in heavenly peace.

Song 7: 'Twinkle, twinkle holy star'

→ Matthew 2.1–11, Luke 2.8–20
→ Tune: 'Twinkle, twinkle, little star' (traditional). Words © Sharon Moughtin-Mumby. For a taster see the Diddy Disciples website.

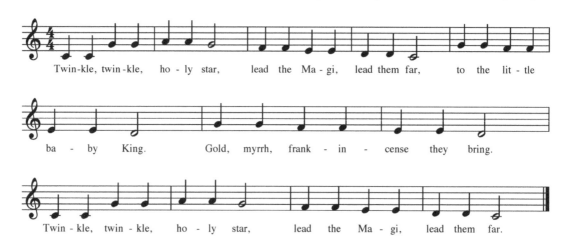

Twin-kle, twin-kle, ho-ly star, lead the Ma-gi, lead them far, to the lit-tle ba - by King. Gold, myrrh, frank - in - cense they bring. Twin - kle, twin - kle, ho - ly star, lead the Ma - gi, lead them far.

Show the children a star on a stick with rounded edges (make sure it is toddler friendly).

That night, there was a special star shining in the dark sky.
The star was telling everyone
that Baby Jesus, the new King, had been born!
Let's sing our song about the star together.

With such young children you may wish only to sing one verse, but I have included all three here.

Twinkle, twinkle, holy star, *Twinkle sign*
lead the Magi, lead them far, *Twinkle sign*

to the little baby King. *Crown on head or point to Jesus*
Gold, myrrh, frankincense they bring. *Count on fingers*
    Or: **1, 2, 3 presents they bring.** *Count on fingers*
Twinkle, twinkle, holy star, *Twinkle sign*
lead the Magi, lead them far. *Twinkle sign*

Dazzle, dazzle angels bright, *Wave arms like wings*
blaze God's love in darkest night!
'Glory in the highest!' sing! *Cupped hands round mouth*
Celebrate the baby King. *Crown on head or point to Jesus*
Dazzle, dazzle angels bright, *Wave arms like wings*
Blaze God's love in darkest night.

Flicker, flicker, lanterns, show *Swing lantern in hand*
wondering shepherds where to go.
Angels sang of peace on earth. *Wave arms like wings*
Shepherds speed to see Christ's birth. *Run on spot*
Flicker, flicker, lanterns, show *Swing lantern in hand*
wondering shepherds where to go. *Point to Jesus*

Song 8: 'Follow, follow, follow the star'

→ Matthew 2.1–11
→ Tune: 'Here we go round the mulberry bush'. Words © Sharon Moughtin-Mumby. For a taster see the Diddy Disciples website.

If your church or school follows the liturgical year, you may like to save this song until after Christmas for the Epiphany season, where it will also appear in Diddy Disciples: January to August.

    Groups that haven't sung 'Twinkle, Twinkle':
    That night, a special star shone in the dark sky,
    telling everyone a special baby was born!

    Hold up a large yellow star on a stick with rounded ends (check it's toddler friendly).

Some clever people, (*If you like:* the Magi/three kings/wise men)
saw a new King had been born.
They followed the star.

    If toddlers are present:
    Let's get up and follow the star together.
    Lead the children in walking in a circle, following the star. You might like to ask toddlers to take turns leading if appropriate.

> ## Tip
>
> If the group includes babies only you can stay seated and move the babies' legs for them like 'cycling', or show two fingers walking around and following the actions. You may wish to cut the song to three verses: normal walking, rowing a boat, and tiptoeing quietly: 'Ssssh!'

[Let's] follow, follow, follow the star,
follow the star, follow the star!

**[Let's] follow, follow, follow the star
to meet the special King.**

Uh oh! It's the desert!
Let's climb on our camels
To help us through the sandy desert . . .

Show how a camel sways as you ride it, or give out toy camels or pictures of camels.
**[Let's] follow, follow, follow the star,
follow the star, follow the star!
[Let's] follow, follow, follow the star
to meet the special King.**

Uh oh! It's the sea!
Let's get in our boats to cross the sea.
Don't forget your camel!

Show the children how to sit down and row a boat as you sing.
**[Let's] follow, follow, follow the star,
follow the star, follow the star!
[Let's] follow, follow, follow the star
to meet the special King.**

Uh oh! A mountain!
Time for some climbing!

Lead the children in pretending to climb a very steep mountain.
**[Let's] follow, follow, follow the star,
follow the star, follow the star!
[Let's] follow, follow, follow the star
to meet the special King.**

Uh oh! A valley. It's a bit dark and a bit scary! Ssssh!
Let's sing really quietly!

Lead the children in tiptoeing round.
**[Let's] follow, follow, follow the star,
tollow the star, follow the star!
[Let's] follow, follow, follow the star
to meet the special King.**

Look! The star's stopped over a stable!

Point to the manger.

What a long journey it's been!
Shall we look inside the stable . . .
Let's tiptoe there . . .
Tiptoe, tiptoe, tiptoe . . .
Tiptoe back to your place around the manger.

It's Baby Jesus! The baby King!

> *If appropriate:*
> Let's kneel down around Baby Jesus.

Song 9: Giving a present to Jesus

→ **Matthew 2.11**

The Magi (wise men/three kings) brought Jesus
special presents.
We can give Baby Jesus a present too!

Show a basket of hearts. Use fabric hearts, or provide new paper hearts each week. If you'd prefer to emphasize the 'light' theme, you could use battery tealights or paper stars.

If you like, you can take one of these hearts/little lights/stars
and give it to Baby Jesus to show your love.

As you sing, encourage the children to place their hearts/candles/stars anywhere they like around Jesus.

Either: 'Away in a manger' by William James Kirkpatrick

Away in a manger, no crib for a bed.
The little Lord Jesus laid down his sweet head.
The stars in the night sky
looked down where he lay,
the little Lord Jesus asleep on the hay.

Or: the refrain only from 'O come all ye faithful', attributed to John Francis Wade, trans. Frederick Oakeley and others

O Come, let us adore him!
O Come, let us adore him!
O Come, let us adore him!
Christ the Lord!

Or: to the tune of 'Here we go round the mulberry bush', like 'Follow the star to Bethlehem', words © Sharon Moughtin-Mumby:

I'll show my love to Jesus,
Jesus, Jesus.
I'll show my love to Jesus,
The tiny baby King!

DIDDY DISCIPLES RESOURCES

Space and environment

Children's groups using Diddy Disciples will generally need their own room to worship in (although for the duration of the session only). This is because Diddy Disciples doesn't involve very much keeping quiet or still, but rather celebrates our voices and body movements and uses them to worship God. The room you use doesn't need to be big: in nursery at school, we hold a Diddy Disciples session within the very small carpet space. However, the size of your room will influence some of the choices that you make. At St Peter's, Walworth, we've found it helpful to divide our room up into two parts, separated by a row of chairs for adults to sit on.

One part is completely empty: this is where the singing and moving and circle time in the first half of the session takes place. This area is clearly sectioned off from the rest of the room with chairs, which cannot be passed by small children (until two chairs are moved to one side later in the session). With toddlers, we've found it particularly important to remove any unrelated toys, books or other items from this area that will inevitably send the wrong signals to the children. In the second half of the session, the babies, toddlers and sensory explorers use this open space for their Creative Response time. We lay out their resources on a large builder's tray before the session, and place this tray in the centre of the space once the other children have moved to their tables as the Creative Response time begins.

The other part of the room is set up with tables and resources for the Creative Responses. We've found that not using chairs makes it easier for everyone to move around the tables more freely and means more children can use each table. However, we do have one table with chairs for the youngest children, who are otherwise not able to reach.

In Chapter 4 of her book, Rebecca Nye provides some very useful thoughts on preparing a space that will help children and adults feel that 'God is here'. They include providing a space that is uncluttered, clean, and cared for. She writes, 'Reflect on the spiritual principles at work in the main building of your church, and you'll find the clues to guide you in creating a helpful kind of space for the children too to do their spiritual work.'[1]

Tip: A helpful exercise by Rebecca Nye

'Stand at the threshold of a space where you meet with children . . . Find at least a dozen adjectives to describe this physical space. Then sit where a child would normally sit in that space: add more descriptors to your list.

Do you think of God as being like any of the things on your list?

Do you think of children as being like any of the things on your list?

What would you most like to change to make this space a better space for children to be with God and God to be with children?'[2]

Resources for the time of Creative Response

We recommend that every group, especially those who are likely to use the print-and-go options, has the following materials to hand. We keep these resources in a separate drawer so they're easy to find each week:

- white paper (different coloured paper is a nice addition)
- coloured pencils (see tip below)
- chunky crayons (for younger children)
- white card (not essential but useful)
- child-safe scissors
- glue sticks (cheap versions are fine)

- PVA glue kept in small lidded pots with spatulas (for younger children)

- straws or lollipop sticks

- masking tape (cheap versions are fine)

- pipe cleaners (not essential but useful)

- string.

> **Tip**
>
> At St Peter's, Walworth, we've found that good-quality pencils are worth the expense. They don't break when dropped and need sharpening less frequently. Over time, this has saved us money and a lot of time and frustration.

Collage materials

These aren't essential, but will always be useful. Many younger children will not spend long with crayons/pencils and are more likely to enjoy glueing and sticking to make a collage. Most units have suggestions for collaging, which requires little preparation if you have suitable materials to hand.

At St Peter's we keep small tubs filled with collage materials arranged by colour. We've found the following tubs particularly useful: yellow/gold/silver, red/pink, shades of green, blue/green, mixed. We tend to continually top up the collage tubs with things we come across here and there – it's amazing the range you can find once you're looking. However, collage sets can also be bought. Asking the children to keep an eye out at home for collage material can really help the group and will resonate with a number of the Diddy Disciples Bible stories, in which God's love for recycling and rubbish is a common theme.

Gathering a range of textures and patterns as well as colours is ideal. Items that we've found useful include:

- scraps of coloured paper discarded by the children when cutting out in the sessions;

- coloured envelopes from birthday cards;

- felt (you can buy offcuts of felt from eBay);

- scrap material (my girls keep us in a constant supply of leggings with holey knees);

- offcuts from people who sew;

- ends of wool from people who knit;

- paper napkins;

- string bags used to hold courgettes or satsumas (depending on the type; some fall apart);

- ribbons snipped into small pieces (Christmas and birthdays are good times to keep an eye out for these);

- tinfoil and cotton wool;

- newspapers;

- broken gift bags or wrapping and tissue paper from presents;

- sweet wrappers or gold chocolate coin wrappers;

- packaging from postal parcels;

- old PVC tablecloths (clear ones can also be great for making telescopes or magnifying glasses);

- leftovers from art and craft sets;

- bark or leaves;

- sandpaper.

If you'd like help in cutting the pieces and sorting them into tubs, you could ask some of the older children who like to lead, or children who enjoy experimenting with scissors, to help. It's one way that these children can serve God, share Jesus' love with other people, and share God's love for recycling.

Interesting media

While pencils and crayons are adequate for many Creative Responses, we've found that encouraging the children to explore using different media can be inspirational. At St Peter's, Walworth, if we introduce a different medium, we tend then to make it available during the whole unit to give the children the opportunity to develop their use of it, while also saving time on planning and preparation.

Ideas of the different media that might be useful include:

- pastels
- chalks
- watercolour paints
- ready mixed paints (using these with shaving brushes can work well for very young children)
- watercolour pencils (for older children, if you have time to show them how they work)
- charcoal
- glitter pens
- dyed string or coloured wool soaked in PVA glue
- sticks and mud
- glitter
- sponges or rollers and paint
- edible cornflour finger paints (see p. 258)
- dyed cooked spaghetti (see p. 257)
- dyed uncooked pasta (see p. 257).

We also encourage the children to draw or paint on different media as well as paper. These might include:

- thick brown or white card
- cardboard from recycling
- stones
- graph paper, lined paper
- pieces of wood (ensure these are free of splinters)
- shells
- fabric, especially pale fabric
- tracing paper or baking parchment
- coloured or textured paper
- patterned wallpaper
- newspaper or magazine cuttings (check these are appropriate before use)
- long rolls of paper taped to the floor with masking tape.

Exploring the possibilities of 'ephemeral' or 'transient' art can give children the opportunity to discover that beautiful things can be fleeting and last only a moment. We don't need to be afraid of the idea that things may not last: we can still celebrate their beauty. Suitable items include:

- things from the natural world, depending on the season: pressed flowers, leaves, grasses, blossom, bark, twigs, sand, berries, stones, shells. Check all these for safety;
- buttons;
- milk bottle tops of various colours;
- dyed cooked spaghetti, or uncooked rice or pasta (see p. 257);
- salt dyed with paint or food colouring;

- edible cornflour paint (see p. 258);
- coloured paper in different shapes: squares, circles, triangles, diamonds, rectangles, hexagons, octagons, etc.

Creative materials from home:

- wooden mosaic shapes
- Etch-a-Sketch
- 'Cordz' sets
- felt sets and boards
- magnetic boards and shapes
- ink pads and stamps
- Post-it pads
- Spirograph
- stencils to use with paint or pencils
- Play Mais.

Recipes

How to make salt dough

Mix 2 cups of flour with 1 cup of salt and 1 cup of water. If you'd like coloured salt dough, add a few drops of food colouring to the water before mixing. If it's too sticky, add more flour; if it's too dry, add a drop more water. If you're making the dough in advance, it can become sticky when stored, so make sure you take extra flour with you and check the dough before use. The shapes that are made with the salt dough will air dry in time (unless they're very thick). The dough can also be dried in an oven (on a low heat for around 3 hours) or in a microwave (check every few seconds).

How to dye cooked spaghetti

Cook the spaghetti according to the packet instructions with a little oil, drain it, then immediately run cold water over it in a colander or sieve to stop the cooking. Divide the cooked spaghetti up into bowls according to how many different colours you would like, add food colouring and mix well. Let the spaghetti dry (this takes an hour or so).

How to dye uncooked pasta

Place the uncooked pasta in a bowl. Mix food colouring with ½–1 teaspoon of vinegar. Pour the vinegar dye mix over the pasta and stir well. Once the pasta is fully coated, spread it out in a single layer on a baking tray to dry.

How to dye uncooked rice

Place the uncooked rice in a bowl. Mix food colouring with ½–1 teaspoon of vinegar. Pour the vinegar dye mix over the rice and stir well. Once the rice is fully coated, spread it out in a single layer on a baking tray to dry.

Tip

If you'd like to make dyed pasta or rice with children, you could use sealed food bags or plastic boxes for the mixing: invite a child to shake them until the pasta or rice is fully coated.

How to make bread

This is a simple bread recipe that has worked for us.

500g strong flour
7g (1 sachet) fast-action dried yeast
1 tsp salt
1 tsp sugar
350ml warm water
sunflower oil to grease
plastic wrap or cling film to cover

To make the dough, put the flour, salt and yeast in a large bowl and form a well in the centre. Pour most of the water into the well and mix to make a slightly wet dough. Add a little more water if needed. Tip the dough out onto a floury surface. Cover your hands with flour, then knead the sticky dough for at least 10 minutes until it's stretchy (you can also do this with a mixer that has a dough hook). Grease a bowl with oil, place the dough in the bowl, cover it with plastic wrap or cling film and leave it until the dough has doubled in size. When handing the dough out to the children, make sure their table top and hands are floured first and that the dough isn't excessively sticky (add a small amount of flour if it's too wet).

To bake the bread: if possible, leave the dough to rise again once the children have shaped it. Place the dough shapes into a preheated oven (220°C/fan 200°C/gas 7) for around 10–15 minutes according to their size (a full loaf will take more like 30 minutes). Tap the bottom of the shapes to check whether they're cooked: they should sound hollow when they're ready.

How to make edible cornflour paint

This paint is completely edible, but its neutral taste means that babies and toddlers aren't encouraged to eat it.

Mix 4 tablespoons of cornflour in a pan with enough cold water to make a medium-thick paste. Pour in 1 cup of boiling water slowly and stir until there are no lumps. Heat the mixture gently on a hob, stirring continually. Once you see clear streaks in the mixture, turn off the heat but continue stirring as the mixture thickens. Divide the mixture up into separate pots according to how many different colours you're planning, add food colouring and mix well. If you place it in the fridge (where it will keep for a couple of weeks), make sure you take it out and let it reach room temperature before use. If the paint needs thinning to use, add boiling water a drop at a time.

Music resources

Music from the Diddy Disciples Building Blocks in alphabetical order:

'The Diddy Disciples little prayers song' Words © Sharon Moughtin-Mumby
From the 'Prayers for Other People' Building Block, Option 2
Tune: 'Frère Jacques' (traditional)

'The Diddy Disciples sorry song' Words © Sharon Moughtin-Mumby
From the 'Saying Sorry to God' Building Block, Option 1
Tune: © Sharon Moughtin-Mumby

With my hands on my head, I re-mem-ber the things _ I've thought to-day, I re-mem-ber the things _ I wish I'd thought a diff'-rent way. I'm sor-ry, I'm sor-ry, I wish I could start _ a-gain. _ I'm sor-ry I'm sor-ry, I wish I could start _ a-gain. _

'We need a new start' Words © Sharon Moughtin-Mumby
From the 'Saying Sorry to God' Building Block, Option 2
Tune: Molly Malone (traditional)

For the things we have thought _____ that we wish we'd not thought, _____ we're sor-ry, _ we're sor-ry. _ We need a new start!

'The Diddy Disciples welcome song' Words © Sharon Moughtin-Mumby
From the 'Welcome' Building Block, Option 1
Tune: 'Glory, glory, alleluia' (traditional)

Wel-come Name 1 to St Pe-ter's. Wel-come Name 2 to St Pe-ter's. Wel-come Name 3 to St Pe-ter's. You are wel-come in the name of the Lord!

'For the love we've shown' Words © Sharon Moughtin-Mumby
From the 'Thank You, God' Building Block, Option 2
Tune: 'All through the night' (traditional)

For the love we've shown with our hands, thank you, God! For the love we've shown with our feet, thank you, God! When we love all those a-round us,

259

DIDDY DISCIPLES • PART 3

ADDITIONAL INFORMATION AND RESOURCES

Diddy Disciples resources

it's the same as lov - ing Je - sus. For the love we've

shown with our voice, thank you, God!

'God loves to give me a new start!' Words © Sharon Moughtin-Mumby

From the 'Saying Sorry to God' Building Block, New Start Action, Option 4

Tune: 'Give me oil in my lamp' (traditional)

Yes, my God loves to give me a new start! How a - ma - zing God's love for me! Yes, my

God loves to give me a new start! How a - ma - zing is God's love for me! Sing ho - sa - nna!

Sing ho - san - na! Sing ho - san - na to the King of kings!

Sing ho - san - na! Sing ho - san - na! Sing ho - san - na to the King!

'Jesus, hear our prayer!' Words © Sharon Moughtin-Mumby

From the 'Prayers for Other People' Building Block, Option 1

Tune: 'Brown girl in the ring' (traditional)

For the world: Je - sus, hear our prayer. For the Church: Je - sus, hear our prayer.

For our place, Wal - worth*: Je - sus, hear our prayer. Lord Je - sus, hear our prayer, A - men.

For the sick and lone - ly: Je - sus, hear our prayer. For our friends and fam - i - ly:

Je - sus, hear our prayer. For our-selves: Je - sus, hear our prayer. Lord

Je - sus, hear our prayer, A - men. Take our prayers: Je - sus, hear our prayer.

260

* Insert local area/school/church/community/parish

Make them ho - ly: Je - sus, hear our prayer. Make them beau - ti - ful:

Je - sus, hear our prayer. Lord Je - sus, hear our prayer, A - men.

'Jesus, hear our prayer!' Words © Sharon Moughtin-Mumby **Alternative tune**
From the 'Prayers for Other People' Building Block, Option 1
Tune: 'He's got the whole world in his hands' (traditional)

For the world and all peo-ple: hear our prayer. _ For all Chris-tians in all pla-ces:

hear our prayer. _ For the place that we live in: hear our prayer. _ Lord _

Je - sus, hear our prayer. _ For the sick and the lone - ly:

hear our prayer. _ For our friends and our fam' - ly:

hear our prayer. _ For _ me and my life: _ hear our prayer. _ Lord _

Je - sus, hear our prayer. _ Je - sus, take our prayers: _ hear our prayer. _ Je - sus,

make them ho - ly: hear our prayer. _ Je - sus, make them love - ly:

hear our prayer. _ Lord _ Je - sus, hear our prayer. _

'Jesus, open up my eyes' Words © Sharon Moughtin-Mumby
From the 'Getting Ready for Bible Storytelling' Building Block, Option 2
Tune: 'Michael, row the boat ashore' (traditional)

'My hands were made for love' Words © Sharon Moughtin-Mumby
From the 'Thank You, God' Building Block, Option 1
Tune: 'HIckory, dickory dock' (traditional)

'You are welcome in the name of the Lord!' (traditional)
From the 'Welcome' Building Block, Option 2
Tune: traditional

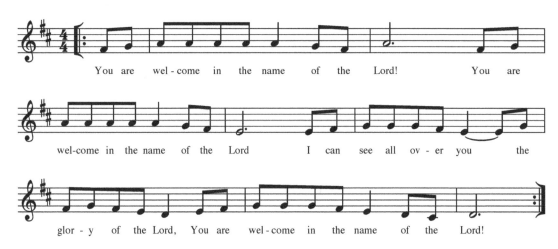

Photocopiable templates

The templates on the following pages are for use with the Creative Response starter ideas at the end of each unit. They are listed here.

Body (p. 264)
Sheep (p. 265)
Circle (p. 266)

Instructions for finger puppet template

1   Cut the finger puppets out along the thick lines.
2   Fold the flaps along the dotted lines, folding away from you.
3   Again folding away from you, fold the puppet in the middle where the arrow is.
4   Tape the flaps to the other half of the puppet.

Instructions for crown template

1   Cut along zigzag line.
2   Sellotape the two halves together with 1 cm overlap so that you have one long strip.
3   Put the strip round your head so that you can measure where to sellotape the ends.
4   Sellotape the ends together to make a crown.

Instructions for paper angels template

1   Cut along the line marked with the scissor symbol.
2   Fold each piece of paper into four along the lines marked 'Fold'. Make sure the angel figure is at the front.
3   Cut round the angel figure, but do not cut where the line is broken at the top of the wings. Be careful not to cut the folds.
4   Unfold the paper. You should have four angels linked together at the top of their wings.

Julia (6) drew this body. What can you make from it? Or would you like to draw your own?

Anastasia (8) drew this sheep. What can you make from it? Or would you like to draw your own?

Abigail (6) drew around a plate to make this circle. What can you make from it? Or would you like to draw your own?

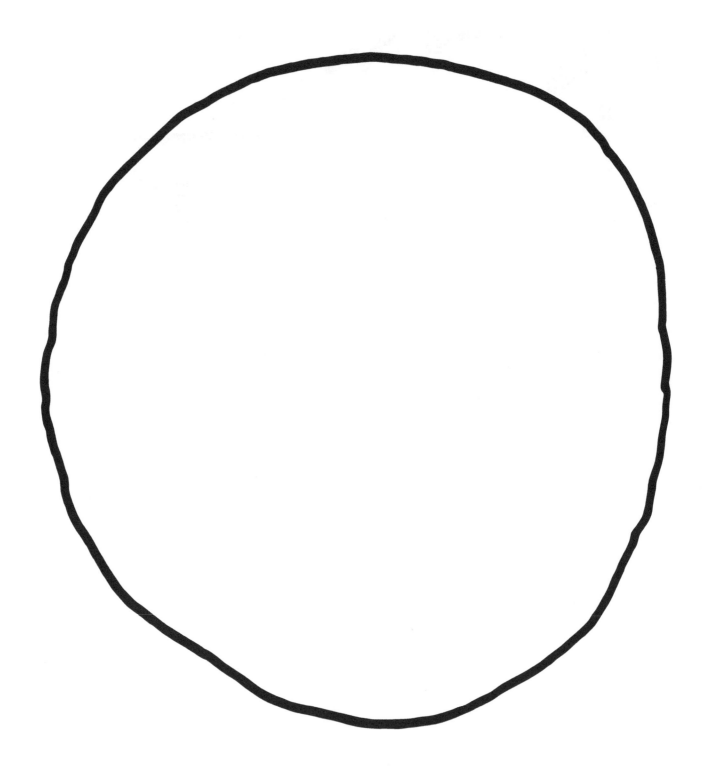

Elijah (6) drew this face. What can you make from it? Or would you like to draw your own?

Isabella (7) drew these finger puppets. Would you like to make them into people? Or would you like to make your own?

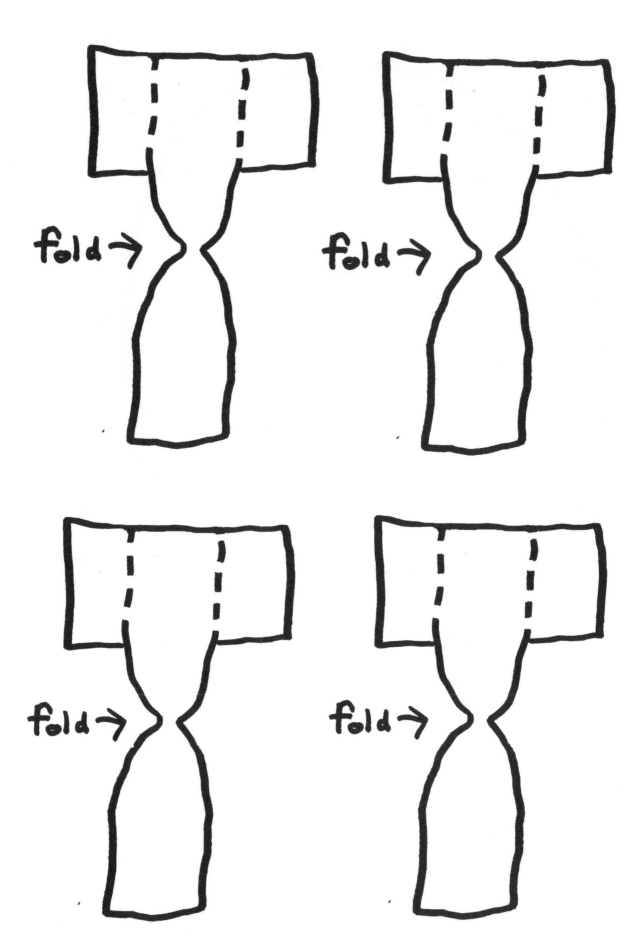

Anastasia (8) and Gavin (6) drew these candles. What can you make from them? Or would you like to draw your own?

Zoe M.-M. (7) drew this heart. What can you make from it? Or would you like to draw your own?

Anastasia (8) drew this postcard. What can you write or draw on it? Or would you like to draw your own?

Mitchell (6) drew round two circles to create this magnifying glass. What can you do with it? Or would you like to draw your own?

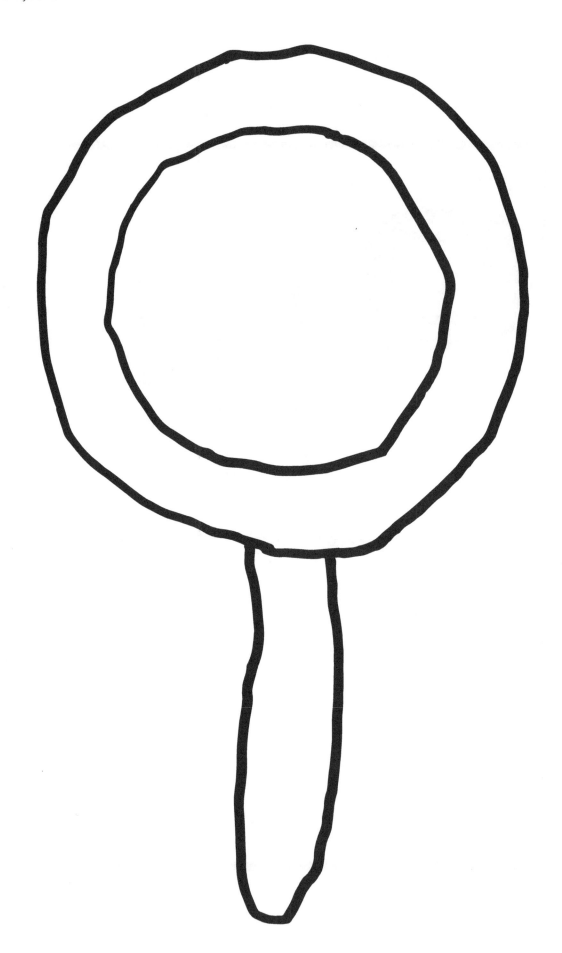

Gavin (6) drew these flowers. What can you make from them? Or would you like to draw your own?

Harry (7) drew around a circle shape to make this chart and Amelia (6) drew the arrow. What can you make with it? Or would you like to draw your own?

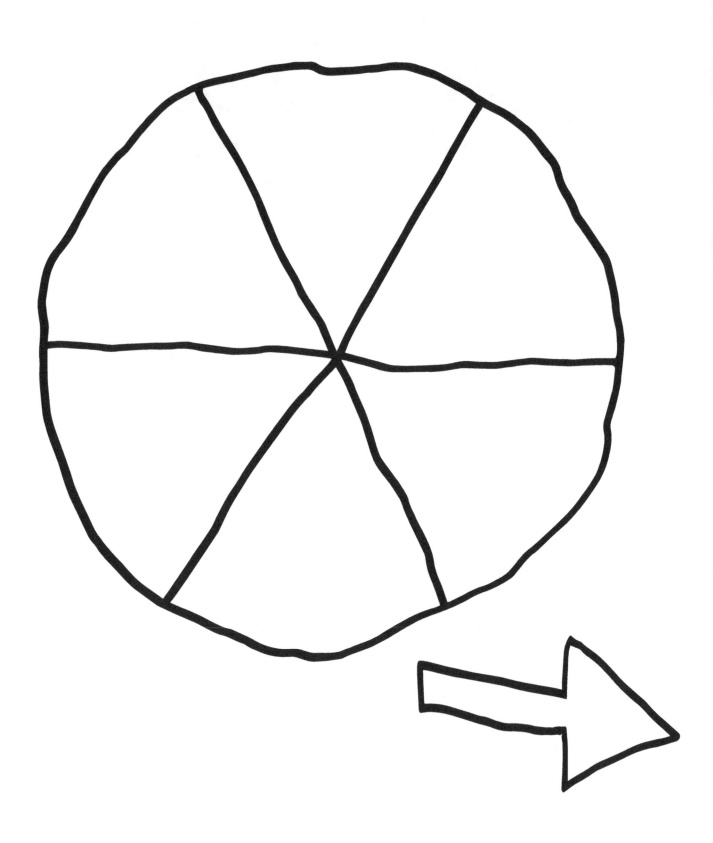

Isla (5) drew this picture frame. What can you draw in it? Or would you like to draw your own?

Nancy (6) made this picture frame. What can you draw in it? Or would you like to draw your own?

God the maker made this!

Joy (8) drew this tree. What can you do with it? Or would you like to draw your own?

Zoe G. (7) drew these poppies. What can you make from them? Or would you like to draw your own?

Philip (6) drew this zigzag line. Can you cut down it to make a crown?

Zoe G. (7) drew this chalice. Would you like to decorate it? Or would you like to draw your own?

Zoe M.-M. (7) drew this cross. What can you make from it? Or would you like to draw your own?

Mitchell (6) drew round a star shape to create this star. What can you make from it? Or would you like to draw your own?

Julia (6) drew this angel. What can you make from it? Or would you like to draw your own?

Joy (8) drew these angels. Can you fold the paper at the arrows, then cut round the angels and open them out to make a chain of 'paper angels'? Or would you like to make your own? *Full instructions on p. 263.*

fold →

fold →

fold →

fold →

fold →

fold →

NOTES

Diddy Disciples: Seven principles

1 See Rebecca Nye, *Children's Spirituality: What It Is and Why It Matters* (London: Church House Publishing, 2009, pp. 51–2; Jerome Berryman, *The Complete Guide to Godly Play: Volume 1* (Denver, CO: Living the Good News, 2002).

2 See Nye, *Children's Spirituality*. Nye also provides three approaches to defining the notoriously elusive concept of 'children's spirituality' in her first chapter.

3 Rebecca Nye, 'Spirituality' in Anne Richards and Peter Privett (eds), *Through the Eyes of a Child* (London: Church House Publishing, 2009), p. 75.

A guide to the Building Blocks

1 Rebecca Nye, 'Godly Play', *The Reader*, Winter 2009.

2 Bill Prevette, 'The Disturbance of God: Holistic Mission and Children in Crisis: Lessons from a Study of Partnership in Romania' in Bill Prevette, Keith J. White, C. Rosalee Velloso Ewell and D. J. Konz (eds), *Theology, Mission, and Child: Global Perspectives* Regnum Edinburgh Centenary Series 24 (Eugene, OR: Wipf and Stock, 2014), p. 98.

3 Henri J. M. Nouwen, *The Only Necessary Thing: Living a Prayerful Life* (Danvers, MA: The Crossroad Publishing Company), 2008.

4 Rebecca Nye, *Children's Spirituality: What It Is and Why It Matters* (London: Church House Publishing, 2009), pp. 49–50.

5 Rebecca Nye suggests 'warm-up' exercises such as this in *Children's Spirituality*, p. 50.

6 Walter Brueggemann, *Prophetic Imagination*, revised edition (Minneapolis: Augsburg Fortress, 2001).

7 Søren Kierkegaard, *Three Discourses on Imagined Occasions* (1845).

8 Henri Nouwen, *Spiritual Formation: Following the Movements of the Spirit* (New York: HarperCollins, 2010), p. 27.

9 Philip Yancey, *What's So Amazing About Grace?* (Grand Rapids: Zondervan, 1997), p. 262.

10 James Martin, SJ, *The Jesuit Guide to (Almost) Everything: A Spirituality for Real Life* (New York: HarperOne, 2010), p. 12.

11 Richard Rohr, *A Lever and a Place to Stand: The Contemplative Stance, the Active Prayer* (New Jersey: Hidden Spring, 2011), p. 42.

12 Rowan Williams, *Resurrection: Interpreting the Easter Gospel* (Cleveland: Pilgrim Press, 2003), p. 32.

13 Rowan Williams, *Ponder These Things: Praying with Icons of the Virgin* (Norwich: Canterbury Press, 2002), p. 37.

14 Williams, *Ponder These Things*, p. 53.

15 Philip Yancey, *Prayer: Does It Make Any Difference?* (London: Hodder and Stoughton, 2006).

16 Rebecca Nye, 'Spirituality', in Anne Richards and Peter Privett (eds), *Through the Eyes of a Child* (London: Church House Publishing, 2009), p. 73.

17 Rob Bell, *Velvet Elvis* (Grand Rapids: Zondervan, 2005), pp. 87–8.

18 Henri J. M. Nouwen, *Sabbatical Journey: The Diary of His Final Year* (New York: The Crossroad Publishing Company, 1998), Monday 4 December.

19 Henri J. M. Nouwen, *Letters to Marc about Jesus* (London: Darton, Longman and Todd, 1988).

20 For instance, see Jerome Berryman, *The Complete Guide to Godly Play: Volume 1* (Denver, CO: Living the Good News, 2002), p. 71.

21 Henri Nouwen, *Peacework: Prayer, Resistance, Community*, reprint edition (New York: Orbis Books, 2014), pp. 22–3.

Diddy Disciples resources

1 Rebecca Nye, *Children's Spirituality: What It Is and Why It Matters* (London: Church House Publishing, 2009), p. 43.

2 Nye, *Children's Spirituality*, p. 46.

Flo's Story

A little story about prayer

After I was widowed, my daughter Jo persuaded me to go to this tea dance in a church hall, a bus ride away from where I live. It was a way to keep fit and meet a few people and really cheered me up, but I still felt empty inside.

One day Dot, the lady who runs the dances, was handing out these little *Prayers on the Move* booklets, so I took one. I hadn't been to church for years and I hadn't prayed for a long time, but reading this little book, by myself, in my own time, the prayers really spoke to me. I realized what had been missing.

The next week, I told Dot that I'd really enjoyed the book and said I thought it would be nice to go to church. Dot said she'd give me a lift. Now I'm going to church every Sunday, I've found my faith again and I'm so happy. That empty feeling inside has gone away and it's all thanks to a little booklet called *Prayers on the Move*.

Inspired by a true story. Names and places have been changed.

Help us to tell more stories like Flo's. Sign up for the newsletter, buy bags, books and travelcard wallets, and make a donation to help more people like Flo find God through a book. www.prayersonthemove.com.